POLICE STAFF COLLEGE

0970959

THE POLICE STAFF COLLEGE
BRAMSHILL HOUSE
BRAMSHILL
HOOK, HAMPSHIRE
RG27 0JW

DISCARDED

NATIONAL POLICE LIBRARY

D1342669

# ANTI-DISCRIMINATION LAW ENFORCEMENT

# Research in Ethnic Relations Series

**Going West: Soviet Jewish Immigrants in Berlin since 1990**
*Jeroen Doomernik*

**Culture, Identity and Politics**
*Edited by T. Ranger, Y. Samad and O. Stuart*

**Communities, Networks and Ethnic Politics**
The leaders and the led
*Ken Hahlo*

**Migration, Citizenship and Ethno-National Identities
in the European Union**
*Edited by Marco Martiniello*

**Housing, 'Race', Social Policy and Empowerment**
*M. L. Harrison*

**Religion, Class and Identity**
The state, the Catholic church and the education
of the Irish in Britain
*Mary J. Hickman*

**Through Different Eyes: The Cultural Identities
of Young Chinese People in Britain**
*David Parker*

**Ethnicity and Development in Nigeria**
*Okwudiba Nnoli*

# Anti-Discrimination Law Enforcement

## A Comparative Perspective

*Edited by*
MARTIN MacEWEN

POLICE
STAFF
COLLEGE
NATIONAL LIBRARY
LIBRARY
BRAMSHILL

# Avebury

Aldershot • Brookfield USA • Hong Kong • Singapore • Sydney

© M. MacEwen 1997

All rights reserved. No part of this publication may be reproduced, stored in a retrieval system, or transmitted in any form or by any means, electronic, mechanical, photocopying, recording or otherwise without the prior permission of the publisher.

Published by
Avebury
Ashgate Publishing Limited
Gower House
Croft Road
Aldershot
Hants GU11 3HR
England

Ashgate Publishing Company
Old Post Road
Brookfield
Vermont 05036
USA

**British Library Cataloguing in Publication Data**

Anti-discrimination law enforcement : a comparative
    perspective. - (Research in ethnic relations)
    1. Discrimination - Law and legislation
    I. MacEwen, Martin
    342.4

**Library of Congress Catalog Card Number:** 96-79945

ISBN 1 85972 404 3

Printed in Great Britain by the Ipswich Book Company, Suffolk

Acc. no. DISC 0970959 RARY
Classmark 344 . 011 3 RY
NATIONAL
MAC

# Contents

# Figures and tables

# Acknowledgements

To all the reluctant contributors, the victims of my own sustained campaign of harassment, I owe a particular debt. It is their knowledge and understanding of the activities and experiences of enforcement agencies that provide the informed commentary without which this book would be much less authoritative.

In particular the personal experience and knowledge of chairpersons, chief executives, legal directors and deputy directors of enforcement agencies, all of whom are contributors to this volume, in addition to specialist academics, provide a poignancy to the description and analysis of a broad band of experience located in different countries but sharing the same concerns.

This book was largely born from contributions made to the Second International Symposium on Anti-discrimination Law held at the Edinburgh College of Art, Heriot-Watt University in September 1995 organised by myself and my colleague, Donna Murray to whom a particular acknowledgement is due.

The first chapter of this book was given a trial run in abbreviated form in the *International Journal of Discrimination and the Law*, (1995,Vol. 1, No. 1) with the permission of this publisher, Avebury.

While I must assume a large responsibility for my own typing and the typesetting of the work of other contributors, a task I handled with little skill and less enthusiasm, I should record my thanks to my secretary Mrs. Nancy Douglas for helping me out with a number of apparently insurmountable problems.

# List of contributors

**Chris Boothman** was born in London of Trinidadian parents and after schooling undertook a BA in Business Law, graduating in 1979. He was admitted as a solicitor in 1982 and practised with Gordon and James Morton, the London Borough of Camden, the Greater London Council and the London Borough of Hackney where he was Principal Solicitor (special projects) before he joined the Commission for Racial Equality in 1991 to become Legal Director. Formerly he was Chairman of the Society of Black Lawyers (1987-1991) and has been a Council member of the Law Society of England and Wales from 1990.

Chris has played a critical role in the development of Legal Services at the Commission for Racial Equality and in developing new strategies and approaches under the current chairman, Mr Herman Ouseley. He has spoken at national and international conferences and has published widely.

**Sarah Christie** who graduated BA(Hons) and LL.B. at Rhodes has focused much of her research interests on labour dispute resolution, employment, equity policy formation and mediating employment discrimination. She is a member of the Independent Mediation Service of South Africa and the alternative Dispute Resolution Association of South Africa.

Sarah has given papers at a number of conferences in southern Africa and Europe: her recent publications include 'Women and the Law', Human Rights and Labour Law Yearbook 1992, Oxford University Press, 1993: Capetown and 'Majoritarianism, Collective Bargaining and Discrimination' (1994), 15 Industrial Law Journal 708.

**Bob Cooper, CBE** was educated at Foyle's College, Londonderry and Queen's University Belfast where he read Law. He was Assistant Secretary (1963-1967) and later Secretary (1967-1972) of the Engineering Employers Federation.

Having served as General Secretary of the Alliance Party of Northern Ireland (1972-1973), he was a member of the Northern Ireland Assembly (1973-1975) and then the Northern Ireland Constitutional Convention (1975-1976). He served as Minister of Manpower Services for Northern Ireland in 1974.

From its inception in 1976 Bob Cooper has been Chairman of the Fair Employment Agency (later Commission) in Northern Ireland. Bob has played a critical role as Chairman in promoting the aspirations for equal treatment for both communities in Northern Ireland, particularly the Catholic minority.

**Professor Brian Doyle** read law at the University of London, Queen Mary College, obtaining a degree of LL.B. (1976), an LL.M (1978). He was called to the bar in 1977 and obtained a PhD in 1993. He worked in the Law School at the University of Salford from 1980 becoming a senior lecturer there in 1988. In October 1995 he took up his present appointment as Chair of Law at University of Liverpool. He is a part-time Chairman of Industrial Tribunals and Research and Education Director to a firm of solicitors.

He has a specialist interest in employment and Discrimination Law and has researched and published widely in these areas. Recent publications include 'Disability, Discrimination and Equal Opportunities', by Mansell Publishing (1995) and 'Disability, Discrimination: The New Law', Jordans (1996).

**Professor Jenny Elisabeth Goldschmidt** graduated with an LLM from the University of Leiden where she completed her doctorate on the National and Indigenous Constitutional Law in Ghana in 1981. In that year she was appointed senior lecturer in Comparative Constitutional and Administrative Law at the University of Leiden where she became Associate Professor in 1984. Between 1989 and 1994 she was Associate Professor for Women and Law at the

University of Utrecht. In 1984 she was appointed Chairperson at the Equal Opportunities Commission for the Netherlands.

Jenny has served on the Board of the Dutch section of the International Commission of Jurors (1975-1979) and has lectured extensively both in the Netherlands and abroad. She is a member of the Judicial Committee of the National Institute Against Racism and between 1989 and 1993 was editor of the Netherlands Periodical on Labour Market and Social Policy Matters. Her publications include several books and articles, mostly in Dutch.

**Lilian Goncalves  Ho Kang You** was born in Paramarido in Surinam and graduated at the University of Leiden in Holland. She served as Legal Adviser to the cabinet of the Prime Minister in Surinam from 1971 to 1973; she was Secretary to the State Council, Vice-President of the Electoral Council and Member of the Government Commission on the Abolition of Married Women's Contractual Incapacity. Between 1973 and 1984 she practised as an attorney but then moved as a political refugee to the Netherlands since when she has practised law. She was appointed Vice-President of the Equal Treatment Commission in September 1994.

Lilian has held a number of additional posts including Chair of the Foundation of Disabled Children, Secretary of the Surinamese Bar Association, Member of the Foundation New Theatre in Amsterdam and Chair of the National Bureau against Racial Discrimination in the Netherlands.

**John Hucker** was born and educated in the United Kingdom obtaining a law degree from the University of Wales, Aberystwyth in 1962 and has undertaken postgraduate work at LSE and Yale Universities. He was Professor of Law at Queens University, Ontario, Canada from 1966 to 1971 and subsequently 1973-1974. In the intervening period he was a senior lecturer in law at the University of West Indies, Jamaica. Mr Hucker has acted as a legislative consultant to the government of Canada (1974-1976) heading a working party which drafted the Canadian Immigration Act of 1976.

John held a series of senior positions in the Canadian Public Service and was appointed Secretary General to the Canadian Human Rights Commission in 1988. His recent publications include 'Towards Equal Opportunity in Canada: New Approaches, Mixed Results' Vol. 26, St Mary's Law Journal, pages 841-855 (1995).

**Alice Leonard** was born and educated in the United States. Before moving to England in 1983 she worked in the US Office of Human Rights in Boston. In 1986 Alice was appointed Deputy Legal Adviser of the Equal Opportunities Commission in Manchester.

Alice has both researched and published widely in the area of anti discrimination law. Her publications include a recent study with Rosemary Hunter 'The Outcomes of Conciliation in Sex Discrimination Cases' (1985) published by the Centre for Employment and Labour Relations Law at Melbourne University at which the research had been undertaken.

**Martin MacEwen** graduated (LL.B.) from Aberdeen University and worked as a District Officer in the Solomon Islands and then with Dunfermline Town Council and the Race Relations Board in London before returning to his native city at the Edinburgh College of Art to lecture in Planning, Housing and Equal Opportunity Law. He is a Director of the Scottish Ethnic Minorities Research Unit and Vice-Principal of the College.

Martin has researched and published widely on race and law issues, including 'Housing, Race and Law' (Routledge, 1990) and 'Tackling Racism in Europe (Berg, 1995).

**Michael O'Flaherty** is the Secretary of the United Nations Committee on the Elimination of Racial Discrimination, a post he has held since December 1994. He graduated (BCL) in Dublin and undertook further studies in Rome (PPH, STB) and Amsterdam (A.S.I.R., MPhil) before qualifying as a solicitor in Ireland. Previously Michael was Co-ordinator to the United Nations Centre for Human Rights Field Operation in Bosnia and Hergosnovena based in Sarejevo and Geneva.

Michael has published widely on the subject of human rights and anti-discrimination law, including 'The International Covenant on Civil and Political Rights: International Human Rights Law in Ireland' (with L Heffernam): Dublin 1995 and 'The Reporting Procedure under Article 40 of The International Covenant on Civil and Political Rights', (1994) 16 Human Rights Quarterly 515.

**Peter R. Rodrigues** has been a lawyer with both the Dutch Anti-Racism Agency (LBR) and the Equal Treatment Commission with whom he now works. Peter was a research worker at the Molengraaff Institute of Private Law at Utrecht University and has recently completed a PhD on Racial Discrimination and Consumer Affairs.

Peter has published widely and contributed to the First International Symposium on Anti-Discrimination Law, an adaptation of his paper there presented 'Racial Discrimination and the Law in the Netherlands' being published in New Community, Vol. 20, no 3 of April 1994 (pages 381-391).

**Meredith Wilkie** is an Australian legal researcher with an interest in Aboriginal affairs and human rights issues who now lectures in Human Rights and Equal Opportunities at the Law School of Murdoch University. Meredith has previously worked with the Aboriginal Legal Service (1978), a Parliamentary Committee of Enquiry into Aboriginal Land Rights and Socio-Economic Conditions (1979-1981) and the Australian Human Rights and Equal Opportunities Commission (1987-1989).

Meredith spent three months at the Danish Centre of Human Rights, the result of her research 'Victims of Neutrality: Race Discrimination in Denmark' being published in the Nordic Journal of International Law (1990) 59.4. She has published on Aboriginal Land Rights and Aborigines in the Criminal Justice system, as well as multi-culturalism and anti-discrimination Law in Australia.

# 1 Promoting equal opportunity: the enforcement agency

*Martin MacEwen*

## Introduction

*Selecting the case studies*

This book comprises a collection of essays on enforcement agencies in the area of discrimination law. The purpose is to highlight commonality and difference of law and practice of enforcement in a selection of countries with a view to teasing out what works effectively, and why, and gauging to what extent there are lessons which are transnational and which may apply in more than one area of discrimination.

The majority of countries chosen for this study share a common law base. Thus the laws in the UK, excepting Scotland to a degree, and Northern Ireland, in Canada and in Australia share the same 'English' common law tradition. It should be noted, however, the differing constitutional position of the various states and their distinctive approaches to aspects of discrimination illustrate that a shared tradition is not a useful indicator of common development or approach.

In common with these countries is the Netherlands in the sense of being part of the economically developed world, in having a dominantly white population but with significant black minorities and in adopting civil legislation against both race and gender discrimination. As the UK but exceptionally in the context of the

1

European Union, the Netherlands have a state agency, the Equal Treatment Commission, to police the laws relating to discrimination on the grounds of both gender and race.

South Africa like Scotland has a hybrid law system sharing an influence from both the Romano-Dutch and the English common law traditions but its new constitutional provisions attempt to entrench equality as a norm in the same manner as apartheid sought to entrench racial difference. More than anything, one suspects, it illustrates that the state needs more than formal structures to dismantle not merely the social processes and personal mind-sets that sustained discrimination but also to tackle the economic and cultural disadvantage of the social underclass, which the system underpinned. It is also a reminder, if one is still needed, that systemic discrimination may have both intended and unintended consequences. The failure to require public transport to cater for the wheelchair user, the restricted access to both private and local authority housing to disabled persons and ethnic minorities and the encouragement of low pay to part-time, second income and dominantly female employees has ramifications which no state agency can in itself disentangle or control in its role of promoting equal opportunity.

Discrimination is multifaceted. We make important decisions by discriminating in favour of one option as against another. The practice is necessary and legitimate. What is open to challenge is arbitrary and stereotypical judgements based on prejudice. By definition prejudice involves a prejudgment, a conclusion as to the suitability of an applicant, for example, on the basis of gender, ethnicity or some physical characteristics unrelated to the job. Not all such arbitrary judgements are rendered unlawful by any country although some attempt more comprehensive coverage than others. Thus in the UK it is generally acceptable in law to discriminate on religious grounds, except in Northern Ireland, on the basis of class or accent, on grounds of age or sexual orientation, on income, on place of residence or even on the basis of a person's diet, clothing or appearance provided such prejudice is not linked indirectly or directly to unlawful grounds such as race of gender. The enforcement agencies examined in this book illustrate the more central areas of arbitrary discrimination, disability, religion, gender and race.

While the focus of this book is a comparative view of the role of enforcement agencies, it is evident that domestic legislation may be influenced not only by the experience of others, the Race Relations Act of 1968 was reflective of a comparative study of legislation in the USA and Canada in particular[1], but also by international conventions. The International Convention Against All Forms or Racial Discrimination of 1965 [ICERD] predates all the municipal or state legislation against racial discrimination to which this study makes reference and has informed much of these provisions. Unusually, in the context of UN conventions, a specialist 'enforcement' committee was established [CERD]. Not only does this committee receive reports every two years from the countries that have ratified the convention, and frequently offers trenchant criticism in response, but it also receives individual complaints from the minority of countries who permit such reference through signatory of Article 14. Chapter 11 describes the work of CERD and in examining the role of one UN agency in the field of human rights, illustrates the actual and potential influence of international obligations on the activities of domestic enforcement agencies.

## The challenge of change

Anti-discrimination legislation is a product of the post-second world war period of reconstruction.[2] One facet of this period was the process of decolonising dependencies, a process affecting both the UK and the Netherlands and the promotion of a professed racial equality in a 'multicultural era'[3] which represents an attempt to deconstruct a history of racism. Similarly the rights of women were reassessed not only in respect of the changing labour market and gender segregation in employment but also in respect of education and life chances. There was a growing acceptance that the formal equality in the law, symbolised in the UK by the voting rights for women conferred in 1918 and 1928, failed to promote equality in practice as reflected in the UN Declaration of Human Rights of 1948. Social barriers of gender demarcation in work, in the home and in recreation and leisure were under threat. Less evident were the changing attitudes to other forms of prejudice, particularly against disabled persons where the medical as opposed to the social definitions of rights and opportunities took longer to contest. But cumulatively the period of reconstruction presented an effective challenge to the primacy of accepted dominant norms which have formed the real or hypothetical benchmark against which the acceptability of diversity (or social deviance) is tested. Such norms

3

are pervasive and include the way we look, behave, talk, react, socialise and mediate, conciliate and even judge. The law to promote equality, therefore, faces a significant challenge which extends to the institutions and processes which are established to enforce the observance of non-discrimination.

## Types of agency

In many common law countries today, as exemplified by provision in the US, Canada, UK, Australia and New Zealand, specialist agencies have been established for the purpose of promoting and/or enforcing anti-discrimination law.[4] Some of these agencies, such as the Commission for Racial Equality and the Equal Opportunities Commission in Britain have a responsibility for one subject area but combine promotional and enforcement functions, while others, such as the Human Rights Commission set up under the Human Rights Act 1993 in New Zealand, encompass a broader responsibility in attempting to police the law relating not only to race and sex discrimination but also to religion, political opinion, family and marital status, sexual orientation, age and disability. A number of regulatory agencies such as the Equal Employment Opportunities Commission in the United States have a responsibility confined to one sector [employment]. In most federal jurisdictions there are regulatory agencies at both the federal and state level (as in Quebec in Canada and as in New South Wales and Victoria in Australia) but the existence of federal legislation may not be replicated at state level, as in Tasmania, or the separate federal state provision may enable the appointment of one enforcement agency in respect of the enforcement of both state and federal provision as in Western Australia in relation to gender and race discrimination.

It is also fairly common for government offices or departments, advisory and regulatory, to be created such as the Commonwealth Office of Multicultural Affairs and the Office of Equal Employment Opportunity (OEEO) in Western Australia. The principal function of the former is to promote good practice and to effect change through the provision of advice, guidance, counselling and policy review.[5] The responsibility of the OEEO for Western Australia is to assist public authorities to meet their legal obligations and to evaluate the effectiveness of statutory EEO management plans.[6]

Perhaps a more fundamental division in the responsibilities of

4

regulatory agencies relates to their powers of enforcement. Commonly, as with the Commission for Racial Equality and the Equal Opportunities Commission in Britain and the Human Rights Commission in New Zealand, the agency has power to initiate complaints and to support complainants in the pursuit of remedies either before the courts or before tribunals. Exceptionally, some regulatory agencies perform the function not only of police and prosecution but also of judge and jury as exemplified by the federal Human Rights and Equal Opportunity Commission in Australia. Most regulatory agencies have a conciliatory function in that they can negotiate extra-judicial settlements for the parties in dispute. Some of these agencies are obliged to go through the process of conciliation before seeking a judicial remedy while others have no such requirement. Moreover, certain agencies, because of their conciliatory function, are not permitted to represent complainants directly or indirectly before tribunals or courts. In some jurisdictions there are specialist tribunals, such as the Complaints Review Tribunal in New Zealand, which deal exclusively with discrimination complaints while in others such as the UK judicial remedies are only available from the courts or generalist employment tribunals.

Clearly then the range of regulatory agencies deployed in the area of anti-discrimination law is widespread and from the above description it might seem difficult to construct a rational explanation for such diversity. But a preliminary question to address is 'Why create a specialist agency in the first place?'

## The purpose of the agency

A study by Baldwin and McCrudden (1987) articulated concern about the increasing use of such agencies by government and the acute problems that they pose for public law. Because they act on behalf of central government but are yet not of central government, they raise constitutional problems. They expend resources in deciding disputes between parties, in interpreting a particular body of law and on occasion in enforcing it: the public may be concerned about their maverick qualities as they are about the broader family from which they stem. That family is referred to as non-departmental public bodies, quangos and public corporations. While it is not intended to question the efficacy of regulatory

5

agencies themselves, it is important at the outset to identify their particular advantages and to relate these to the particular responsibilities of the agencies in the field of anti-discrimination law. Perhaps the most obvious reason for creating a regulatory agency by central government is to off-load work onto a specialist body with a single function which may be more effectively pursued because it is the central interest of the organisation and not merely one of a number dealt with by an organisation confronted with a multiplicity of competing demands, the most urgent of which may be elsewhere.

In addition to the benefit of having an agency which will hone its particular expertise unencumbered by other demands, there is the consideration that some responsibilities may be quasi-judicial in combining rule-making, decision-making or adjudicative functions, and they may be inappropriate for a government department. Insofar as the regulatory agency does act as a tribunal or court, it may be as economic to develop the specialism required for effective adjudication within a single purpose agency rather than to expand the membership of existing courts and tribunals in order to accommodate new legislative requirements. In the UK the Franks Committee on Courts and Tribunals (Franks 1957) concluded that the advantage of specialist tribunals over courts was that they were cheap, informal, accessible and provided specialist expertise. While most of the agencies referred to above do not have the powers of tribunals, they do have responsibility frequently conferred on them in the conciliation process to determine a fair resolution of a complaint, to seek a settlement which will be binding on the parties and to resolve matters in a professional and skilled manner: to that extent their processes are akin to those of informal adjudication and the advantages may be similar to the attributes Franks gave to the tribunal.

Clearly one of the central criticisms of regulatory agencies is their lack of public accountability, the minister responsible for the sector being able to disown before parliament any responsibility for day to day management of such agencies. While that criticism may be significant, the obverse side is that those appointed to oversee the day-to-day administration of the agency are likely to be selected because of their specialist knowledge and skills or experience in the area. It is true that the government of the day may often reflect its own prejudices and preferences in its selection of commissioner or board members. In so doing it may influence the direction in which the regulatory agency may move and exercise indirect control or guidance as to not only the general policy and approach but also its operational management style. But the fact that the agency is not directly controlled by a department, does mean that there is a buffer between the government of the day and the institution which should provide some protection against the vagaries of party political priorities: moreover an agency from time to time[7] may investigate the practices of central and local government itself in a manner foreclosed to a sister department. There are a variety of ways in which agencies may act as 'insulators' between government and the public.[8]

Firstly, where an independent agency such as the Commission for Racial Equality or Human Rights Commission in New Zealand has power to bring proceedings against the public sector and to enforce protective legislation against breach by government departments, then the government may, with some credibility, claim that it has complied with the legislation with greater conviction than where the enforcement agency was an arm of government itself. Consequently the arms-length factor of the regulatory agency gives both a legitimacy and a credibility to government's own undertakings in the area of anti-discrimination provisions.

Secondly, there may be a number of unpopular, yet necessary activities which the regulatory agency may wish to pursue and from which the government would wish to distance or dissociate itself at least insofar as denying that it had a direct responsibility for the day to day activities of the agency. Such distance might not only free government administration from partisan politics and party political influence but it may also, in the constitutional sense, appear more appropriate for an agency rather than government to be examining certain issues: thus CRE formal investigations into local authority housing or educational provision would have been further inflamed had it been central government who were undertaking the investigation.[9]

Lastly, in respect of policy, deliberation and formulation, an independent administrative agency may be seen to bring a greater sense of independence and objectivity to its deliberations and recommendations which a Department of State might be accused of lacking. Moreover it may be able to consult interest groups, agencies and individuals whether formally or informally, set up consultative machinery and deploy quick, flexible and innovative approaches that central government would find difficult to replicate.[10] Its

7

deliberations may also be seen to hold an objectivity in support of government policy as well as in opposition to it.[11]

In addition to the 'added value' which an agency may hold in the eyes of central government, there may also be less open reasons for central government to value the work of an agency. Katznelson (1973) in his critique of the then Community Relations Councils (a non-statutory local network of voluntary councils associated with and part funded by the CRE) suggested that the role of 'insulator' was also that of buffer in the sense that it enabled central government to distance itself from the legitimate political aspirations of the black community by creating a 'representative' agency which was in fact a colonial outpost of central government. While that assertion was not effectively substantiated[12], to the extent that regulatory agencies in the anti-discrimination field are there to pursue implicit and/or explicit objectives set by government either within the legislation or by way of directives or instructions which may be given from time to time, then the principal objective of promoting racial equality and counteracting racial discrimination may be qualified by other objectives such as defusing social tension.[13] Agencies may also be used as part of the government's repertoire of illusion from its box of magic tricks to disguise its real concerns, for example giving the impression of taking firm action on an issue of public concern by referring it to the agency.

Frequently the criticism made of regulatory agencies are the mirror of their supposed attributes. Thus they are accused of being slow and inefficient, unfair, predictable, corrupt, ill-managed and unresponsive to changes in political opinion and of lacking those very specialist skills and knowledge which were supposed to justify their existence.[14] Moreover, like all aspects of bureaucracy the agencies will desire growth and, in seeking new business to justify such growth, they may sideline or pervert the primary purpose or purposes for which they were appointed. It is claimed from time to time that particular agencies 'go native' and become too closely identified with the interests of the client group to which they have become captive.[15] There is also a risk that specialist agencies marginalise the importance of mainstream central and local government initiatives by diverting responsibility elsewhere.

## The limits of the law

The historical legacy of systematic and systemic discrimination against individuals and groups on the basis of disability, sex, race, religion or class, has impelled legal measures to protect both individual and occasionally group interests. These anti-discrimination provisions are selective - in large measure they eschew remedial action for historical disadvantage and they deny recognition of group rights - and assume that economic amelioration will flow from the provision of a complaints mechanism. They are likely, therefore, to be deficient and leave the goal of equal opportunity unrealised.

In commenting on the failure of the Civil Rights legislation in 1964 to deliver substantial improvement to the economic circumstances of blacks in America, Fiss (1971) has observed that the limited nature of legal strategies was not just a function of the circumstances of politics but reflected a deep commitment to the values of economic efficiency and individual fairness which, in turn, made little if any impact on the historical legacy of class or group disadvantage: the question for Fiss was whether or not that commitment should be moderated so as to yield through enactment or construction, a more robust strategy.[16]

The difficulty with a more restricted and classically liberal view of the extent to which the law should be interventionist is its failure to acknowledge the nature of discrimination. In Gunnar Myrdal's study 'The American Dilemma' (Myrdal 1944) racism was characterised as a simple anomaly in a society committed to equality; it was the repairable failure of liberal, democratic practices in respect of black rights to coincide with liberal, democratic theory. Bell (1992) challenges that view by reference to Hochschild's re-examination of Myrdal's 'anomaly thesis'.[17] It was Hochschild's view that the continued viability of racism within the United States demonstrated that it was not simply an excrescence on a fundamentally healthy, liberal, democratic body, but was part of what shapes and energises that body Thus liberal democracy and racism were historically, and even inherently, reinforcing. As a consequence the American dilemma was not the supposed tension between liberal democratic theory and liberal democratic practice, but was a fundamental problem of reconciling liberalism with democracy. Heilbroner (1971) has suggested that the merging of racial issues with that of neglect serves as a rationalisation for the policies of inaction that have characterised so much of the American response to need. Programmes to improve slums are seen by many as programmes to subsidise blacks and initiatives to improve prison conditions are measures to coddle black criminals with a consequence that the fear and resentment of black people takes precedence over the social problem itself. Crenshaw (1988) suggests that because whites believe

that blacks are unambitious or inferior they also believe that the
black predicament is deserved. In that belief, it becomes much
harder for whites to be convinced that something is wrong with the
entire system. Similarly a challenge to the legitimacy of continued
racial inequality would force whites to confront myths about
equality of opportunity that justify for them whatever measures of
economic success they may have attained. There is a 'property
right' in being white in respect of class differentiation but even the
dirt poor southern white will thank God for his colour as an
emblem of membership of a dominant group. For these reasons,
the system which has created its own white and black
underprivileged is protected from radical challenge.

While Bell (1992) contextualises the above arguments in the
historical experience of the States in respect of slavery and the
unifying experience of the U.S. immigrant oppressing the black
American, there are few, if any, countries which can point to a
racist-free past: setting aside the explicit racism of Apartheid in
South Africa, the British exploitation of its colonial empire and the
racist attitudes towards post-war immigration, the Australian
decimation of the Aboriginal population, the Canadian indifference
to the culture of the Inuit and the oppression of the Japanese
indigenous population during the Second World War and the New
Zealand lip-service to the cultural identity of the indigenous Maori,
all point to the universality of white racism against blacks and the
comparability of distinctive historical experience.

Given the ingrained persistent and pervasive nature of racism, it is
clearly optimistic to expect that an anti-discrimination law, in itself,
will have anything other than a marginally ameliorative impact on
improving the real life chances of black and ethnic minority
communities. While there may be significant differences regarding
the forms and experience of discrimination on other grounds such
as religion, sex and disability, there is commonalty regarding its
persistence and its linkage with cultural, economic and social
norms set by non-members of the disadvantaged group.
Accordingly, at best anti-discrimination laws may provide
protection against the worst abuses and facilitate a remedy where a
wrong has been identified. Unless they are accompanied by
government policies and strategies which imbed the legislative
provisions in a more holistic approach to discrimination,
substantial change is unlikely to be effective.

Consequently in examining the role of enforcement agencies, it is important to acknowledge on the one hand the limited sphere in which they are operating and on the other the importance of contextual policies and practices which may either enhance or inhibit their ability to achieve stated or implicit objectives. For this reason it is necessary to go beyond their 'agreed' objectives in assessing the efficacy of their performance. Nonetheless, an awareness of such objectives and the strategies adopted to achieve them, will form part of an overall approach and are worthy of examination because of it.

It is also relevant to consider whether the location of an individual sex or race discrimination law within a more general statute dealing with human rights - preferably reflecting constitutional guarantees - is likely to enhance the profile, status and impact of an enforcement agency. One argument, beyond those of rationalising resources, unifying approaches and sharing experiences, is that people are more likely to support a statute with which their own interests as one oppressed may be identified by reference to gender, age, disability or marital status, for example. The generic approach to arbitrary discrimination may consequently have educational, social and psychological advantages over the agency with a one subject remit.

## Objectives of legislation: the policy framework

At one level it may be fairly straight forward to seek common goals or purposes both for anti-discrimination law and the agencies which have been set up to facilitate their observance. Thus anti-discrimination law legislation may have the following aims:-

a)    to form part of a governmental strategy to promote equality of opportunity for  historically disadvantaged groups in society by securing equal treatment in education, in employment, in housing and other major facets of life.

b)    to provide remedies and redress where such opportunities are denied.

c)    to enforce provisions against incitement, harassment and victimisation; and

d)    to promote codes of good practice in the public and private sector, to monitor observance of the legislation and to make recommendations for its improvement.

Whilst it may be likely that many or all of these objectives are implicit in all anti-discrimination legislation, the particular emphasis and the inclusion of other objectives may well influence the priorities adopted by an enforcement agency and its operational methodology in securing compliance. As an example, I now turn to three enactments and the purpose which may be said to lie behind them.

The British Government's White Paper on Racial Discrimination which preceded the 1976 Act (HMSO 1975) was emphatic regarding the need for complementary social policy in recognising that legislation provided a framework for actions but was limited in what it could achieve.

> ..Government fully recognises that this (the legislative framework) is only part of the subject; that the policies and attitudes of central and local government are of critical importance in themselves and in their potential influence on the country as a whole (HMSO, 1975: 6).

In respect of enforcement the White Paper observed that it was hoped that most institutions and individuals would respond to the government's positive lead in promoting equality of opportunity and would change their practices voluntarily.

> However, it is essential in those cases where this does not occur that the law should be capable to providing adequate redress for the victim of racial discrimination as well as eliminating discriminatory practices which are against the public interest..the government proposes to adopt the new and radical approach reflected in the enforcement provisions of the Sex Discrimination Bill. It would combine the right of individual access to legal remedies with the strategic functions of a powerful Race Relations Commission (to become the conjoined Commission for Racial Equality) responsible for enforcing the law on behalf of the community as a whole (HMSO, 1975: 20).

The House of Commons Home Affairs Committee appointed a Sub-Committee on Race Relations and Immigration which was responsible for an enquiry into the Commission for Racial Equality in Session 1981-82 (HMSO, 1981). The report included a Summary of Recommendations and Conclusions. It concluded that the Commission should continue in its dual role as an investigative and promotional body provided that its promotional work was solely dictated by the need to eradicate racial discrimination. It warned the Commission that in making a public intervention in matters of controversy, it should bear in mind the risk that public confidence in it as an enforcement agency would be undermined by what may be seen to be partisan intervention in public debate.

Apart from making a number of recommendations in respect of management, staffing and research, it criticised the emphasis of the Commission in respect of investigations wanting a sharper focus.

> In future the Commission should take stock of its available staff resources before plunging into a major new investigation (para 59).

It added that the Commission should act more in the manner of other specialist law enforcement and advisory commissions and should shed some of its multifarious functions which had been taken on.

> ..by rushing ahead with promotion work unrelated to law enforcement, the Commission have put an unwieldy cart before an admittedly ponderous horse.. [18]

In Australia the Commonwealth Racial Discrimination Act of 1975 states that it is enacted pursuant to the need to give effect to the Convention on the Elimination of All Forms of Racial Discrimination of 1965 which forms the first schedule to the Act. The preamble to the Convention makes reference, inter alia, to the principles of dignity and equality in the UN Charter, the right to protection from discrimination and incitement, a condemnation of segregation, colonialism and apartheid as well as the 'false,.. unjust and dangerous' doctrines of racial superiority. It states that discrimination is an obstacle to peaceful and friendly relations between nations and is capable of disturbing the harmony of persons living side by side 'even within one and the same state.'

The references to colonialism, segregation and policies of apartheid may be of greater historical than contemporary significance and the preamble is more an invocation of goodness than a manifesto for its achievement. But given that Australia has passed municipal legislation in respect of equality on the grounds of race, gender and civil and political rights to implement its ratification of international conventions it may be unfair to suggest that the broad generalisations which inevitably underpin the these reflect domestic priorities. A usual starting place in searching for a legal expression of state priorities is the constitution.

The Commonwealth of Australia Constitution Act of 1900 has been amended on a number of occasions, the last of which (as at October 1993) was the Australia Act of 1986. However, despite the fact that most modern constitutions or those which have been updated, contain provisions relating to human rights, the Constitution of Australia is decidedly silent in this area. Chapter 5 of the constitution, dealing with the powers of the states, does provide under section 116 that the Commonwealth will not legislate in respect of religion and 117 provides that a subject of the Queen, resident in any state, shall not be subject in any other state to any disability or discrimination which would not be equally applicable to him if he were a subject of the Queen resident in such other states. It may also be worthy to note, at least in passing, that section 127 provided, until repealed in 1967, that Aborigines would not be counted in reckoning the population. Accordingly the formal recognition of Aborigines as members of the Australian population worthy of being counted, is of less than thirty years longevity.

Although evident in the Australian situation there may be a more general truth that the purposes of anti-discrimination law and the perceived role of the enforcement agency are better elucidated by reference to broader equal opportunity position statements than those reflected in constitutional provision. Two are exemplified.

In November 1993 the Human Rights and Equal Opportunity Commission, in response to a request from the Federal Government in 1992 prepared a report 'State of the Nation Report on People of non-English speaking Background' being the first of a series that would be presented on an annual basis. However, because the report was largely a position statement and descriptive as to the present circumstances of this section of the community, it did not provide a critique either of the effectiveness of the existing race discrimination provisions nor of the performance of the enforcement agency itself. While it noted the particular difficulties and needs of the community in respect of employment, the provision of English language training, the needs of the aged, youth, refugees and asylum seekers, its recommendations for action were remarkably thin. The report showed that there were marked disadvantages in the labour market for certain ethnic communities, especially the recently arrived ones who have a disproportionate number of young people seeking to establish themselves in the workforce. It also revealed that the endeavours of young people of non-English speaking background as shown by their school retention rates and entry into post-school education institutions were not being transformed into gains in the employment market.

This must lead to questions on whether there is some systemic discrimination on the grounds of race.

More optimistically the report commented that despite the astonishing diversity of Australia's population at this time there was remarkably little overt friction. Nonetheless there were worrying signs that some ethnic communities had not been able to establish themselves in an equitable fashion and there was a danger that a visibly different ethnic underclass might be developing. The report observed that the question of racism was not being addressed in any systematic way (page 255) although it acknowledged that there were a number of initiatives which had been taken at federal, state and local level to combat racism and an increasing awareness that community education campaigns needed to operate at many different levels: an effective programme required integrated strategies across all institutions, media access and equity provisions by all aspects of government and the active co-operation of unions, employers, churches and religious organisations. The report referred to the study by Price, 1993 'Ethnic Intermix in Australia' which indicated that 40 per cent of Australians will be the product of a *mixed marriage* (parents of different ethnic groups) by the year 2000. Charles Price had contended that, unlike the ethnic and racial strife in some multi-cultural societies such as Yugoslavia, USSR, India and elsewhere, these ethnic inter-marriage rates are a major insurance policy that multiculturalism will have a happy future in Australia. While that conclusion may demonstrate a particular view of what multiculturalism may mean (by implication it seems to be akin to an assimilationist norm in this context), it also demonstrates a not uncommon view of community development objectives.

15

A report 'Social Justice for Indigenous Australians, 1993-94' was published by the Minister for Aboriginal and Torres Strait Island Affairs (the Hon. Robert Tickner, MP) in 1993. The report observed that following on the High Court's judgment in the Mabo case, the debate on social justice, while recognising for the first time in Australian Law the realities of the occupation and possession of Aboriginal land before European colonisation, tended to be overshadowed by the potential impact of the judgment on land tenure. The designation by the United Nations of 1993 as the international year of the world's indigenous people had been strongly supported by Australia and many activities associated with the year had done much to increase knowledge and appreciation of the cultures, the problems and the aspirations of Aboriginal and Torres Strait Island people. The year 1992-93 was the first year of operation of most of the enlarged programmes flowing from the Commonwealth governments' response to the report of the Royal Commission into Aboriginal Deaths in Custody. That report, it was observed, had brought home to Australians as never before, the harshness and alienation that characterised daily life for so many Aboriginal and Torres Strait Island people.

Amendments to the Aboriginal and Torres Strait Island Commission Act 1989 further strengthened the role of the Commission. New bodies were also established in 1992-93, the Office of Indigenous Affairs within the Department of the Prime Minister and Cabinet, and the post of Social Justice Commissioner within the Human Rights and Equal Opportunity Commission. The 'State of the Nation Report on Aboriginal and Torres Strait Islanders' will be produced shortly by HREOC to mirror that on non-English speaking people of non-English speaking backgrounds and will include observations on the enjoyment and exercise of human rights by Aboriginal and Torres Strait Islanders in Australia. When that report is produced it may provide a better means of judgment with regard to the activities of the HREOC as an enforcement agency in respect of meeting such rights. However the Social Justice Report does refer to the development of training and information packages for community workers to assist Aboriginal and Torres Strait Island communities to address human rights abuse. There is a package of measures being promoted through ATSIC and other Aboriginal and Torres Strait Island networks.

The Report is a conscious attempt to bring together in one

document descriptions of the activities of all Commonwealth departments and agencies designed for, or of particular relevance to, the 'most disadvantaged of Australians', the Aboriginal and Torres Strait Islander peoples. In depicting the social, economic, cultural and historical setting for such policies and programmes and in identifying the resources allocated, it also claims to set a standard of accountability. In theory both reports provide the policy context within which the provisions of anti-discrimination law on the grounds of race and the relevant enforcement agencies operate. But for the purpose of comparison unless like reports are available in the countries concerned, an evaluation of the contextual reference points remains problematic.

Neither the State of the Nation Report nor the 'Social Justice' Report attempt an analysis of the performance of the Human Rights Commission as an enforcement agency, although clearly an self-critique is provided by the HREOC itself in its annual reports (see HREOC, 1993). Like most annual reports, however, the commentary is largely descriptive and, to a large extent, cannot make any claim to be critically evaluative.

The New Zealand Bill of Rights Act of 1990 requires by section 19 that other legislation is construed, where not contrary to its terms, consistently with the right to be free from discrimination in situations not covered by the anti-discrimination laws (Mai Chen, 1994: 464). This is of limited impact but from the year 2000 the Human Rights Act of 1993 will be able to override other statutes which have discriminatory provisions. The 1993 act is the most radical reform of New Zealand's anti-discrimination laws since the Human Rights Commission Act was passed in 1977; a Human Rights Commission Report to the Minister of Justice in 1987 recommended significant changes to the Human Rights Commission Act.

One of the aims of the Human Rights Act 1993 is to implement more fully the obligations of ICERD which New Zealand ratified in 1971. In its ninth periodic report to the Committee for the Elimination of All Forms of Racial Discrimination (CERD) dated 19 June 1990, the New Zealand Government expressed itself as being committed to the complete elimination of racial discrimination in all its forms.

The multi-racial and multi-ethnic composition of New Zealand society demands that no form of discrimination

17

based on colour, religion, race, ethnic or national origin be tolerated. New Zealand law specifically prohibits racial discrimination and there is strong and active government commitment to the promotion of racial harmony. Since July 1984 when the Labour Government assumed office, there has been a new impetus to raise and improve the status of the indigenous Maori people in New Zealand society. Emphasis has been placed on encouraging Maori economic development, educational advancement and the greater use of Maori language. There has also been a positive policy of appointing Maoris to positions on committees where they can represent the Maori point of view and influence policy.

The report went on to enunciate a number of principles associated with the Treaty of Waitangi. In respect of the Race Relations legislation the report observed:-

The Race Relations Act of 1971, as amended in 1977 and 1989, continues to provide the legal framework within which the obligations laid down in the Convention are observed in New Zealand. The provisions of the Race Relations Act operate within the same administrative framework as the Human Rights Commission Act 1977 which covers other forms of discrimination.

There have been two reviews of the law, the one on the Human Rights Commission Act and the other on the Race Relations Act which led eventually to the adoption of the Human Rights Act of 1993. While the special relationship of the Maori people to government policy and legislation to promote equality of opportunity emanates from their indigenous status, there may well be a danger that this focus detracts from the existence of racism against other minority groups (see Mai Chen, 1994). To some extent that priority, of promoting Maori aspirations before other minority groups, has been modified by the creation of a Ministry of Pacific Island Affairs from 1986 to promote the development of Pacific Island people in New Zealand in a way which recognises and reflects Pacific Island cultural values and aspirations and promotes their full participation in New Zealand's social cultural and economic life (ICERD, 1990).

According to the New Zealand Government, the Bill of Rights of

1990 was intended to serve three primary functions. The first was to provide a set of standards by which the government would be guided for the enacting of laws. It would thus provide a safeguard in that any departure from these principles would be apparent to all. Secondly, it would be an important step in New Zealand's evolution towards constitutional maturity. Thirdly, it would be a source of education in that it would provide inspiration about the importance of human rights and the values which underlie them. Both the Maori Council and a large majority of submissions received by the Justice and Law Reform Committee which considered the draft bill, opposed its entrenchment in part because it was seen to detract from the Treaty of Waitangi.

From the above discussion it appears to be commonly accepted that the law on anti-discrimination is but one facet of a necessary strategy to counteract racism and racial discrimination. But there is no explicit reference to the agency concerned being the lead institution in deployment and development of the broader strategy. The actual powers of the agency, however, may constitute an implicit pointer to where the agency is located within the broader scheme of things.

Agencies are likely to be involved in the following activities:-

a. The investigation of individual complaints
b. Strategic investigations [or pattern and practice or formal investigations] pursued on behalf of the agency
c. Promotional work : this might include 1. the issuance of guidance and codes of practice [statutory and non-statutory], 2. education and training, 3. networking and 4. research
d. The provision of advice to government on law and practice: this might include a critique of current anti-discrimination law: a commentary on the impact of existing legislation: a preview of proposed legislation: and advice on the impartiality or otherwise of the criminal or civil justice systems.

In the UK while the CRE has power to initiate its own formal investigations, we have noted how the Home Affairs Committee wished the CREs promotional activities to be firmly linked to enforcement and how it wished a narrower range of investigations to be pursued. In Australia the powers vary but the emphasis is on individual complaint based investigations frequently without accompanying power conferred on the agency to initiate its own strategic investigations. It is possible to construct a theoretical approach to complaint based investigations which, by class action, broad coverage, prioritisation and close contact with the communities affected, impact on strategic issues such as indirect and systemic discrimination, but the reality is different. With such limited resources devoted to complaint based investigations, the strategic impact is minuscule and is not aided by the vast geographical areas covered by a single jurisdiction.[19] In New Zealand the functions of the Complaints Division of the Human Rights Commission is set out in section 75 of the 1993 Act. This enables self initiated investigations where there appears to be a breach of the Act [subsection d] or, even if there is no apparent breach, there is suspicion of differential treatment on racial grounds [e]. Clearly the impact of the 1993 Act remains to be tested over time but if the New Zealand Courts follow the British in their construction of like provisions there is a danger that self-initiated investigations will be declared ultra-vires unless there are reasonable grounds to suspect a breach or differential impact. In the UK this has effectively stymied broad ranging investigations into named respondents where the source of information seeks non-disclosure although, in contrast to the position in New Zealand, the CRE has power to investigate 'for any purpose connected with the carrying out of its statutory duties' in respect of thematic inquiries in which there are no named respondents [s.48(1) of the 1976 Act]. Accordingly the strategic role of investigations in New Zealand may be limited.

## The conciliation process

In contrast with the situation in the UK, where the obligation to seek a conciliated settlement in the Race Relations Act 1968 was abandoned in the 1976 Act in respect of race discrimination, was never applied to gender discrimination and is not a feature of the Disability Discrimination Act 1995, in both Australia and New Zealand the law requires the relevant agencies to attempt, or at least to consider, conciliation. The New Zealand model requires the Conciliator [in the UK this was a Conciliation Committee] to form an opinion as to whether the complaint has substance and, if so, then to seek a settlement and an undertaking against repetition. According to the 1993 Annual Report of the Human Rights

Commission and the Office of the Race Relations Conciliator (1994: table 6), two thirds of the 142 race complaints were dealt with in the reporting year, suggesting an average conciliation time of not less than three months and possibly much longer.[20] According to that report 12% of those investigations established substance, in 9% the evidence was inadequate, in 26% no case was found and in 19% the investigation was discontinued. These percentages appear to compare with those of the UK where of 1,640 complaints those settled on terms in 1993 were 7% and those successful after a hearing were 6.3%, a total of 13.3% satisfactory formal resolutions for the complainant: but the former figures ignore those which were neither conciliated nor successful determined informally or before a tribunal.[21] What neither the official reports from New Zealand nor those aggregated from the Australian states show are the percentage success rates of all race cases settled in favour of the complainants by courts or tribunals after conciliation has failed.

There is, however, some criticism of the conciliation model. The final report of the Review of the Victorian legislation (Scrutiny of Acts and Regulations Committee, 1993:74) states that there are a number of problems if not with the model of conciliation then at least with the way it is working in practice identifying three major criticisms, some matters taking twelve months or more to settle, the perceived bias of the Commission in favour of the complainants and confidentiality inhibiting effective evaluation.

In New South Wales a major criticism of the Anti-discrimination Board's operation is the delay in investigating and conciliating a complaint[22] : in 1992/1993 64% of complaints were dealt with in nine months, the rest taking longer. But in the submission of the Board to the NSW Law Reform Commission's Review of the Anti-discrimination Act of 1977 (May,1994:190) one reason for delay was said to be the lack of resources. The advantages of the model were emphasised in response to :-

Question 206. The priority given to the process of conciliation irrespective of the grounds of discrimination is also seen as a problem...[In the case of racial discrimination] the process treats racism as an individual, personal act and overlooks the institutional racism which impacts profoundly on society.

Should conciliation continue to be given priority irrespective of the grounds of discrimination?

> The Board believes that the parties should continue to be given the opportunity to conciliate....regardless of the grounds of discrimination.

It should be noted, however, that in NSW s92(1) of the 1977 Act gives the President of the Board a discretion whether to conciliate and the complaint may thus be referred directly to the Tribunal without an attempt at conciliation. The Board suggests that direct reference should only be made with the complainant's agreement, apparently now standard practice but not a legislative requirement. The Board offered no observations to the question in respect of institutional racism. Moreover the Board were not concerned about their own neutrality in the process nor the lack of a defined procedure [190], the lack of legal representation [192], the power imbalance nor the lack of legal aid.

> Conciliation is an alternative method of dispute resolution and the philosophy is to allow [settlement of the complaint].. in as non-legalistic way as possible.[192]

From the above discussion, which itself is clearly illustrative and attempts no more than give a flavour of the kinds of debates which take place concerning the purposes and functions of such enforcement agencies, it is important to appreciate that purposes are distinguishable from functions which comprise, to a large extent, the means or mechanisms whereby the aims may be achieved. To that extent it is not inconsistent to have common stated objectives but very different mechanisms prescribed by legislation, including the power and competence of enforcement agencies by which the purposes are to be pursued. It is also a truism that the legislative definition of functions is one thing but the context in which it is placed, the operational style which is deployed and the emphasis and interpretation given to functions by the agency concerned may be responsible for shaping very different products.

The study by Mayhew (1968) of the Massachusetts Commission against Discrimination concluded that the Commission's function could not be interpreted strictly as law enforcement within well defined parameters but was more accurately depicted as a function of negotiation between opposing interests and pressures for the purpose of establishing compromises. It was apparent that the power exercised by the dominant norms which were challenged by the Civil Rights legislation, including those exercised in the job and housing markets and the values of elite administrators and judges, determined the acceptability of change to such an extent that civil rights groups felt frustrated by the methods of the Commission and came to view them all as a facade behind which the black minority were mislead into believing that the majority cared about them (Hepple, 1992: 28).

Accordingly it is not merely the legislation which is a product of compromise between the civil rights proponents and the power elites in opposition (Abrams, 1982: 15) but also the actual day to day functioning of the agencies established to secure its enforcement. With that understanding a statistical analysis of the extent to which any given enforcement agency receives, negotiates and concludes complaints, conducts formal investigations and promotes equal opportunities in the public, voluntary and private sectors, is likely to prove an inadequate pointer to the merits of the legislation by which the agency was established and the powers and methods it is enabled to deploy in the achievement of its objectives.

## Observations

There are significant methodological and analytical problems associated with drawing conclusions from the kind of crude comparison of enforcement agencies reflected in this book, even if the comparative position of ethnic minorities both in terms of population size and position in the particular social, economic and political dominant 'cultures' are taken into account and there is an assumption that the experience of discrimination on the grounds of sex, religion or disability share a common core  That does not challenge the legitimacy of making comparisons between the kinds of enforcement agencies employed in different jurisdictions and the relative success or failure of particular aspects of their function, while acknowledging that any conclusions can only be tentative and indicative.

This introduction does suggest, however, that one or two observations about such enforcement agencies can be made. Perhaps the most obvious is that the kind of agency created by Federal or State legislation does not reflect any objective assessment of aspirations and needs peculiar to the country or state in question although elements within the powers of the enforcement agency - such as the creation of an Aboriginal and Torres Strait Island Social Justice Commissioner - may do so. Consequently there appears to be a fair degree of arbitrariness in the decision to make an agency a single focus e.g. race or a multi-focus encompassing all aspects of discrimination: whether to make the agency single sphere e.g. covering only employment or only the public sector, or comprehensive: whether to oblige the agency to conciliate or not: whether to enable the agency to represent complainants or not and whether to charge the same agency with the responsibility for an adjudicative function. That observation does not preclude the view that particular forms of agency may be more suited to the needs of particular states than others, but merely that legislatures never bothered to assemble and analyse the evidence which would support that conclusion.

Secondly, while there may be some benefits in having a multiplicity of agencies in its provision or customer choice, the advantages of a one stop shop provided by the agency which deals with matters whether Federal or State and whether public or private, employment or housing, appears to outweigh the limited and marginal advantage of having more than one agency competent to provide advice in the pursuance of a complaint. Similarly, while we have only touched on the issue of networking, those enforcement agencies which do have established links with advisory bodies such as the Race Equality Councils, Neighbourhood Law Centres or the Aboriginal Legal Service may prove more successful not only in attracting different complaints but in providing necessary support to complainants during investigation.

Third, the obligation imposed on certain enforcement agencies to go through a process of conciliation before reference to a body for adjudication is more likely to cause unnecessary delay than when this competence is discretionary and not obligatory. Moreover the representation of the public interest to protect civil rights may appear under threat in some circumstances where conciliation appears to be the norm as it may conjure up concepts of negotiated compromise where this may be inappropriate.

In all jurisdictions there is a considerable amount of evidence to demonstrate that complainants are likely to initiate individual complaints from a weak power base: thus employees may be reluctant to challenge the authority of an employer because of the continuing reality of the power relationship even where a complaint is successfully pursued through the enforcement agency. It would, therefore, seem appropriate to explore whether privately negotiated conciliation safeguards the vulnerability of the complainant more effectively than the publicly adjudicated pronouncements of a tribunal or court.

Fourth, where conciliation fails or is deemed to be inappropriate, the traditional expectations of the system of justice would point to the requirement for there to be an independent body to which the matter is referred. It seems difficult to reconcile that principle with the powers of certain enforcement agencies such as the Human Rights and Equal Opportunity Commission in Australia to go on to adjudicate references when its own internal processes of conciliation have failed.

That said, it is clearly in keeping with this discussion of the power base of disadvantaged minorities both at an individual and at a group level that a specialist tribunal be established for determining such complaints. There are two major qualifications to that observation. Firstly, whatever tribunal is established it must have the power to impose an appropriate settlement within a reasonable period of time. Secondly, its authority must not be unreasonably curtailed by the countervailing adjudication of a mainstream appeal system. If we accept that discrimination is systemic, where is there evidence to suggest that it does not lie in the Courts of Appeal and the Supreme Courts? While it may be true that the Supreme Courts have protected human and civil rights, in few jurisdictions have their judgments been sensitive, informed and unchequered.

Fifth, the relationship between the enforcement responsibilities of regulatory agencies and their promotional activities is relatively unexplored and unresolved. While in the UK experience the Home Affairs Committee was highly critical of the Commission for Racial Equality because of its failure to link its promotional activity effectively with its enforcement powers, few would deny the legitimacy of the educative function of enforcement agencies. There must be value in the promotion of good practice guides provided they change practice. The question remains as to how best to achieve that objective.

Last, in evaluating the relative effectiveness of enforcement agencies, some consideration must be given to the debate over a human rights approach and the tension between the promotion of group and private rights. Because the statistical base of information is so ambiguous, there is little empirical evidence to suggest that a human rights approach is necessarily beneficial: there is an evident tension between the logic of rationalising approaches to discrimination under the unifying civil rights umbrella and the counter-advocacy of the advantage of specialisation and, perhaps of equal importance, the implicit hazard of marginalising the dominant concerns of discrimination on the grounds of race, gender and disability by their association with other significant but arguably less socially demanding concerns in respect of age, sexual orientation and, in dominantly secular societies, religious affiliation. The clear advantage of the civil rights approach is that it should be an effective mechanism for promoting a consistent philosophy towards civics - that while any decision is, by its nature, discriminatory, it should not be based on arbitrary criteria.

Traditionally, right wing governments have proved antipathetic to extending the role and impact of anti-discrimination law enforcement agencies, not infrequently suggesting that the supposed equity of the market place should not be encumbered with the distorting influence of regulation inhibiting genuine freedom of choice. But the truth is seldom that simple. Malcolm Cross (1993) in his critique of the Thatcher government's promotion of equal opportunity policies has demonstrated that equal opportunity at a structural level has been significantly undermined by the regulation imposed by central government on local authorities in their allocation of resources from whatever source. The cumulative impact on those urban authorities with the highest ethnic minority group concentrations in the UK has been to starve them of infrastructure resourcing and consequently undermined the various community development initiatives supported by the urban programme, partnership initiatives and projects associated with local economic regeneration. There appears to be a mind set to equality of opportunity which accepts the desirability of its formal delivery but denies the legitimacy of any holistic strategy delivering substantive and measurable improvement in the economic circumstances of minority groups. The best that an anti-discrimination law enforcement agency can achieve in such circumstances is to secure that economic disadvantage reflects that of class and socio-economic group which, despite its coincidence with racial origins, is not an unbreakable linkage in every particular.

If it is the nature of quangos and enforcement agencies not to be truly accountable to central government, it may be some compensation if they prove accountable, at least indirectly, to the

26

groups which they are designed to serve.

[1] See Street, H., Howe, G. and Bindman, G. (1967) 'Report on Anti-discrimination Legislation', the Home Office : London

[2] Much of the following discussion in this chapter is based on the material first published in the 'International Journal of Discrimination Law' vol.1 no.1, 1995, '

[3] See Thornton, M. (1990: 54)

[4] See generally MacEwen et al (1994) 'Anti-discrimination Law on the Grounds of Race: a Comparative Literature Survey of the provisions in Australia, New Zealand, Canada and the USA', CRE/SEMRU; London

[5] See OMA (1993)

[6] OEEO (1993) 'The Office of Equal Employment Opportunity Annual Report 1992-93' [p8], OEEO, Perth, Western Australia

[7] see CRE (1985)

[8] See McCrudden & Baldwin (1987:6)

[9] see Liverpool (CRE 1984a and 1989), Tower Hamlets (CRE 1988), Hackney (CRE 1984b)

[10] see CRE (1992) 'Second Review of Race Relations Act 1976'

[11] see Federal Race Discrimination Commission of Australia (1993)

[12] see MacEwen, M (1986), Banton, M (1985) [Promoting Racial Harmony, Cambridge University Press, Cambridge], Commission for Racial Equality (1988)

[13] PSI, (1991); MacEwen (1991)

[14] see McCrudden & Baldwin (1987:9)

[15] see critique of Commission of Racial Equality by Home Affairs Committee [HAC] in HMSO (1981)

[16] Fiss O. (1971) 'A Theory of Fair Employment Laws', 38 University of Chicago Law Review 235: see also Bell, D. (1992) 'An Allegorical Critique of the United States Civil Rights Model' in Hepple, B and Szyszczak, E. (1992) (Eds) 'Discrimination: the limits of the law', Mansell: London

[17] Hochschild, J (1984) 'The New American Dilemma', Newhaven, Yale University Press.

[18] see discussion in Baldwin and McCrudden 1987: 251 et seq.

[19] a point expanded on by Thornton (1990:158).

[20] The report does not state average times for conciliation; the four month average assumes that two thirds were dealt with within two months and one third within five, perhaps this is more generous than is warranted.

[21] From Table 1 (page 9) Commission for Racial Equality Annual Report 1993, (1994), CRE: London.

[22] See generally New South Wales Law Reform Commission Discussion Paper No. 30 'Review of the Anti-discrimination Act 1977' (NSW), February, 1993.

# 2 The role of the British Equal Opportunities Commission in combating sex discrimination

*Alice Leonard*

## The Equal Opportunities Commission

The EOC was created by the Sex Discrimination Act in 1976 with all-party support. Although it is funded entirely by Government, the statutory role means that the Commission is genuinely independent of Government.

Up to 15 Commissioners are appointed by the Minister for Employment. These Commissioners are women and men from different backgrounds who cover a broad spectrum of society.

The Commission employs 170 staff at its Headquarters in Manchester in small offices in Scotland and Wales, and a Press Office in London. Its budget is £6m: that is 1p per month per person resident in Great Britain.

The Commission has three statutory duties:

- To work towards the elimination of discrimination
- To promote equality of opportunity between men and women generally
- To keep under review the working of the Sex Discrimination Act and the Equal Pay Act, and to submit proposals for

amending both Acts to the Secretary of State when necessary.

The Commission uses its legal powers, its promotional work, and its research both strategically and comprehensively to carry out these duties.

*Legal  powers*

There are many ways in which the EOC aims can be achieved, but without doubt a strong legal base has been the significant and unique factor in enabling it to work towards achieving equal opportunities. It can:

- *Assist individuals:*  the EOC can advise individuals in taking claims of sex discrimination and equal pay to industrial tribunals on appeal.
- *Bring Judicial review proceedings*: the EOC can bring judicial review proceedings to challenge a decision or policy of a public authority.  One legal action can change the situation for many and, if properly targeted, can be extremely effective.
- *Conduct Formal investigations:*  the EOC also has the power to conduct formal investigations, either based on a specific belief that an employer is discriminating, or a more general review of a sector or type of service.  These can be very successful in generating changes in attitudes and practices.

*Promotional work*

The EOC uses its persuasive powers, often in co-operation with employers. It publishes good practice guidelines, sponsors conferences, and networks with employers.

*Research*

The EOC is well-known for its leading-edge research. It attempts to keep abreast of the issues, and also ahead of them! The EOC's innovative and forward-looking research provides a sturdy underpinning for its policy and legal work.

## The EOC's legal powers

*Advice and assistance to individual complaints*

The Sex Discrimination Act 1975, as amended, (SDA) gives the EOC the specific ability to advise, assist, and represent individuals who are contemplating, or are taking, sex discrimination and equal pay claims to the industrial tribunals and the county courts. The Commission is aware of the importance of this role, and devotes the time of approximately 30 casework staff and six in-house lawyers - as well as funds for legal representation by out-house solicitors and barristers - to this and related work.

The EOC recognises that, for most individuals, taking a discrimination claim can be daunting, and realises that they need:

- expert advise and guidance, easily available on the practical meaning of the law
- the ability to prepare a legal claim, obtain evidence, evaluate defences
- the ability to effectively present a claim to a tribunal or court
- financial support if legal representation is needed
- remedies which fully compensate them for the effect of the discrimination
- protection from victimisation

Individuals are advised by specialist units with knowledge of specific case law, precedent, and tribunal and court procedures relating to the individuals' specific complaint: pregnancy and maternity issues; equal pay issues; general employment issues (recruitment, promotion, dismissal, sexual harassment); pensions; education and training.

Initial advice to an individual includes information on the relevant law; whether they appear to have a good legal claim; the time limits for filing a claim; obtaining the necessary evidence; the relevant tribunal or court procedure; and the remedies available.

Individuals who wish to proceed to tribunal receive help with:

- *Obtaining evidence: the statutory questionnaire.* Knowing the importance of obtaining evidence to support a sex discrimination claim, Parliament established a questionnaire procedure (s74 of the SDA) whereby an individual can ask questions to his/her employer (or other potential respondent) to determine whether or not discrimination has occurred. It is a method for "pre-litigation discovery'. EOC staff have 'model' questions for each issue and tailor them specifically to an individual's case.

- *Preparing the application to the tribunal.* This application, called'the IT1' sets out the individual's claim. EOC staff advise on the proper way to state the claim, on the relevant information needed and the statutes to refer to,

- *Analysing the respondent's answer.* The 'IT3' states the employer's defence. When the individual complainant receives it, EOC staff will advise them on the case as a whole, in light of the information provided in the IT3 and in the response to the s74 questionnaire. At this point, the individual will often decide whether or not to proceed further with the claim, and whether to request full representation by the EOC.

This is done for all individuals who request this assistance: several hundreds each year. Where the EOC does not assist them further, it can provide specific guidance on progressing their case to the tribunal in the *Step by Step* Guide.

## EOC Legal Representation for Individuals

Even with its considerable resources, the EOC is not able to provide representation to every individual who requests it. To make the most of its resources, it has in recent years adopted criteria for those cases it will assist. There are two types of criteria :

*General criteria*, for example, cases likely to clarify important points of law or principle; cases likely to affect large numbers of people; cases likely to have maximum impact; cases likely to have potential for follow-up.

*Issued Based Criteria*, selected, for example, from among the following: pregnancy and maternity; equal pay/equal value; recruitment, promotion, dismissal; victimisation; remedies; hours of work/part-time work. These priorities change from time to time in accordance with employment trends and legal developments.

*Nature of Assistance*

The EOC can provide:

- full legal representation by a solicitor and/or barrister. The Commission takes cases in-house where there is a significant policy or legal issue on which the Commission has particular expertise or which the Commission wishes to keep under close control;
- a letter of advice on presenting the individual's case to the tribunal;
- a skeleton argument for the individual to present to the tribunal.
- any other form of assistance it deems suitable.

*The EOC's impact through individual cases*

EOC-assisted cases have been highly successful in bringing about change: both in employers' practices and in the law itself. 1995-96 was an illustrative year.

Fifty six cases were concluded, of which 6 (11%) were successful at the industrial tribunal; 8 (14%) were unsuccessful at tribunal; 42 (75%) were settled.

By comparison, in 1992 - 1994, only 46% of cases settled; so the percentage was much higher in 1995. This is likely to be due at least in part to the lifting of the compensation limit on sex discrimination cases after the ECJ decision in *Marshall v Southampton and South West Hampshire Area Health Authority (no.2), [1993] IRLR 445 (CA).*

Other results were:
- 65 applicants in the 56 cases received a total of £369,421 in compensation. The vast majority of this (£324,455) was from settled cases. There were only three cases of compensation awards by the tribunal (total £21,966) and a further two cases were successful at tribunal with total compensation of £23,000 agreed in subsequent settlements.
- There were changes to respondents' policies or practices in 30 of the 48 cases which were successful at tribunal or were settled. Interestingly, in only one instance was the change in policy or practice as a result of a case which went to a tribunal hearing; all

others resulted from cases which settled.

- Many of the cases which settled involved major employers: the Ministry of Defence, Abbey National Building Society, ICI Chemicals, The Crown Estate, The Home Office, Bellwoods Chartered Accountants, B & Q plc, and The Rugby Football Union, plus several county councils. The undertakings included respondents' agreements to:
  - adopt an equal opportunities or sexual harassment policy
  - have independent consultants review their payment systems
  - issue revisions of policy to all branches
  - implement a new pay policy based on the EOC's draft Code of Practice
  - issue a staff manual on sex discrimination, equal pay, and maternity-related issues
  - provide training for all managers on sex discrimination and equal pay issues
  - train all employees involved in recruitment in equal opportunities issues
  - introduce comprehensive non-discriminatory selection procedures
  - introduce a code of conduct for councillors and an effective complaints procedure.

In addition, several settled or successful cases put considerable pressure on respondents to make wider changes: the MOD's concession on *Hollingworth et al* ( Case 30076/94, Southampton Industrial Tribunal) that Article 119 applied to the Armed Forces made it virtually inevitable that the MOD would move to remove the Equal Pay Act exemption for servicemen and women, which it has now done in the Armed Forces Bill. The EAT decision in *Gillick v British Petroleum Chemicals Ltd (1993) IRLR 437* has helpfully clarified the applicability of s9 of the Sex Discrimination Act on contract workers, and the recommendations in *Hoare v The Home Office* (Case 20516/94, Manchester Industrial Tribuanal) should have significant impact on equal opportunities in the Prison Service.

*Access to Justice initiative*

25,000 people a year now contact the Commission for advice, many to ask for support to take legal proceedings. A string of successful high-profile discrimination cases has encouraged individuals to come forward with complaints of discrimination, as has the removal of the 'cap' on compensation for discrimination claims. Obviously, the Commission does not have the resources to assist every individual case, but without such support many individuals feel unable to go ahead on their own, daunted by the prospect of legal proceedings.

But there are few organisations who have the expertise to advise and represent applicants on sex discrimination cases, and many of these are under threat from inadequate funding. Legal aid is available to few. As a result, the EOC is facing ever-increasing demands for its services. For all of these reasons, it has launched a programme to transfer knowledge and expertise on discrimination issues out to individuals and to other organisations which can assist them. This programme includes:

- Helping individuals with self-help publications providing information and guidance. The EOC guide *How To Take Your Case to Industrial Tribunal,* is directed towards the individual, in clear and simple language, with illustrations from those types of claims which individuals can take by themselves. A new edition of the EOC's comprehensive casebook, *Towards Equality,* is of use to both individuals and advocates.
- Advisory and training agencies which can themselves advise and represent individuals. The EOC provides nationwide training sessions for law centres, advocates, solicitors and trade unionists, on sexual harassment, maternity rights, equal pay and indirect discrimination.
- Information packs on difficult issues. The Commission also publishes briefing notes and information on certain recurring issues, such as compensation levels, and statistics for certain claims of indirect discrimination.

*Major legal developments: the impact of European Community law*

In recent years, the EOC has had notable success in litigation by invoking European Community law, particularly Article 119 and the Equal Treatment and Equal Pay Directives. These instruments, drafted in broad terms to assume equal treatment of women and men in pay, and other aspects of access to employment, have been powerful tools in challenging restrictive provisions of domestic anti-discrimination law.

- *European Court judgment in the Marshall case.* 1994 finally saw the conclusion of the long-running case of Helen Marshall, in which the central issue was whether the upper limit on compensation for sex discrimination claims was in accordance with European Community law. After the industrial tribunal decision in Miss Marshall's favour, there were appeals, until the House of Lords referred this issue to the European Court of Justice. The ECJ decided emphatically in Miss Marshall's favour.

  It was then a matter for the UK Government to take steps to implement the European Court decision. The EOC was pleased that the Employment Department act quickly and decisively to fully implement the *Marshall* decision. The statutory maximum on compensation has now been abolished for both sex and race discrimination claims, and for claims of religious discrimination in Northern Ireland.

- *Increase in Tribunal Awards.* The removal of the limit has begun to take effect: award by tribunals are getting higher. Examples include:
  - an award of £36,000 to a purchase ledger supervisor, for a claim of victimisation and selection for redundancy;
  - an award of £28,000 to a sales account manager for her treatment after returning from maternity leave, and her ultimate dismissal;
  - an award of over £24,000 to a young woman for discriminatory refusal to offer her a job of apprentice car technician;
  - an award of £22,000 to a nursing assistant, for discrimination in retirement age.

These cases largely reflect compensation for lost wages, even where they have accumulated over a considerable period of time. But The EOC is also seeing quite substantial awards for injury to feelings: awards for £8,000 and more in sexual harassment cases, and awards for £4,000 and £5,000 in claims other than sexual harassment.

The EOC's message since *Marshall* is that the cost of discrimination is increasing, and that companies certainly need to take this seriously. To discriminate will now cost money and promote a negative image for employers. Employers now need to:
  - systematically assess existing employment policies, procedures and practices, to identify and remove elements of sex and/or

marriage discrimination.

- integrate equality into any new policy initiatives.

- devise comprehensive programmes to train supervisors and managers on legal requirements.

- ensure they have sensitive internal grievance procedures, so that complaints can be resolved at an early stage, to the satisfaction of aggrieved employees.

- *The MOD pregnancy dismissal cases.* Perhaps the most high-profile impact of *Marshall* has been on the pregnancy dismissal claims by ex-servicewomen against the Army, Navy and RAF. The history of these claims goes back to November 1991, to the EOC's judicial review proceedings challenging the MOD policy of discharging women when they became pregnant.

The challenge to the policy and to the exception of the Armed Forces from the Sex Discrimination Act were essentially conceded by the Ministry of Defence; and the Ministry agreed to compensate women who had been discharged on grounds of pregnancy back to 1978. Over 5,000 women applied for compensation, with about 2,000 filing tribunal claims. A network of 350 solicitors was formed to advise and represent these women, a fine example of the legal profession working in a co-ordinated way to help a large group of litigants.

Many of the service women waited until the ECJ gave its decision in *Marshall* before they settled their claims or went to tribunals and, because of the advantageous benefits of service in the armed forces and the substantial interest due they have received substantial awards of compensation. These claims represent a serious loss to the individuals involved, and the Commission is pleased that they have been appropriately compensated.

The EOC's strategic reasons for taking the cases at the outset were to challenge the exemption in the Sex Discrimination Act and to change the practice. This has been achieved: as a result of the judicial review, the several thousand women in the Armed Forces now have rights to maternity leave equivalent to those of women in civilian life. And the MOD is generally giving equal opportunities issues a much higher priority.

- *Compensation for indirect discrimination.* A second important impact of the *Marshall* decision is its impact on indirect discrimination claims. The Sex Discrimination Act provides that in cases of indirect discrimination, compensation may not be awarded unless the respondent intended to discriminate; a point notoriously difficult to prove.

The EOC had taken cases to challenge this provision - unsuccessfully, and it had also proposed to the Secretary of State that this restriction be removed - also unsuccessfully. But after a number of industrial tribunals in Great Britain and in Northern Ireland held that this provision was contrary to the Equal Treatment Directive, and contrary to the rationale of *Marshall*, the Government has introduced regulations which provide for compensation to be awarded for unintentional indirect discrimination where that is appropriate to adequately compensate an individual.

Complaints of indirect discrimination have been fairly infrequent in the past, no doubt in part because there was little possibility of financial compensation. The availability of compensation will be an encouragement to individuals with indirect discrimination claims.

- *P. v. S. and Cornwall County Council (1996) IRLR 437.* This was a ground-breaking case, raising the question whether discrimination against transsexuals come within the Sex Discrimination Act. P, while employed as a man, had been offered a renewed contract giving a substantial salary increase and other benefits. After he informed his employer of his intention to undergo a change of gender, the contract was not ratified. P alleged that her subsequent treatment and redundancy resulted directly from her gender change from male to female.

  The industrial tribunal held that a transsexual had no remedy under domestic legislation, but that the scope of the Equal Treatment Directive might be wider. This was because the Directive states that there should be no discrimination whatsoever 'on grounds of sex'. The tribunal referred this issue to the European Court of Justice, which held that P's claim did fall within the scope of the Directive.

  In a subsequent case, *R v C* (Case 60986/94, London South Industrial Tribunal), in which a transsexual claimed sex discrimination against a private sector employer, the industrial tribunal took the issue a step further holding that the Sex Discrimination Act itself, could be read to include a claim of discrimination against a transsexual, even where the Equal Treatment Directive itself was not directly applicable.

- *Judicial Review.* One of the most significant cases the EOC has ever taken was its judicial review against the Secretary of State for Employment of the thresholds for part-time workers' entitlement to redundancy pay and protection against unfair dismissal.

At the time, whereas full-time workers qualified for those benefits after 2 years' continuous employment, part-timers qualified only after 5 years, and those who worked less than 8 hours a week never gained entitlement, regardless of the years they worked. It was accepted by the parties and the court that these thresholds were indirectly discriminatory against women, as the great majority of those who work part-time (less than 16 hours a week) are women. The House of Lords ruled that the Government had failed to offer sufficient evidence to justify this discrimination, and that it was therefore unlawful. The Government's defence was based on economic grounds - that removal of the thresholds would reduce the availability of part-time work; and therefore of employment opportunities for women. The EOC's evidence was that the price of these basic employment protection rights for part-timers does not mean employers will not hire them. The judicial review was successful, and after the March 1994 judgment, the Government in 1995 equalised entitlement for part-time and full-time workers for all employment protection rights.

The House of Lords judgment was important for two reasons:

> First, it has served as the foundation for the equalisation of rights for part-timers. The UK now has 5 million part-time workers, over 80% of them women. Part-time work is seen as marginal and is frequently low status and low paid. A part-time worker is seen as dispensable, and so is valued less than the full-timer. The Commission believes that the judicial review is a major step in the process of equalisation of rights for part-timers. Subsequently it has urged employers to review the benefits and opportunities offered to their part-time employees, to ensure that they conform with the requirements of the law. The EOC itself has taken the matter further by issuing guidelines on the employment of part-time employees, 'Part-time workers, not second class citizens', which cover matters from pay and benefits to conditions of service.

Second, the House of Lords has clearly ruled that the EOC has the power to use judicial review to challenge sex discrimination in domestic legislation which is incompatible with European Community law. It held that as the enforcement body set up by Parliament to work towards the elimination of sex discrimination, the EOC has a sufficient interest to permit it to bring its own proceedings against the Secretary of State.

*Formal investigations*

The EOC's formal investigation powers have been used to great effect. The *Southern Derbyshire Health Authority* investigation was a prime example of an EOC formal investigation. A midwifery course for the non-clinically trained refused to offer places to women with family responsibilities, who were not allowed to apply until their children were of school age. The Commission found this was indirect discrimination and was unjustifiable. The FI was followed up with a questionnaire to all health authorities in England and Wales, the responses to which were produced in a booklet 'Equality Management in the National Health Service', which identified where improvements were needed. This contributed to the process of change in the NHS which has resulted in equal opportunities being pushed higher up the agenda and a blue print for action being produced. Today, the Department of Health is a leading Government department on equal opportunities for women, in both employment and service delivery.

In March 1995 the EOC published the report of its first ever investigation into the recruitment practices of an employment agency. A formal investigation into Yorkshire-based *Workforce Employment Agency Ltd* found that the agency had discriminated against both men and women following complaints to the EOC from men who had been refused jobs as packers because it was regarded as 'women's work'.

The growth in employment agencies in the last decade has been dramatic and there are now approximately 15,000 in Great Britain supplying 5 million workers a year into permanent and temporary jobs.

The EOC used the lessons learned in the Workforce Investigation to write guidance on how to stay within the law for job agencies and the people who use them. Free copies of the leaflet were sent out to every licensed jobs agency in Britain.

Since the investigation ended, the Federation of Recruitment and Employment Services, the largest representative body for the industry, has been working closely with the EOC to draw up a code of practice for members.


**Promotional and development work**

While it has its law enforcement powers, the EOC also has a very positive experience of working with employers. Two examples are the Equality Exchange and the Fair Play for Women initiative.

*EOC Equality Exchange*

The Equality Exchange is the forum and network which the EOC has established for employers and trainers, to accelerate the pace in the design and implementation of effective equal opportunities policies. With a membership of over five hundred, the Equality Exchange covers all major employment sectors and most geographical regions of England, Ireland Scotland and Wales. Its three main objectives are:

- to encourage and help employers exchange information and experience on the design and implementation of good practice in employment procedures;
- to ensure the effective delivery of the EOC's messages to the employment community;
- to provide a mechanism for the employment community to voice their concerns, and where appropriate, to influence national policy development in relation to sex equality.

The Equality Exchange uses various means to meet these aims, including an informative monthly mail shot to members, associated regional and sectoral networks, and conferences and training seminars on legal developments and other topical issues.

*Fair Play for Women*

In 1994 the EOC launched an important initiative in co-operation with the Secretary of State for Employment, the first ever joint Government-EOC partnership. The project brings together employers, voluntary organisations, local governments, TECs, and others, to promote equality of opportunity for women in economic and social life, at the regional level. The EOC is working with the Employment Department to promote 'Fair Play for Women' at work, in public appointments, in education and training, in enterprise, in the benefit system, under the law, in transport, as care providers, in health, in tackling crime, in sport, in the Civil Service, in public service employment and internationally.

For the EOC, a major objective is to improve the quantity and quality of women's participation the workforce and decision-making processes. This joint initiative with the Employment Department will help to remove obstacles to equality of opportunity, and to unleash the skills, talents, and creativity which are still too often fettered and constrained by traditional attitudes and stereotypes of both men and women.

## EOC research

The Commission is widely known and respected for its position at the leading edge of research on equal opportunities issues. Research is an important tool for the EOC in anticipating trends and developing well-founded policy proposals.

The important areas of recent research projects are:

- The economics of equal opportunities
- Double discrimination against ethnic minority women
- Gender and low pay

### The economics of equal opportunities

Increasingly, the Commission is met - both in policy discussions and in its legal cases - with the argument that equal opportunities involve costs to employers. It has recognised the need to develop further information in the area of 'the economics of equal opportunities' - to inform and stimulate a much-needed debate on the economic costs and benefits of gender equality: within the policy community, that is the political parties, employers, trade unions, economists, and also within the research community.

The Commission has now undertaken a substantial programme of work on the 'Economics of Equal Opportunities', commissioning over a dozen expert papers from economists and political scientists. Their topics ranged from an analysis of the shortcomings of traditional economic analysis in taking on a gender prospective, to far more specific analysis of the changing face of the labour market, with the increased casualisation and fragmentation of the workforce, and the implications for both social and economic policy.

This important research was published in 1995, and it has led to the commission defining 'the business case' for equal opportunities. The EOC argues that there is a very strong business case for equality, and is working with companies of all sizes to promote this message.

The EOC cost benefit analysis shows that the benefits of equality are:

- best use of human resources
- flexible workforce to aid restructuring
- Workforce representative of local community
- improved corporate image with potential employees and customers
- attract ethical investors
- managers integrate equality in corporate objective
- new business ideas from diverse workforce

The costs of inequality are:

- inefficiency in use of human resources
- inflexible workforce limiting organisational changes
- poor corporate image with prospective employees and customers
- management time on grievances and tribunal claims

The EOC has a strong tradition of working to help employers to promote equality. It continues to build on its partnerships with employers to identify and tackle new problems as they arise. The EOC is working to ensure that equality is built into new working patterns. A particular challenge for the EOC is to communicate its messages to small and medium sized employers who represent the biggest growth area of employment. For the EOC, the business case has always complemented the fundamental human right to equality. The EOC is finding that the combination of these arguments is proving to be a powerful lever in achieving equality between the sexes.

## Double discrimination: ethnic minority women

The issue of the phenomenon of 'double discrimination' against ethnic minority women falls between the remits for two different bodies: the EOC and the Commission for Racial Equality. It has been has recognised for some time that there was need for specific research on ethnic minority women, and the opportunity to undertake it arose after the 1991 Census, which was the first to collect comprehensive and accurate information on the ethnic composition of the UK population.

The EOC commissioned two separate pieces of research:

- A comprehensive analysis of black and ethnic minority women and the labour market, based on the 1991 Census, and
- A review of all known research on ethnic minority women in Britain.

The research - published in June 1994- showed that ethnic minority women do face 'double discrimination' in the workplace:

- Women from ethnic minorities face discrimination because of their gender and also discrimination because of their race. For example, they tend to be in the lower status jobs within occupations such as nursing and medicine. 'Double discrimination' may take the form of longer hours, lower pay, and poor working conditions.
- White women earn on average 20% less than white men, but women from ethnic minorities tend to earn up to 25% less again. Overall, ethnic minority women earn a staggering 63% less than the male weekly wage.
- Future job losses are predicted in urban areas where the majority of the ethnic minority population live, and in sectors which traditionally employ ethnic minority women -- the textile industries, manufacturing and catering.
- Ethnic minority women are twice as likely to be unemployed as white women.
- Many more ethnic minority women are unemployed despite

45

the fact that they are much more likely to continue in higher education after school-leaving-age than are white women, and they are therefore better qualified.

The EOC is making the important point that UK businesses are under-utilising ethnic minority women. Businesses are paying the price of not using a talented and well-educated potential workforce. British business has awakened to the commercial benefits of employing women, but appears to be extraordinarily slow in extending their equal opportunities policies towards ethnic minority women. Businesses would gain in effectiveness by employing a workforce which more accurately reflects the society in which we live.

The disadvantages experienced by black and ethnic minority women raise issues which the EOC cannot tackle alone. The EOC is now urging other agencies and other people to use the findings in its research reports to inform and develop their own solutions. The EOC will be working in partnership with the voluntary sector and in particular groups representing black and ethnic minority women, to take this work forward.

One specific way the Commission built on the research was in its 1994 edition of 'Women and Men in Britain'. 'Women and Men' is the EOC's annual publication with data on women and men and education, training, employment, etc. In 1994, the EOC teamed up with the CRE to publish data on gender and race: to produce a joint special edition of 'Women and Men' which reviewed the position of those women and men in Britain who may face double discrimination.

*Women and low pay*

The Commission has also published important new research on women and low pay. The research reveals that at least 4 million women in Britain are low paid -- over one-third of all female workers. It also shows that low pay is an issue central to the failure to achieve equality between the sexes.

The research identified several important causes of low pay:

- Lack of access to training and education, combined with gaps in employment and lack of affordable childcare;

- Concentration of women in low paid sectors of employment, low paid occupations, and the lowest levels of grade in industry;
- Different payment systems for men and women with shorter pay scales for women's jobs and less access to overtime, shift pay, bonuses, and performance related pay;
- Gender definitions of men and women's skills resulting in jobs with lower status and pay;
- The operation of the Income Tax and National Insurance systems, which encourage some employers to keep pay below contribution thresholds, leading to increased dependency on the state; and
- The absence of a statutory minimum wage.

Some of these are of course not surprising, but it is important to have established them soundly.

The Commission now has identified things which Government, employers, and trade unions can all do to address these problems:

- The Government should evaluate and address the disparate gender impact of the National Insurance and Tax systems and
- Ensure that equal pay legislation is effective and accessible.
- Employers should regularly review their pay structures to check they are not discriminatory, including auditing pay systems and job evaluation. They should re-evaluate job evaluation schemes to make them fair and free of sex bias.
- Employers should adopt positive attitudes towards equal opportunities for women, including equal access to training provision, more childcare facilities, and family-friendly policies.
- Trade unions should develop strategies to increase membership in non-unionised areas where low pay is prevalent, including membership of black and ethnic minority women.

**The challenge for the future**

Like all other Government-funded bodies, the EOC faces a considerable challenge in meeting continuously increasing demand for its services while facing little if any increase in its funding.

One way the Commission has responded is to set itself specific aims and objectives. It has defined its longer term aims: what it has called '13 milestones on the road to equality'. These are:

- simplified and accessible laws and procedures for those who complain of sex discrimination
- an effective mechanism in place to evaluate policy options and proposed legislation for any disproportionate impact on one sex
- an improved system of maternity rights and a national strategy to provide good quality, affordable childcare available to all
- an education and training system in which significant inequalities in access and opportunity have been eliminated
- a significant increase in the numbers of women in decision-making, particularly where they have traditionally been under-represented
- equal status for part-time workers; in statute, job contracts and in practice
- publication of all official statistics by gender and, where possible, ethnicity, age and disability
- a substantial decrease in the number of jobs segregated on the basis of sex
- continuing increases in the numbers of men sharing caring responsibilities and in the value society places on this work
- an expansion in statutory and contractual paternity, parental and family leave provision
- a substantial narrowing of the earnings gap between women and men
- structural changes to the state pension system to increase the numbers of women able to achieve a full entitlement in their own right
- reform of the social security system to meet more closely the future patterns of me's and women's working lives

It has also developed a Corporate Plan to the year 2000, which defines core tasks following from its statutory remit and recognises that the Commission's key audiences are Government, other politicians, policy makers, the public sector, the European institutions, the employment community and individuals.
These key audiences are being asked:

- to seek compliance with the law
- to provide guidance and information to individuals
- to promote and disseminate EOC policies on equal opportunities and equal treatment

- to produce authoritative and independent information on sex discrimination and equality of opportunity
- to campaign for equal opportunity and to increase public support on key sex equality issues.

The Commission sets annual plans for its work, defining the main targets - such as small and medium sized businesses, the benefits system, and the issue of job segregation, as well as development projects, for example on equal pay, multiple discrimination, and the changing world of work; and dissemination projects such as the Fair Play initiative and the Equality Exchange.

As it celebrates its 21st year in 1997, the Commission seeks to achieve the maximum effect in all it does. There has been tremendous progress on gender equality in the past twenty one years but the EOC recognises that it has to continue to use both the remedial and preventative approaches of its work towards achieving its statutory objectives of eliminating sex discrimination and promoting equality of opportunity between the sexes.

# 3 The Dutch experience of enforcement agencies: current issues in Dutch anti-discrimination law

*Peter R. Rodrigues*[1]

## Introduction

This chapter explores the experiences of enforcement agencies in the Netherlands in the legal battle against discrimination on the grounds of race. The author has focused here mainly on racial discrimination, so as to provide a more compact view of the current issues in Dutch anti-discrimination law, which are also relevant to discrimination on other grounds. In the Netherlands enforcement agencies against racial discrimination have been active for several years, although the history of organizations against gender discrimination goes further back. Another reason for this focus is the author's field of expertise: he worked for four years at the National Bureau against Racial Discrimination.

After a brief overview of Dutch law against racial discrimination and the Equal Treatment Act, the most important enforcement agencies are described.[2] Enforcement, means the law in action. This paper not only examines legal norms, but also the effectiveness of legal measures. Consequently the results of enforcement in criminal, administrative and civil law have to be compared. The roles of complaint boards and codes of conduct are also of importance. The complexity of enforcement will be illustrated with a case of cross-border racism. Conclusions are then drawn from this analysis.

50

## Anti-discrimination law

The provisions of 1971 in the Criminal Code constituted the first anti-discrimination legislation and were introduced implemet of the International Convention on Elimination of All Forms of Racial Discrimination (ICERD).[3] With the amendment of the Criminal Code in February 1992, these provisions were revisited and expanded. The Criminal Code penalizes racial insult, incitement to xenophobia and discrimination on grounds of race as well as publication and dissemination of these notions. It is also a criminal offence to take part in or to support, in any way, activities which discriminate against people on racial grounds or to exercise discrimination in the public service or in the practise of a profession or trade. The definition of discrimination can be found in Article 90quater of the Criminal Code. This definition repeats Article 1 ICERD. Direct discrimination (the intended objective) as well as indirect discrimination (the effect) is prohibited. The Supreme Court decided in 1976 that the term 'race' in Dutch criminal law had to be interpreted in accordance with the definition of Article 1 ICERD, so race also means colour, descent and national or ethnic origin.[4]

In 1983 the principle of equal treatment and non-discrimination was introduced into the first article of the Dutch Constitution. The significance of the principle of equal treatment is expressed in the first sentence: 'persons shall be treated equally in equal circumstances'. The preparatory work and explanatory memorandum indicate that a difference of treatment may be permitted on reasonable and objective grounds only.

The principle of non-discrimination in the second sentence of Article 1 prohibits distinctions made on grounds of religion, belief, political opinion, race[5], religion, sex, or any other ground. The Constitution applies only in cases between the government and civilians, and not in cases between civilians.

Until September 1994, there was no specific regulation in civil law to combat racial discrimination. The enforcement of the Equal Treatment Act (*Algemene Wet Gelijke Behandeling*) brought an end to that situation.[6] This Act will be discussed in paragraph 3 (see appendix I for the text). The absence of specific provisions on racial discrimination has resulted in the use of Article 162 Book 6 of the Civil Code on tort (unlawful act). The norms from the ICERD, art. 1 Constitution and the criminal legislation were used to interpret the general clause to tort or delict. The same has happened to general clauses in labour and contract law.

To encourage the recruitment of members of ethnic minority groups, employers have been required to submit annual reports on the number of ethnic minorities employed in their enterprise[7]. The reguirment was laid down in the Equal Employment Act (*Wet Bevordering Evenredige Arbeidsdeelname Allochtonen*), which came into force in July 1994, despite very strong opposition against the legal provisions from trade and industry.[8]

The purpose of the Act is to require individual employers to strive for equal representation of people from ethnic minorities within the workforce. The percentage of those from ethnic minority groups within a certain company are required to be equivalent to the percentage of ethnic minorities in the workforce of the region in question. The main provisions of the Act include: (a) a registration of individuals from ethnic minorities among the staff; (b) a written public report on the representation of ethnic minorities within the company's staff and; (c) a plan to improve participation of ethnic minorities on all staff levels. There is a penalty for failing to comply with the requirments of the Act.

**Equal Treatment Act**

The principle of equal treatment and non-discrimination works is the same fashion as human rights, in the relationship between the government and the individual. This is also true for art. 1 of the Constitution, that is not directly applicable in lawsuits between civilians. Nonetheless, human rights can have effect in the relations between individuals. This so-called horizontal effect is explaind in the Equal Treatment Act (*Algemene Wet Gelijke Behandeling*). The Act specifies the non-discrimination principle as laid down in the constitution for civil law relations. Its aim is to prevent discrimination on grounds of religion, belief, political opinion, race[9], sex, nationality, hetero- or homosexual preference or civil status in the following areas (Article 5-7):

* employment and professions (advertisement, selection procedure, commencement of an employment relationship, terms and conditions of employment including salary, on the job training, promotion and dismissal);

52

* supply of goods and services and the conclusion of agreements in the course of conducting business or exercising a profession, by the public service and institutions working in housing, welfare, health care, culture and education;
* public supply of goods and services and the conclusion of agreements concerning these matter by private persons;
* school and career advice.

The Act provides for only two penalties: standard terms that violate the Act are void (Article 9) and termination of an employment contract in defiance of the Act is also void (Article 8). The intention is to enable a party whose rights have been violated to initiate tort proceedings.

The legislation also provides for the establishment of a Equal Treatment Commission, vested with powers to investigate, mediate and judge. This body now provides victims of discrimination with an important avenue for redress (see the contribution of Golschmidt and Goncalves, chapter 7).

The Act explicitly prohibits direct and indirect discrimination, except in a number of specified cases in which unequal treatment is considered to be objectively justified.

Affirmative action on grounds of race and sex is permitted. However, religious, philosophical or political organizations are allowed to incorporate special requirements in their employment policies concerning the respective religious, philosophical or political beliefs of their employees if these beliefs constitute a genuine occupational qualification for a particular job.

The Act does not provide for a shift of the burden of proof and only solves few of the problems of victimization in employment cases.

Significantly, the Act does not cover all forms of discrimination. For example, incitement to racial hatred, scientific research and private clubs are not included. Possible discrimination in those areas still may be punished by tort procedure in civil law.


**Enforcement agencies**

At present there are about forty Anti-Discrimination Bureaux, spread throughout the Netherlands. These bureaux were either established by private initiative (e.g. action groups) or set up and subsidized by the local authorities. Most bureaux are formed by the cooperative efforts of action groups and local authorities. The services offered by these bureaux include handling cases of discrimination reported to them by victims and mediators, giving information on how to prevent racial discrimination, and conducting local research. They offer an easy-access for people who are victims of discrimination. The local network of Anti-Discrimination Bureaux, have a staff consisting primarily of volunteers, but sometimes including a professional. One of the problems is to provide sufficient expertise which enables local Anti-Discrimination Bureaux to play their role. The number of complaints handled annually by the forty Bureaux is about 2,000[10].

The National Institute against Racial Discrimination (LBR) is an independent organization funded by the Department of Justice. The general aim of the Institute is to prevent and combat all forms of racial discrimination in the Netherlands, using the available legal means. The institute priorities include discrimination on the labour market, housing and consumer and police affairs. The National Institute against Racial Discrimination maintains close contact with local lawyers, local organizations against racism and organizations of ethnic groups. Its activities include:

* conducting research on structural forms or patterns of racial discrimination;
* suporting the adoption of codes of conduct;
* advising the government on anti-discrimination legislation;
* training and advicing lawyers and workers of local Anti-Discrimination Bureaux;
* publishing its own bi-monthly magazine (LBR-Bulletin);
* initiating law-suits and test cases;
* providing aid to plaintiffs.

Numerous Dutch organizations work actively to prevent and combat racial discrimination, as well as to offer help to victims of it. In addition to the local Anti-Discrimination Bureaux, the Netherlands Centre for Immigrants (NCB), the Dutch Refugee Council, the Anne Frank Foundation and the Centre for Information and Documentation on Israel (CIDI) are the most important organizations.

Of the enforcement agencies, the Equal Treatment Commission plays the most significant role, mainly due to its legal basic and complaint procedure for victims. The contribution by Goldschmidt and Goncalves discusses the tasks and powers of the Commission in more detail (chapter 7).

One of the main problems facing enforcement agencies is how to keep a fine balance between maintaining an open dialogue with the government and the business community and serving as the mouthpiece for the agencies' grassroots. The role of action group come lobbyist, is difficult to play.

## Criminal, administrative or civil law?

In both common law and civil law countries, legal provisions against discrimination are found in criminal, administrative and civil law. Analysis of the effectiveness of legal measures, requires examination of the results of enforcement into the different areas' of law.[11]

In the Netherlands, the first anti-discrimination legislation was introduced in criminal law (1971). The different terms used in the description of crimes often leads to problems of interpretation and renders proof of discrimination very difficult. The revised articles of the Criminal Code have failed to change that. Victims of racial discrimination are often reluctant to file complaints because they lack confidence in the legal apparatus. The unpreparedness of the police and justice officials to act swiftly against discriminatory behaviour after complaints have been filed also plays a major role. This is one of the reasons that the number of sentences against violations of discrimination provisions of the criminal code is so low. To improve this situation, a new instruction to the Public Prosecutors and police officers was introduced in September 1993. This lays down procedures to be followed in cases of racial discrimination. The effectiveness of these instructions depends to a large extent on how familiar these officials are with them and how willing they are to implement them.

In this respect, it is significant that the Netherlands has been twice accused by Dutch plaintiffs concerning cases where the criminal proceeding failed on the bases of the ICERD individual complaint procedure.[12] In both cases, the ICERD Committee reprimanded the State. When the Netherlands signed and ratified ICERD (1972), the Dutch government could not have imagined that it would ever be the accused party in a ICERD procedure. Although seldom used,

ICERD could become an important tool to fill gaps in Dutch anti-discrimination policy. Although the criminal case load of discrimination cases increased from 60 in 1991 to 182 in 1993[13], the figures still reveal that the criminal procedure is not used often in the Netherlands. Recent research shows that in criminal cases, discrimination stands on the top of the list of acquittals: 27% during the years 1989-1993.[14] The average rate of acquittals in criminal cases is 4.5%. Those figures confirm the considerable ineffectiveness of anti-discrimination provisions in criminal law.

Administrative law is not often used to prevent racial discrimination. There is a provision that bars and restaurants can lose their liquor licence if they are convicted of racial discrimination in their service to the public. But in comon with experience in Australia, for example, this provision has yet to be applied.

The new Equal Employment Act is also an administrative measure. This Act requires employers of organisations with 35 or more employees to examine the extent to which their policies on appointment, promotion and dismissal as well as the terms of employment and working conditions obstruct the participation of individuals from ethnic minority groups. Employers are required to file a public report on the representation of ethnic minorities in their organization[15] and to take measures to remove the obstacles and to encourage the participation of the target group. These obligations are to be carried out through drawing up a plan with goals and targets, in consultation with the works council (a mandatory requirment for all large employers). Employers and governmental organizations have put up remarkable resistance to reporting the figures for ethnic minorities and fulfilling other requirments of the Act. One year after the Act went into force (July, 1995), this opposition lead to an almost collective refused to cooperate: only 1.8% of the employers had fulfilled the requirments. They prefer collective violation of the law to the risk of losing goodwill on the personal level. Of the 15 government ministries, only four provided the information in time. The fear of negative publicity may became a new tool for redress. If corporate or governmental accountability is too inadequate to protect equal rights, the most effective sanction is consumer pressure: the boycott.[16]

In civil law, the pursuer sits in the driver's seat. He initiates, organizes and plans the lawsuit. However the pursuer in civil lawsuits concerning discrimination faces four problems, three of which are very common: (a) the costs of the lawsuit; (b) the time it takes before a final decision is made and; (c) the inconveniences involved in taking a case to court. In addition to these three, the fear of victimization in discrimination cases is a major consideration in decisions to refrain from launching legal proceedings.

Advantages of civil law include the kinds of procedures available. An important instrument to eradicate racial discrimination is the summary proceedings *(kort geding)*.[17] The court is free to decide the shifting of the burden of proof is concerned and can pass judgement in a very short time.

Another commonly used instrument is group action. The right to sue for interest organizations was incorporated into Dutch legislation on July, 1994.[18] The Act gives a right of action to legal persons representing the interest of other individuals.

Article 305a Book 3 Civil Code provides for an association (vereniging) or foundation *(stichting)* to take legal action in civil suits to protect the interests of other persons, as far as these interests are in accordance with the association's or foundation's articles of incomparaties or estabishment.[19] No such right exists where the interests are too incongruous or if, considering the circumstances, the plaintiff has not conferred sufficiently with the defendant prior to starting the lawsuit.

The new provisions do not allow plaintiff association/foundation to seek monetary damages. If an individual person who was injured by a certain act does not wish this act be used to file a complaint, the act may not be used in a lawsuit. Furthermore, an individual may resist a ruling consisting of an order or prohibition. He or she is then not bound by this ruling.[20]

Regulations in civil law seems to be the most effective manner to combat discrimination. Probably, the best way to tackle the main obstacles blocking access to justice, is to combine civil law provisions and a non formal complaint procedure.

**Hard or soft law**

Analyses of case law shows that the use of complaint board procedures in discrimination cases is substantial. The advantage of those procedures is that they minimize the normal obstacles: costs, time and trouble. If the boards meet the standards of a decent complaint procedure (objective, hear both sides, fair play), it is a serious alternative to courts. Examples in the Netherlands are the Board for Journalism (*Raad voor de Journalistiek*), the Advertisement Code Board (*Reclame Code Commissie*) and the Ombudsman.

Another example is the self-regulation of the agencies for temporary work. After publication of the results of a research project into discriminatory practices of employment agencies for temporary work, a code of conduct for these employment agencies was drawn up by the Confederation of employment agencies for temporary work (*Algemene Bond Uitzendondernemingen*) in consultation with the National Bureau against Racial Discrimination[21]. This code contains directives for the staff of these agencies on equal treatment of all job seekers. Racial characteristics of job seekers are not to be registered and mediating services are to be refused when discriminatory, i.e. non function-related, requirements are imposed by an employer seeking a temporary worker.

Complaints of discrimination against the temporary employment agencies can be filed with the complaint board of the Confederation. In 1991 the Ministry for Social Affairs and Employment commissioned a study into the effectiveness of the code of conduct.

The report revealed that almost all of the agencies were aware of the existence of the code and all claimed to comply stictly with it. A practical test, however, revealed that 90% of the agencies still gave in to the discriminatory preferences of employers. The results of the research prompted a direct revision of the code, which went into force in February 1994 and a new training programme for employers in agencies for temporary work.

Codes of conduct are not themselves law, but they do set the standards by which individuals can be judged if they have to defend themselves in a lawsuit.[22] Even if the boards and codes are not often used, they can still help to enforce the non-discrimination norms, because people can appeal to it in conflict situations.

Codes can also be found in the following fields.

In November 1992, the Association of Insurers in the Netherlands (*Verbond Verzekeraars in Nederland*) issued a code of conduct to prevent discrimination in the entire insurance sector. Not just racial discrimination, but all kinds of discrimination are dealt with in the code of practice.

The association for employers and trade unions for the hotel, recreation and catering industry (*Bedrijfschap Horeca*) published a code of practice against racial discrimination for the sector. The code seeks to prevent and combat racial discrimination. Both the staffing policy as well as the sale of goods and services are dealt with in the code. The code is supposed to give clarity and (legal) certainty to the entrepreneurs, the employees, the guests and the clients with regards to the meaning of the legal requirments concerning racial discrimination in the hotel, recreation and catering industry. The code went into force in May 1993. Hardly any complaints have been filed, because the complaint board fails to meet the standards for a decent complaint procedure. The members of the complaint board, by example, are all representatives of the hotel, recreation or catering industry.

Dutch politicians have refrained for many years from making minority issues and immigration of party political concern. Unfortunately, this attitude has rebounded, since politicians occasionally discuss publicity ideas and statements on issues of immigration and minority policies which generate more and more public debate with racist overtones. Criticism of this tendency by minority and anti-discrimination organizations, prompted the introduction of a code of conduct for politicians and minorities in April 1993.

## Cross-border discrimination

The Verbeke case, a case of cross-border discrimination, illustrates the kind of problems that internationalization causes for enforcement organizations.[23] The defendant was Belgian and the plaintiffs were Dutch anti-discrimination organizations.[24] The dispute related to pamphlets which denied the holocaust ('the Auschwitz lie'), a 'view' held by so-called revisionists. The leaflets were being distributed by the defendant in Belgium who intended as large a dissemination as possible in the Dutch speaking countries. The papers ended up (unrequested) in the letter boxes of people with Jewish sounding names in various places in the Netherlands, including The Hague.

As this case was pending, the anti-discrimination provisions in the Belgian Criminal Code did not forbid denial of the Holocaust.[25] A civil suit was not an option, as experience had shown that courts had always ruled in favour of free of speech in anti-discrimination cases.

In June 1992, the anti-discrimination organizations filed a criminal complaint in the Netherlands. To prevent Verbeke from continuing to disseminate these pamphlets the plaintiffs started a group action under civil law based on the Brussels Convention of 1968. This Convention has a *forum delicti* provision, which provides court access for the place where the harmful event occurred.[26]

The plaintiffs launched summary proceedings to obtain an injunction on pain of a recognizance. The ruling was in favour of the plaintiffs in so far as the defendant was forbidden to distribute the pamphlets directly or indirectly in the Netherlands. He was also ordered to refrain from propagating revisionist views in the future in a manner offencive to the Jewish inhabitants of the Netherlands.[27]

Two years after the criminal complaint was lodged, the Dutch Public Prosecutor had taken no further action. The threat of an official complaint resulted in the response that nothing could be done, because of the inadequacy of Belgium's legislation.

The defendant had temporarily stopped disseminating revisionist leaflets. By the time the case came before the Court of Appeal in The Hague, Verbeke recommenced distributing revisionist materials in the Netherlands. On 16 June 1994, the Court of Appeal confirmed the prior ruling of 4 November 1992 by the district court in the civil case against Verbeke.

The Court of Appeal concluded that the manner in which Verbeke was denying the Holocaust was offencive in terms of private law. However, the court stated that this denial of the Holocaust was not a criminal offence, as were racist insult or incitement to xenophobia and discrimination. Neither the defendant, nor the plaintiffs appealed the ruling to the Supreme Court.

In the spring and summer of 1994, Verbeke was sending new revisionist documents such as like 'the Rudolf Expertise' to news papers and libraries. In the fall of 1994, he sent them to secondary schools. Despite the ruling of the Court of Appeal, the anti-discrimination organizations could not prevent this. After much public pressure and questions asked in the House, a criminal prosecution was finally launched. On 16 March 1995, Verbeke was convicted for his acts and suffered a penalty of 6,000 Dutch gilders and 6 months suspended imprisonment, with a probationary period of two years.

The Verbeke case cleary shows the differences between civil law and criminal law. It took two and a half years and intensive lobbying before the Public Prosecutor started prosecution. Especially in international law cases, the intervention of the own government is necessary, partially because enforcement of international law cases is complex, very costly and time consuming. Harmonization of the anti-discrimination law in the European Union appears to be necessary or racial activities can be based in the Member State which has the lowest dominator with respect to anti-discrimination law. The experience with the European legislation against sex discrimination has shown very clearly just how effective an instrument can be as a harmonizing Community Directive in forcing the pace of change, even among the most reluctant Member States.

## Concluding remarks

On a scale of effectiveness, civil law does have the highest score than administrative and criminal law, because the initiative to start and organize a procedure is left to the victim or persuer. The equal opportunities provisions in administrative and criminal law do have an impact, but are less important to enforcement agencies.

The effectiveness of civil law provisions depends not only on the norm, but also on procedural measures like the burden of proof, group actions and summary procedures. Group actions and summary procedures are well developed and useful redress tools in Dutch civil law and play an important role in the structural legal aid of enforcement agencies. If legal instruments are inadequate, the consumer boycott may provide an effective instrument to change the attitudes on equal rights.

The main problems involved in enforcing the anti-discrimination norm in civil law are fear of victimization, costs and the time and trouble of filing a lawsuit. Especially in cases where the victims have no financial interest, but an immaterial claim, enforcement is rare. The retrenchment of the government budget for legal aid also serves to obstruct access to justice.

Enforcement of anti-discrimination law would be optimum if civil law regulations provided for less formal complaint procedures for victims and their interest organizations. The new Equal Treatment Act (1994) provided for civil law procedures and complaint procedures handled by the Equal Treatment Commission. Banton was correct when he stated that the Equal Treatment Act will greatly improve protection against racial discrimination in Dutch law. However, much will depend on how the provisions, are applied.[28]

Anti-discrimination law should be combined with self-regulation (soft law). Codes of conduct implement the norm in a more practical way than law does. Moreover, complaint boards based on soft law, have a higher degree of acceptance because they are chosen more or less voluntarily. To be effective, the boards should meet the standards of a decent complaint procedure.

For victims the enforcement agencies are often the first step to start legal action. The agencies file criminal complaints, report cases to complaint boards or start civil procedures. More and more the agencies also find their way to the Equal Treatment Commission.

Besides complaints on behalf of victims, the case load of group actions is growing. The first experience with collective action to the Equal Treatment Commission seems to show that this measure is an important tool for the agencies.

Cross-border racial discrimination, i.e. discrimination transported from one State to another, suggests that the European Commission should develop a directive to harmonize anti-discrimination law in Member States of the European Community.[29] The European regulations and case law in the field of sex discrimination, makes it clear that the challange to discrimination contributes to the welfare in the Economic Union and should be expanded to discrimination on other grounds.

[1]Mr. Rodrigues is member of the Equal Treatment Commission and research fellow at the Molengraaff Institute for Private Law which is part of the Faculty of Law of the University of Utrecht in the Netherlands. This chapter is based on a contribution to the second Edinburgh International Symposium on Anti-discrimination Law and Enforcing Rights 11-12 September 1995.

[2]At the first SEMRU Edinburgh symposium -in 1993- Rodrigues gave an overview of Dutch law against racial discrimination, Racial Discrimination and the law in the Netherlands, *New Community* 1994, Vol. 20, no. 3, p. 381-391.

[3]See N. Lerner, *The U.N.Convention on the Elimination of all Forms of Racial Discrimination*, Sijthof en Noordhoff, Alphen aan den Rijn and Rockville, 1980 and also M. Banton, Discrimination, Open University Press, Buckingham, Philadelpia, 1994, p. 36-41.

[4]HR (Supreme Court) 15 June 1976, NJ (*Nederlandse Jurisprudentie* ) 1976, 551.

[5]Which should also be interpreted according to art. 1 ICERD.

[6]Heringa, *Algemene wet gelijke behandeling*, Kluwer, Deventer, 1994.

[7]See K.W.H. van Beek, *To be hired or not to be hired, the employer decides*, The relative changes of unemployed job-seekers on the Dutch labour market, Amsterdam, 1993 and F. Bovenkerk, M.J.I. Gras and D. Ramsoedh, *Discrimination against migrant workers and ethnic minorities in access to employment in the Netherlands*, International Labour Office, Geneva, 1994.

[8]Peter Rodrigues, *Kleurrijke kansen, Medezeggen -schapsorganen en de WBEAA*, Kort & Bondig, deel 5, FNV Centrum Ondernemingsraden, Amsterdam, 1994.

[9]The Equal Treatment Act also adheres to the ICERD with respect to the definition of the term 'race'.

[10]No. 1 are hate speeches like in pamphlets or written on walls or buildings (25%).

[11]A. Bocker, A Pyramid of complaints: the handling of complaints about racial discrimination in the Netherlands, *New Community*, 1991, Vol. 17, p. 603-616.

[12]Case of Yilmaz-Dogan versus the Netherlands, decision of 10 August 1988, Communication 1/1984 and Case of L.K. versus the Netherlands, decision of 19 March 1993, Communication no. 4/1991.

[13]Tweede Kamer (Second Chamber), 1992-1993, 22 800 hoofdstuk VI, no. 3, p. 81 and Tweede Kamer, 23.900 hoofdstuk VI, nr. 3, p. 52.

[14]Steeds meer strafzaken gaan door vrijspraak "over de kop", *Kwartaalbericht rechtbescherming en veiligheid* (CBS) 1994, nr. 4, p. 6-10.

[15]At the Chamber of Commerce.

[16]P.R. Rodrigues, *Consumer boycotts. New activism in the European Consumer Movement*, Group actions and consumer protection (Th. Bourgoignie ed.), Bruxelles, 1992, p. 319-327.

[17]J. ten Berge Koolen, *The (Ab)use of Summary Proceedings*, 8th World Conference on Procedural Law, Utrecht, 1987.

[18]Before July 1994 group actions were also possible based on judge made law.

[19]N. Frenk and E.H. Hondius, Collective Action in Consumer Affairs: Towards Law Reform in the Netherlands, *European Consumer Law Journal* 1991, no. 1, p. 17-34.

[20]Article 305b Civil Code provides the same rules for 'public' legal persons, such as product boards (*produktschap* ) and industrial boards (bedrijfschap) and municipalities.

[21]The research was done by the National Bureau against Racial Discrimination.

[22]M. Banton, *Discrimination*, Open University Press, Buckingham, Philadelphia, 1994, p. 64.

[23]see also Gerrit Betlem, *Civil liability for Transfrontier Pollution*, Dutch environmental tort law in international cases in the light of community law, Graham & Trotman/Martinus Nijhof, 1993, p. 125.

[24]The organizations are the National Bureau against Racial Discrimination, the Anne Frank Foundation and the Centre for Information and Documentation on Israel.

[25]A special provision is added and in force since March 14, 1995.

[26]Article 5 (3).

[27]Rb Den Haag 4 November 1992, KG 1992, 399; LBR-Bulletin 1992, no. 6, p. 19 note by Tazelaar; Migrantenrecht 1993, 13 note by Rodrigues: NJCM-Bulletin 1993, p. 303 note by Van der Neut.

[28]M. Banton, 1993, *An international dimension, Met het oog op de toekomst*, Tjeenk Willink, Zwolle, p. 12.

[29]Geoffrey Bindman (1994), How can EC law confront racism? *New Law Journal*, March 11, 1994, p. 352-353.

# 4 Disability discrimination and enforcement in Britain: future prospects

*Brian Doyle*[1]

## Introduction

The reputation and authority of disability discrimination laws (as with anti-discrimination legislation generally) rest very much upon how the law is enforced and what effective remedies are available for transgressions of its letter. The ultimate failure of the British disabled workers quota scheme in the Disabled Persons (Employment) Act 1944 might be largely explained by the inability of the authorities adequately to police and enforce the legislation, and the paltriness of such penalties as have been exacted from employers in breach.[2] The failure to provide disabled persons with an individual right of action to enforce their rights, such as they are, under the existing law, and the choice of the criminal justice system as the forum for executing the law, have both contributed to the resulting futility of the legislation.

The setting of a new agenda for disability employment rights in Britain via the Disability Discrimination Act 1995 must also address the manner in which (and the means by which) the new discrimination or equal opportunity legislation is to be enforced. This will in turn raise questions concerning institutional and individual enforcement strategies, the role of judicial enforcement and the appropriateness of remedies. In this chapter we look at the establishment of the National Disability Council under the new legislation and the rivals claims under the Civil Rights (Disabled Persons) Bill of a Disability Rights Commission with institutional powers to enforce, administer and implement new legal objectives.

## Institutional enforcement

From time to time, it has been suggested that the Equal Opportunities Commission (EOC) and Commission for Racial Equality (CRE) should be merged to produce one body responsible for the overview and enforcement of equal opportunities legislation.[3] The obvious parallels are with the Equal Employment Opportunities Commission (EEOC) in the US, or the human rights commissions and councils in Canada, or the anti-discrimination or equal opportunity boards, commissions and commissioners in Australia. Merger has been rightly resisted on the suspicion that it is merely a pretext for public expenditure cuts in the financing of anti-discrimination initiatives. Furthermore, both the EOC and CRE have been lukewarm to any proposals that disability discrimination law, if enacted in Britain, would become part of their individual portfolios.[4] Subsequently, disability rights activists themselves have seen the dangers that such recommendations would hold and that, in particular, disability would have to compete for attention and resources with other prohibited grounds in any grand anti-discrimination enforcement agency.[5] Attention has thus switched more recently to the establishment of a Disability Rights Commission as the centrepiece of a new disability rights statute.

## Civil Rights (Disabled Persons) Bill

Since 1982 there have been numerous attempts to introduce, by means of private members' bills, anti-discrimination legislation covering disabled persons. The enactment by the US Congress in July 1990 of the Americans with Disabilities Act gave British disability rights advocates renewed inspiration to attempt similar legislation in this country. In the 1991-92 session the first of many Civil Rights (Disabled Persons) Bills was presented, patently fashioned after the American model. For the first time, a comprehensive and carefully drafted proposal for disability discrimination legislation was before Parliament. Despite cross-party support the Bill and its successors has failed to progress.

## Disability Rights Commission

The proposal for the establishment of a Disability Rights Commission was at the heart of the Civil Rights (Disabled Persons) Bills and is the favoured strategic legal response of disability rights activists to disability-related discrimination.[6]

Such a Commission would be charged with a number of functions. First, it would work towards the elimination of disability-informed discrimination. Second, it would have powers to carry out general investigations to ensure that the new law was being complied with. Third, the Disability Rights Commission would investigate individual complaints of non-compliance with the law and provide a conciliation service in respect of such complaints. Fourth, it could provide assistance, including legal and financial assistance, to disabled persons seeking to enforce their new rights under the legislation. Fifth, the operation of the legislation would be kept under review and the Commission would be responsible for submitting proposals for statutory amendments. Sixth, the Disability Rights Commission would be responsible for publishing codes of practice directed at the requirements of the legislation.

The Disability Rights Commission, if it had been established, would have been made up of a number of Commissioners. Eight to 15 commissioners had been suggested as the appropriate number, with 4 commissioners holding a full-time appointment. There would have been a full-time chairman of the Commission (it has been suggested that he or she should be a person with a disability, as would be the deputy chairman). It was proposed that 75% of the seats on the Commission should be filled by disabled persons or their authorised representatives, and that Commissioners should hold office for up to 5 years, subject to reappointment. The Commission would be founded as a body corporate but would not be an emanation of the Crown. It would not be subject to Crown immunity nor would its staff be civil servants. However, the Commission would rely upon public funding for its activities, expenses and payroll. Furthermore, the Secretary of State would have to promulgate regulations to address the powers and procedures of the Commission when carrying out individual or general investigations, including the power to issue non-discrimination notices or to take cases of discrimination to the tribunals or courts. The Commission would be expected to report annually to the Secretary of State and to Parliament.

*What makes the Disability Rights Commission different?*

It will be readily recognised that the template for the suggested Disability Rights Commission is that provided by the EOC and the CRE.[7] However, there are two noticeable differences between the proposed model and its progenitors. First, unlike the CRE and EOC,[8] the proposed Disability Rights Commission would not be given express research and education functions. This omission might be more than purely accidental. The 1980s saw the calls for disability discrimination law met with the political response that more research was required to identify the incidence and experience of disability, while the preferred governmental approach to disability discrimination was a policy of education and persuasion. Disability rights activists were understandably suspicious of enshrining this strategy in law and were rightly concerned that the justiciability of these issues might be down-graded. However, not to give any new Commission here a research and education mandate appears short-sighted, whatever the tactical reasons for not so doing.

Second, and more significantly, there is no explicit legal requirement that the CRE and EOC should be constituted so as to represent an appropriate racial or gender mix of Commissioners, whereas disabled Commissioners are proposed to be in the majority on a Disability Rights Commission.[9] Given the symmetry of race and sex discrimination legislation, it would obviously send an undesired signal to employers if the EOC and CRE were to practice racial or sexual quotas or set-asides in their own constitutions. Disability discrimination law, on the other hand, would be asymmetrical and the same objection in principle could not be taken to the reservation of commissionerships for a pre-determined proportion of disabled persons. Furthermore, disabled persons, perhaps more keenly than women and ethnic minorities, have felt themselves to be commandeered by others (primarily the disability professions, charities, and organisations *for*, rather than *of*, disabled people) who have purported to speak on their behalf, and they would now seek a clear voice of their own. Moreover, it can be argued that first hand knowledge and experience of disability and disability discrimination are important qualifications for those who would shape the destiny of any new disability discrimination law.[10]

## Disability Discrimination Act 1995

The Civil Rights (Disabled Persons) Bill had little chance of becoming law and was effectively defeated once again in the 1994/95 parliamentary session. However, the Government's own Disability Discrimination Act reached the statute book in November 1995 and its employment discrimination provisions will come into force on 2 December 1996.[11] The Disability Discrimination Act is the most important civil rights measure in the UK for a generation. The parliamentary process has done much to transform what initially appeared to be a half-hearted measure and reluctant reform into a legal framework in which the rights of disabled persons to full social integration and equal participation may be pursued and achieved. The Act, although much strengthened, still falls short of the comprehensive and universal civil rights legislation demanded by disability rights activists and disabled citizens. Nevertheless, it deserves an opportunity to succeed or fail. Ultimately, the rights of disabled people in the UK will rely more upon society's willingness to observe the spirit, and not just the letter, of the legislative mandate.

### Legislative background

That a government measure addressing (although not fulfilling) the rights and aspirations of disabled persons to full participation in society should have completed the legislative process is remarkable in itself. Political recognition of the phenomenon of disability discrimination is of only recent vintage. Moreover, only two years ago the Prime Minister, Mr John Major, told the House of Commons: 'We have no plans to introduce generalised anti-discrimination legislation because we foresee problems in both approach and implementation'.[12] In May 1994, amid much recrimination and not for the first time, the Government defeated the private members' Civil Rights (Disabled Persons) Bill. Yet during the summer of 1994 the Government recanted and published a Green Paper proposing anti-discrimination legislation.[13]

Then in January 1995 the Minister for Disabled People set forth his proposals for law reform in the shape of a White Paper,[14] supported by a bill - the Disability Discrimination Bill.

Between the First Reading of the Bill in the House of Commons on 12 January 1995 and the Royal Assent on 8 November 1995 the Bill has been substantially revised. Indeed, its progress through the legislature has been an interesting case study in the law-making process. For much of the session, the Government's Bill was shadowed by the reintroduced private members' Civil Rights (Disabled Persons) Bill (hereafter the CRDP Bill), modelled closely after the United States' Americans with Disabilities Act 1990. During the Committee stage of the CRDP Bill in the House of Commons, the Minister was seen more in the role of an opposition spokesperson, tabling substantive amendments designed to test the principles and parameters of the Bill. Although the CPDP Bill has now been killed off, there can be little doubt that it has acted as a catalyst for change and improvement to the Disability Discrimination Bill (now the 1995 Act). Indeed, in the lower chamber, Opposition members waged a campaign consisting of a series of attempted amendments to the Government's Bill to make it more like the private members' Bill (the CRDP Bill). Little if anything was conceded by the Government in the form of substantive amendments to its Bill by this direct route, but the Opposition arguments did not fallen entirely upon deaf ears. While the Government did not accept the Opposition amendments, it did listen in part to the supporting arguments. This resulted in important concessions so as to include new (but ultimately disappointing) measures on disabled access to education and transport within the scope of the statute, as well as a narrowing of defences and some expansion of rights in Part II of the Act (the employment provisions).

*Weaknesses and lacunae*

Nevertheless, although the final version of the DDA 1995 is a much improved and strengthened response to the mischief of disability discrimination, there remains a number of lacunae and weaknesses that may undermine the efficacy of the new legislation when it comes to be tested in the arena of litigation. Concerns have been variously expressed, for example, about the 20 employee threshold for the operation of the employment provisions of the Act and about the role of costs in measuring the reasonableness of adjustments that must be made to accommodate the rights of disabled persons.[15] However, there are three burning issues that continue to be a cause of concern and which ultimately may determine the success or failure of the new law.

First, the definition of the protected class - who is a 'disabled person' and what is meant by 'disability' - remains problematic.[16] The Government intended that the Act should apply only to disabilities and disabled persons as commonly recognised and sought to avoid defining the protected class in a way that flies in the face of an easily understood and recognised commonsense definition. So a 'disabled person' is defined as 'a person who has [or had] a disability', while such a person is one who 'has a physical or mental impairment which has a substantial and long-term adverse effect on his ability to carry out normal day-to-day activities'. This is essentially a medical definition of disability and in contentious cases will call for expert medical evidence to establish the *locus standi* of a plaintiff to bring a complaint of disability-related discrimination. For many years, disability rights advocates and disabled individuals themselves have rejected the medical model of disability, preferring a social model of disability which emphasises the disabling effects of the social and physical environment rather than focuses upon impairment or medically recognised conditions.

Experience in other common law jurisdictions suggests that the definition of disability has to be a broad one. Employers and service providers might otherwise irrationally treat someone as being disabled, and make distinctions and discriminatory classifications accordingly, even though that person may not actually be disabled in a medical sense. This was recognised by the United States Supreme Court in the 1987 landmark decision of *School Board of Nassau County, Florida v. Arline*[17] where a teacher with a previous history of tuberculosis was treated as within the protection of civil rights law because, although she was not currently disabled by a medical condition, she had been discriminated against by an employer who had dealt with her on the basis of its perception of her previous record of illness. While the Government amended its Bill so as to include within the protection of the DDA 1995 individuals discriminated against because of 'past' disability, it steadfastly refused to extend the legislation to outlaw discrimination based upon a person's perceived or reputed status as disabled. As one of the purposes of anti-discrimination legislation is

71

to prevent life opportunities being determined on the basis of irrelevant or irrational criteria, this exclusion of perceived or reputed disability - an exclusion typically not countenanced in other countries with disability discrimination laws - is a disappointing loophole in the new protections to be afforded by the legislation.

Second, the definition of discrimination used in the Act is somewhat novel and untried. A person discriminates against a disabled person if, for a reason relating to disability, he treats the disabled person less favourably than he treats (or would treat) others to whom that reason does not (or would not) apply and the treatment in question is not *justified*. This is a hybrid definition which combines elements of the existing concepts of discrimination as understood in the context of race and gender discrimination law. In the Government's view, the definition is wide enough to encompass both direct and indirect forms of discrimination, but this is achieved at the price of including a justification defence which is not usually regarded as part of the *direct* (as opposed to *indirect)* discrimination formula. Although the Government revisited the defence of justification during the debates and, by amendment to the draft legislation, tightened up its application, discrimination lawyers and theorists will be watching the operation of this novel definition very closely. There is concern in some quarters that this experiment may harbinger the introduction of a justification defence to direct discrimination in race and gender discrimination legislation.

Third, the Disability Discrimination Act has been much criticised, both within and from outside Parliament, for its relatively weak enforcement strategy. The prosecution of the new rights afforded by the draft statute will depend upon the individual complainant. There is no provision for class actions nor for an enforcement agency with powers to aid, finance or pursue litigation in the way that the Equal Opportunities Commission and the Commission for Racial Equality are so enabled under the jurisdiction of sex and race discrimination statutes. The DDA 1995 contains only provision for an advisory body - the National Disability Council - and Opposition members consistently, but unsuccessfully, tried to amend the Bill so as to include a disability rights commission fashioned after the model provided by the EOC and CRE. The absence of a strong enforcement agency or strategic framework is likely to be particularly telling in respect of the employment provisions in Part II of the Act. Legal aid is not available in the industrial tribunals and yet many of the early precedents testing the scope and ambit of the new law are likely to arise in that forum. Unrepresented applicants in the industrial tribunals are at a noticeable disadvantage, despite the supposed informality of the administrative justice system, and that is likely to be a double disadvantage when account is taken of this new and complex legislation.

**National Disability Council**

Part VI of the Disability Discrimination Act 1995 deals with the establishment of a National Disability Council (NDC) and related issues.[18] A separate Northern Ireland Disability Council (NIDC) is also established by the Act.[19] The Council is to be a body corporate. It is not to be treated as a servant or agent of the Crown and does not enjoy any status, immunity or privilege of the Crown. The Council has the power to regulate its own procedure, including the power to determine its own quorum.

*Membership of the National Disability Council*

The NDC will consist of a minimum of 10 members and a maximum of 20 members, including a chairman and deputy chairman. Council members are to be appointed by the Secretary of State, as is the chairman and deputy chairman of the Council, both of whom are members of the Council.[20] Council members are to be appointed from among persons who, in the opinion of the Secretary of State, satisfy one of the following criteria:

(a) they are persons who have knowledge or experience of the needs of disabled persons or the needs of a particular group or groups of disabled persons;
(b) they are persons who have knowledge or experience of the needs of persons who have had a disability or the needs of a particular group or groups of such persons;
(c) they are persons who are members or representatives of professional bodies or bodies which represent industry or other business interests.

The Secretary of State is to be obliged to consult such persons as he or she considers appropriate before appointing a Council member.

73

This does not explicitly include organisations of and for disabled persons, although the Minister of Disabled People has given such an assurance.[21] It is also anticipated that the Council will be representative of the regions, of women and of ethnic minorities.

It is intended that the power of appointment will be used to 'try to secure that at all times at least half' the Council members consist of disabled persons, persons who have had a disability or the parents or guardians of disabled persons.[22] During the passage of the Act unsuccessful attempts were made to raise this proportion from a half to three-quarters. The Minister for Disabled People has indicated that half the Council seats will be set aside for disabled persons or their representatives, but that the functioning of the Council should not become unconstitutional simply because of a temporary imbalance in membership proportions caused by an unforeseen resignation and hence the word 'try' in the sub-section.[23]

The term of office of a Council member shall not exceed five years, but otherwise a member shall hold and vacate office in accordance with the terms of his or her appointment, subject to a right to resign office by written notice to the Secretary of State. There is nothing to prevent a member from serving more than one term of appointment on the Council, whether consecutively or after an interruption of service. Regulations may provide for the removal of a member from office by the Secretary of State in prescribed circumstances.[24]

The Act intends that Council members should be remunerated while in office and it provides that, subject to the approval of the Treasury, the Secretary of State may pay such remuneration or expenses to any member of the Council as is considered appropriate.[25] The DDA 1995 also provides for appropriate staffing of the Council.

*Duties and functions of the National Disability Council*

The primary duty of the Council will be to advise the Secretary of State on its on initiative or at the request of the Secretary of State on the following matters:

(a) matters relevant to the elimination of discrimination against disabled persons and persons who have had a disability;

(b) measures which are likely to reduce or eliminate such discrimination;

(c) matters related to the operation of the Act or of provisions made under the Act (i.e. regulations, codes of practice and guidance).[26]

The Secretary of State may by order confer additional functions on the Council, but this will not include any functions with respect to the investigation of complaints which may be the subject of proceedings under the new legislation. This distinguishes the NDC from the EOC and the CRE. It is clear that the Council is a purely advisory body, enabled only to make recommendations in respect of the matters or measures listed above.

The Council's power to give advice on its own initiative on matters relevant to the elimination of disability discrimination, or measures likely to reduce or eliminate such discrimination, does not include a power to give advice in respect of any matter relating to the operation of provisions of or arrangements made under the Disabled Persons (Employment) Acts 1944-1958 or other employment legislation. The Council is also not empowered to give advice on its own initiative on matters related to the operation of the 1995 Act or of provisions made under it in so far as those matters or provisions arise under Part II of the Act (discrimination in the employment field). The NDC also has no independent power to proffer advice in respect of codes of practice to be prepared by the Secretary of State,[27] or the form and content of the proposed statutory discrimination questionnaire in employment cases,[28] or in respect of arrangements for the provision of supported employment.

However, all these restrictions on the Council's power to give advice on its own initiative will not have effect at any time when there is in existence neither the National Advisory Council on the Employment of Disabled People (NACEDP)[29] nor any person appointed by the Secretary of State under the Act to advise or assist him or her in generally connection with matters relating to the employment of disabled persons and persons who have had a disability.[30] Their responsibilities would then pass automatically to the NDC. The intention of these restrictions, therefore, is to ensure separate spheres of responsibility between the NDC and pre-existing advisory bodies, and to avoid duplication between the work of the NDC and the NACEDP. The Minister for Disabled People has opined that the NDC would not 'be precluded from considering the adequacy of anti-discrimination provisions in employment where that is appropriate as an aspect of its broad overview of anti-discr mination measures.'[31]

The Council is further limited in discharging its primary duties under the Act by a provision which ensures that, in carrying out its duties above, the Council must have particular regard to the extent and nature of the benefits which would be likely to result from the implementation of any recommendations which it makes. Moreover, it must also consider the likely cost of implementing any such recommendations. To that extent, the Council is required when making recommendations, if reasonably practicable, to assess the likely cost of implementation and the likely financial benefits which would result from the implementation of its recommendations.

In exercising its primary advisory functions, and before giving the Secretary of State advice on any matter, the Council is obliged to consult and have regard to any representations made to it as a result of such consultations. There would appear to be nothing to prevent the Council from consulting widely. Indeed, the Act expects the Council to consult with such persons as it considers appropriate. However, the DDA 1995 also requires the Council to consult with any body:

(a) established by any enactment for the purpose of giving advice in relation to disability or any aspect of disability;
(b) established by a Minister for the purpose of giving advice in relation to disability or any aspect of disability;
(c) having functions in relation to the matter to which the advice relates.

This will include specialist bodies such as the NACEDP, the Disabled Persons Transport Advisory Committee and the Health and Safety Commission. It may include (although this is not made explicit) voluntary organisations of and for disabled persons.

Apart from its primary duties and functions adumbrated above, the Council also has a duty, when asked to do so by the Secretary of State, to prepare proposals for a code of practice dealing with matters referred to it by the Secretary of State.[32] In similar circumstances, it may be asked to review a code of practice and, if it considers it appropriate, propose alterations to the code. The Council does not have the power to issue codes of practice of its own initiative. It merely has the power to prepare or to review them when asked to do so by the Secretary of State. The power to issue codes of practice is vested in the Secretary of State, although the Council might suggest to the Secretary of State that he or she instruct it to prepare a code of practice where it has identified such a need. Where the Council has been involved in the preparation or review of codes of practice, the Secretary of State *may* issue those codes of practice in response to the Council's proposals.

## Annual reports

The NDC must make an annual report to the Secretary of State as soon as is practicable after the end of each financial year. The annual report is designed to inform the Secretary of State as to the Council's activities during the preceding financial year. The annual report is to be laid before Parliament and it is anticipated that the report will be published and available in the public domain. It is the Government's intention that the Council should publish its annual report in formats accessible to persons with various disabilities and the Government has suggested that the annual report might be made available in signed and sub-titled video format, audio cassette and Braille.[33] In any event, the Council will be subject to the provisions of Part III of the Act and, as a provider of goods, facilities or services, would be legally obliged to produce the report in alternative formats as far as reasonably possible.

## Supplementary powers of the Council

The Act anticipates that the Council may be granted additional powers or functions in the future. The Secretary of State is empowered to make supplementary regulations to address further provisions. These include the providing of information by the Secretary of State to the Council and the commissioning of research to be undertaken on behalf of the Council.[34] The regulations may also provide as to the circumstances in which and the conditions subject to which the Council may appoint advisers.[35]

## Concluding remarks

Whatever body is charged with responsibility for disability discrimination law, one of its central functions will involve it in investigations of compliance and non-compliance with the legislation. The power to conduct formal investigations into suspected discriminatory activities of individuals or enterprises has been, at least on paper, an important weapon in the armoury of institutional enforcement.[36] However, in practice, both the EOC and CRE have been hidebound in the pursuit of formal investigations and subjected to judicial control that has blunted the edge of this weapon.[37] In turn, this has diminished the role of non-discrimination notices, issued as a result of a formal investigation, addressed to named parties, and requiring them to discontinue identified discriminatory acts or practices.[38] Moreover, little (if any) use has been made of the Commissions' powers to seek injunctive relief against persistent discrimination.[39] Consequently, the burden of the EOC and CRE's main efforts in the enforcement area has been limited to assisting individual complainants (although, importantly, including advice and legal representation).[40]

It is clear that the NDC is not a sibling of the EOC or the CRE. It is a purely advisory body with a limited remit and no powers of enforcement.[41] In particular, unlike the pre-existing Commissions, the Council lacks the power to provide assistance to complainants, to conduct formal investigations into suspected acts or patterns of discrimination or to bring proceedings to enforce the Act on behalf of complainants or in its own name. It also wants for a general power to monitor and review the operation of the legislation. Nevertheless, when empowering a new Disability Rights Commission (or re-empowering the National Disability Council at some future date), account must be taken of the experience of the CRE and EOC and of the limitations placed upon their authority by judicial control.

In the final analysis, carefully drafted discrimination statutes are often only as good as their procedural and remedial frameworks allow them to be, however far-sighted their substantive provisions might be. The ability of disabled persons to challenge incidents and patterns of disability-informed discrimination rests entirely upon those parts of discrimination legislation that provide a cause of action, a route to litigation and an array of enforceable responses to identified unlawful actions, policies or practices. The law's emphasis upon the individual-based complaint process of the British SDA 1975 and RRA 1976 is often blamed for the alleged failure of the legislation to root out systematic and institutionalised discrimination. The want of formal class action procedures in this country also leads to a failure to learn the lessons of discriminatory episodes beyond the confines of the individual case. The treatment of discrimination complaints in isolation, and as being limited to their peculiar circumstances, frequently results in the repetition of unlawful behaviour and the consolidation, rather than demolition, of discriminatory policies and practices. It is unlikely that the new disability-focused anti-discrimination law in Britain will have learnt those lessons.

[1] Professor of Law, Faculty of Law, University of Liverpool. This paper draws from Doyle, *Disability, Discrimination and Equal Opportunities: A Comparative Study of the Employment Rights of Disabled Persons* (1995: London: Mansell Publishing Ltd) and Doyle, *Disability Discrimination: The New Law* (1996: Bristol: Jordan Publishing Ltd).

[2] See, most recently: House of Commons Employment Committee, *The Operation of the Disabled Persons (Employment Act 1944* (HC Paper 389) (1995: London: HMSO).

[3] See for example: House of Commons Employment Committee, *Recruitment Practices: Volume 2: Minutes of Evidence, Appendices and Index* (2nd Report, Session 1990-91: HC Paper 176-II) (1991: London: HMSO) at Q627.

[4] See for example: House of Commons Employment Committee, *The Work of the Equal Opportunities Commission: Minutes of Evidence* (Session 1989-90: HC Paper 364-i) (1990: London: HMSO) at QQ87-92.

[5] See in particular oral evidence given to the House of Commons Employment Committee in *Disability and Employment* (1st Report: Session 1990-91: HC Paper 35) (1990: London: HMSO) at 57-58. Prior to the enactment of the (Northern Ireland) Fair Employment Act 1989, it was suggested that omnibus discrimination legislation, encompassing race, sex, religious conviction and disability, might be adopted in the province, necessitating a merged enforcement agency: Department of Economic Development, *Equality of Opportunity in Employment in Northern Ireland: Future Strategy Options: A Consultation Paper* (1986: Belfast: HMSO). This did not meet with universal approval and did not subsequently feature in the pre-legislative proposals. See the slightly more sympathetic response of the Standing Advisory Commission on Human Rights, *Religious and Political Discrimination and Equality of Opportunity in Northern Ireland: Second Report* (Cm 1107) (1990: London: HMSO) at 74-75.

[6] This has been an essential part of many of the private members' bills of recent years and, in particular, of the recent CRDP Bills. The account below draws, in particular, from the latest versions of those bills without citing individual clauses, so as to avoid confusing references to what is only draft legislation.

[7] See generally SDA 1975 Part VI and Sch 3; RRA 1976 Part VII and Sch 1.

[8] See SDA 1975 s 54; RRA 1976 s 45.

[9] This proposal does not appear to be modelled upon any similar provision in comparative disability discrimination laws elsewhere. In Australia and Canada, disability is part of omnibus discrimination legislation and the human rights commissions and anti-discrimination boards in these countries are not legally required to be representative of the groups for whose protection the law operates. The recent establishment of a federal Disability Commissioner in the Australian Commonwealth does not include disability as part of the job specification: (Commonwealth) Disability Discrimination Act 1992 Part 6. In the US, although disability legislation is separately enacted, it is enforced by the EEOC, which is simultaneously charged with responsibility for civil rights law generally.

[10] This argument, as applicable to race and sex, is implicitly recognised in the actual make-up of the CRE and EOC.

[11] At the time of writing, the commencement order has not been laid, but the Government's intentions were announced on 6 June 1996 in Department for Education and Employment Press Release 185/96. See also: Disability Discrimination Act 1995 (Commencement No. 1) Order 1995 (1995 S.I. No. 3330) and Disability Discrimination Act 1995 (Commencement No. 2) Order 1996 (1996 S.I. No. 1336). The employment provisions of the Act are supplemented by the Disability Discrimination (Employment) Regulations 1996 (1996 S.I. 1456) and the *Code of Practice for the Elimination of Discrimination in the Field of Employment against Disabled Persons or Persons Who Have Had a Disability* (1996).

[12] HC Deb Vol 217 col 485 (22 January 1993).

[13] *A Consultation on Government Measures to Tackle Discrimination Against Disabled People* (1994: London: Department of Social Security).

[14] *Ending Discrimination Against Disabled People* (Cm 2729) (1995: London: HMSO).

[15] See generally: Doyle, *Disability Discrimination: The New Law* (1996: Bristol: Jordan Publishing Ltd).

[16] Disability Discrimination Act 1995 ss 1-3 and Schedules 1-2; Disability Discrimination (Meaning of Disability) Regulations 1996 (1996 S.I. No. 1455); *Guidance on Matters to be Taken into Account in Determining Questions Relating to the Definition of Disability* (1996).

[17] (1987) 480 US 273.

[18] See in particular: DDA 1995 s 50 and Sch 5. The NDC was effectively established on 1 January 1996 by virtue of Disability Discrimination Act 1995 (Commencement No. 1) Order 1995 (1995 S.I. 3330) reg 2. See further: National Disability Council Regulations 1996 (1996 S.I. No. 11) and National Disability Council (No. 2) Regulations 1996 (1996 S.I. No. 1410).

[19] DDA 1995 Sch 8 paras 33 and 52.

[20] The first Chairman of the NDC is David Grayson of Business in the Community.

[21] HC Deb Standing Committee E col 404: Mr. W. Hague.

[22] The NDC has been initially established with 16 council members (plus the Chairman of the NIDC). Of the 16 council members, 9 are either a disabled person or the parent or guardian of a person with disabilities. Nine members are drawn from organisations of or for disabled people, 5 from commerce or industry, 1 from the trade union movement and 1 from public service.

[23] HC Deb Standing Committee E col 403: Mr. W. Hague.

[24] See National Disability Council Regulations 1996 (1996 S.I. No. 11) reg 2 (in force on 29 January 1996).

[25] Provision for the payment of the expenses of the NDC is made by the National Disability Council Regulations 1996 (1996 S.I. No. 11) reg 3 (in force on 29 January 1996).

[26] Among the NDC's first acts was to issue a consultation package on proposals for a code of practice about rights of access to goods, facilities, services and property under the Act. This was issued in March 1996 in tandem with the Government's consultation documents on regulations relating to the initial rights of access to goods, facilities and services, and on the timetable for implementing the remaining non-employment provisions. The consultation period has resulted in the *Code of Practice on Rights of Access to Goods, Facilities, Services and Premises* (1996).

[27] Under DDA 1995 ss 53-54.

[28] DDA 1995 s 56.

[29] Established under Disabled Persons (Employment) Act 1944 s 17(1)(a). The existence, remit and constitution of the NACEDP is to be reviewed by the Government in 1997.

[30] Under DDA 1995 s 60.

[31] HC Deb Standing Committee E col 397: Mr. W. Hague.

[32] Under DDA 1995 ss 51-52 which came into force on 1 January 1996 by virtue of Disability Discrimination Act 1995 (Commencement No. 1) Order 1995 (1995 S.I. 3330) reg 2.

[33] HC Deb Standing Committee E cols 407-408: Mr. W. Hague.

[34] See: National Disability Council (No. 2) Regulations 1996 (1996 S.I. No. 1410) reg 2.

[35] See: National Disability Council (No. 2) Regulations 1996 (1996 S.I. No. 1410) reg 3.

[36] SDA 1975 ss 57-61; RRA 1976 ss 48-52.

[37] See, in particular: *R v CRE, ex parte Cottrell and Rothon* [1980] IRLR 279 Div Crt (CRE is discharging a quasi-judicial function and must observe natural justice and fair process); *Hillingdon London Borough Council v CRE* [1982] AC 779 HL (CRE may not carry out a formal investigation unless it has genuine belief, and not mere suspicion, that the party subject to investigation has committed discriminatory acts); *CRE v Prestige Group plc* [1983] IRLR 408 QBD (CRE must inform the party to be investigated so that representations can be made before any investigation commences). See also: *Science Research Council v Nass* [1979] 3 All ER 673 HL.

[38] SDA 1975 ss 67-70; RRA 1976 ss 58-61.

[39] SDA 1975 ss 71-73; RRA 1976 ss 62-64.

[40] SDA 1975 ss 74-75; RRA 1976 ss 65-66.

[41] Arguably, the establishment of the NDC and the lack of a disability rights commission under the DDA 1995 means that the enforcement strategy of the 1995 Act falls short of the expectations placed on nation states legislating in this field by the United Nations Standard Rules on the Equalization of Opportunities for Persons with Disabilities (December 1993). See: Doyle, 'Disabled workers' rights, the Disability Discrimination Act and the UN Standard Rules (1996) 25 *Industrial Law Journal* 1-14.

# 5 Australia's Human Rights and Equal Opportunity Commission

*Meredith   Wilkie*

**Overview of Australian enforcement agencies**

The first Australian anti-discrimination legislation (concerned with race discrimination only) was promulgated not by the national, or 'federal' government, but by a State government (the South Australian Prohibition of Discrimination Act 1966).   The first national legislation was the 1975 Racial Discrimination Act which established the office of Commissioner for Community Relations with power to attempt conciliation of discrimination complaints.

All States and Territories now have anti-discrimination legislation (or 'equal opportunity' legislation) administered by a State Equal Opportunity Commission (or equivalent) or jointly with the federal agency.  It is important to appreciate that the State Commissions are not branches in any sense of the national Commission.  While they can be, and are, contracted as agents of the national Commission (as described within), the State Commissions operate pursuant to State legislation and are independent.

*Grounds and areas*

Each State and Territory covers a slightly different range of discriminatory 'grounds'.  The core grounds of race, sex, marital status and disability are universally covered (with the exception of Tasmania which covers sex and related discrimination alone), while age, sexual preference, religious conviction and family responsibilities are not always included.

There is considerable uniformity across jurisdictions as to the 'areas' in which discrimination is made unlawful: employment, education, access to places and facilities, accommodation and land, provision of goods and services. Moreover, all Australian legislation prohibits both direct and indirect discrimination, usually defined by identical formulae.

## Definitions

Direct discrimination is less favourable treatment of the complainant in an area covered by the Act on a prohibited ground (or 'status') than would be received by a person not of that status otherwise similarly circumstanced. Indirect discrimination in most jurisdictions involves proof of four elements:

1   The respondent imposes a term, condition or requirement on all, e.g., job applicants or clients.

2   A substantially higher proportion of people of the complainant's status are or would be unable to comply with that term, condition or requirement.

3   The complainant herself/himself is unable to comply.

4   The term, condition or requirement is unreasonable in all the circumstances.

The second element - the 'proportionality test' - imposes a difficult data collection task upon complainants and, in practice, operates to mask discriminatory practices in all but the most extreme cases. Perhaps as a consequence, few cases of indirect discrimination have been pursued. Indeed, a recent study of sex discrimination complaint files in three jurisdictions found apparent instances of indirect discrimination were significantly 'under-detected', not only by complainants but also by the officers of the Equal Opportunity Commissions involved (Hunter and Leonard, 1995, p.9).

It should be noted, too, that a practice having a discriminatory effect will not be unlawful if it is 'reasonable'. Proof that it is not reasonable rests with the complainant in most jurisdictions.

These two features of the standard formula of indirect discrimination have encouraged the Federal Government to initiate an amendment to the definition of indirect discrimination in the *Sex Discrimination Act 1984* (SDA). The proportionality test will be deleted and the burden of proof of (un)reasonableness will be transfered to the respondent. The proportionality test is omitted in the definition of indirect race discrimination in the Federal *Racial Discrimination Act 1975*. Section 9(1A) of that Act provides: Where:

(a) a person requires another person to comply with a term, condition or requirement which is not reasonable having regard to the circumstances of the case; and

(b) the other person does not or cannot comply with the term, condition or requirement; and

(c) the requirement to comply has the purpose or effect of nullifying or impairing the recognition, enjoyment or exercise, on an equal footing, by persons of the same race, colour, descent or national or ethnic origin as the other person, of any human right or fundamental freedom in the political, economic, social, cultural or any other field of public life; the act of requiring such compliance is to be treated, for the purposes of this Part, as an act involving a distinction based on, or an act done by reason of, the other person's race, colour, descent or national or ethnic origin.

*Enforcement*

Just as Australian jurisdictions have established similar anti-discrimination jurisdictions, so too have they adopted the same model of enforcement. Discrimination, including harassment, is not criminalised in Australia. It is made unlawful by legislation, creating a 'statutory tort'. A complaint must be made to the Commission administering the legislation creating the 'tort'. The Commission, having determined that the complaint is within its jurisdiction, 'investigates' the complaint and attempts to reach a conciliated settlement.

The investigation's first step will be to inform the respondent - the alleged discriminator - of the allegations and invite a written response. The majority of complaints are 'resolved' - either by withdrawal or by settlement - in this process of 'mediated correspondence' or 'mediation' (Pentony, 1986, p.10). Delays in processing complaints may account for higher rates of complainant 'drop-out' in some jurisdictions - which must be distinguished from 'withdrawal' of the complaint. In one office surveyed by Hunter and Leonard (1995, p.17) almost 30% of all complaints initially accepted were 'finalised' by loss of contact with the complainant. This high proportion contrasts with the 10% observed in another jurisdiction.

The complainant may withdraw the complaint at any stage of the process. One-quarter of the sex discrimination complaints surveyed by Hunter and Leonard (1995, p.17) were withdrawn. A major reason for withdrawal was that the parties had reached a private settlement (23%). Another 10% withdrew for fear of reprisals or damage to their reputations and 13% determined they did not have enough evidence on which to pursue the complaint. Delay was a factor in only 5.5% of withdrawals.

If necessary a conciliation conference will be convened. This will occur, for example, where the respondent has failed to co-operate fully in the investigation or where the complainant does not accept the respondent's explanation. (It is possible for the Commission to by-pass the conciliation conference if satisfied that a settlement is unlikely to be reached. In this situation, the complaint is referred directly to the tribunal.)

The conciliation conference is presided over by an officer of the Commission - a conciliator. The parties are not entitled to be legally represented, although the proscription may be waived. Hunter and Leonard (1995, p.4 and p.8 respectively ) found that 15% of complainants and 24.8% of respondents were legally represented at the conciliation conferences in their survey (sex discrimination complaints only). Unlike respondents, complainants were more likely to be represented instead by their trade union or other association (5.7%) or to be accompanied by a family member or friend (14.5%) (p.4). The conciliation conference is a confidential process.

Commissions vary widely in their investigation and conciliation practices (see generally Hunter and Leonard, 1995). This is particularly evident in the extent of their employment of conciliation conferences. Hunter and Leonard (1995, p.14) found these were used in only 19.5% of cases in one jurisdiction compared with 69.4% in another.

A negotiated settlement of a discrimination complaint - whether at a conciliation conference (46.7% in Hunter and Leonard, 1995, p.14) or otherwise (53.3%) can include any lawful terms consistent with the objects of the legislation. The terms of the settlement are not otherwise constrained by legislation (e.g. as to the amount of monetary compensation). 30% of settlements surveyed by Hunter and Leonard included an apology, almost 30% involved payment of compensation and 30% involved a commitment to policy change. Much less common terms included reinstatement in employment (2.7%), action against the perpetrator where the respondent is vicariously liable (3.4%) and the introduction of a workplace EEO program (8.8%) (Hunter and Leonard, 1995, p.18).

Where the processes of investigation and conciliation are unsuccessful in resolving the complaint, it must be referred to a tribunal established under the Act. Nothing said or done during conciliation may be introduced in evidence before the tribunal. Rather, that phase of the complaint process is sealed.

The tribunal is typically a quasi-judicial specialist tribunal - often called the Equal Opportunity Tribunal or Board. The tribunal is usually part-time and will be presided over by a practising lawyer (commonly a QC). Other members may include non-lawyers. Typically the tribunal will be constituted by a panel of three.

Although not bound by the rules of evidence and directed to deal expeditiously according to justice, tribunal hearings largely mirror more formal court proceedings. Considering their constitution, the fact that legal representation is the norm, that the unsuccessful party has a right of appeal and that the proceedings are generally open to the public, this formal adversary style is perhaps not surprising.

As in other respects, jurisdictions vary in the proportion of complaints referred to a tribunal (between 1.4% and 17.8% of complaints accepted in Hunter and Leonard's survey, 1995, p.17).

*Remedies*

The range of remedies which can be awarded by Equal Opportunity Tribunals varies little across Australian jurisdictions. All are authorised to award damages for both economic loss and for hurt and humiliation (a ceiling of $40,000 is imposed in two States). Exemplary, or punitive, damages are not available. Damages are by far the most common remedy. Others which can be awarded, instead or in addition, are:

1 an injunction prohibiting continuation or repetition of the unlawful conduct;
2 an order that the respondent perform any reasonable act such as reinstatement, promotion, publication of an apology;
3 cancellation or variation of a contract or agreement which contravenes the legislation.

State tribunals, in contrast to the federal tribunal, make enforceable determinations and awards. Unsuccessful parties are entitled to appeal, but generally only on a question of law, to the State Supreme Court and thence, if leave is granted, to the High Court of Australia.

## Federal-State relations

Before turning to a detailed investigation of the agency of particular interest, it is necessary briefly to address the issue of the inter-relationship of the State/Territory and federal legislation and their administering Commissions. Ordinarily the effect of the Australian Constitution would be to invalidate (and thus render inoperative) State legislation purporting to enter a field covered by federal legislation. The federal anti-discrimination Acts, however, exclude this effect, permitting State anti-discrimination laws to operate as well, provided they do not offend the spirit of the federal laws. Many reasons commend this approach, including the better accessibility of State Commissions, the ability of State tribunals to make binding decisions (denied to the federal tribunal on constitutional grounds) and the freedom of the States to cover grounds not available to the federal government (again due to constitutional restrictions, the federal power to legislate at all on this topic being largely dependent on the scope of Australia's international treaty obligations).

Federal legislation may bind State governments (and does so in the case of the *Racial Discrimination Act 1975* ). State legislation, however, may not bind the federal government. Thus a complainant in Victoria whose discriminating employer is a federal government department or agency, must seek redress under the relevant federal legislation. In most other cases,[1] the complainant may choose whether to pursue a State or a federal complaint. For complainants of race or sex discrimination, the remoteness of the federal agency (head office in Sydney, New South Wales) will not be a deterrent to pursuing a federal complaint. The federal Commission, HREOC, has regional offices in Queensland, Tasmania, the Australian Capital Territory and the Northern Territory. In addition, State Commissions in Victoria, South Australia and Western Australia are contracted as agents to receive, accept or otherwise, investigate and attempt to conciliate all local complaints under the *Racial Discrimination Act 1975* and the *Sex Discrimination Act 1984*. The HREOC only becomes involved when the complaint must be referred to the federal tribunal. Even at this stage, the tribunal will be convened in the complainant's own State or Territory.

## The Human Rights and Equal Opportunity Commission

Australia does not have a bill of rights. Limited citizen rights are protected by the Australian constitution. Prior to Australia's ratification of the International Covenant on Civil and Political Rights (ICCPR), it was felt that a national bill of rights would enable the administration to affirm the ICCPR in good conscience. However, all proposals for a bill of rights have failed to date. (For a detailed history see Bailey, 1990, pp.50-58.) Instead the Federal Parliament passed the *Human Rights Commission Act* in 1981, merely scheduling the ICCPR to it. This has not had the effect of 'incorporating' the ICCPR (in Australian law a treaty has no domestic effect until 'incorporated' by legislation[2]).

*Administrative arrangements*

The *Human Rights Commission Act* was replaced in 1986 by the *Human Rights and Equal Opportunity Commission Act* which established the HREOC and the office of Federal Human Rights Commissioner. The Human Rights Commissioner administers the human rights jurisdiction which is defined by the instruments scheduled to the Act: the ICCPR, ILO Convention 111 Concerning Discrimination in Respect of Employment and Occupation, the Convention on the Rights of the Child, and three UN Declarations.[3] Simultaneous amendments to their respective Acts brought the Race Discrimination Commissioner (who succeeded the

90

Commissioner for Community Relations) and the Sex Discrimination Commissioner under the auspices of the HREOC. The Commission is headed by a part-time President without portfolio.

The Race Discrimination Commissioner is responsible for handling complaints under the *Racial Discrimination Act* (incorporating the International Convention on the Elimination of All Forms of Racial Discrimination [ICERD]), while the Sex Discrimination Commissioner administers the *Sex Discrimination Act* (incorporating the Convention for the Elimination of Discrimination Against Women). They have been joined by a Privacy Commissioner, a Disability Discrimination Commissioner and the Aboriginal and Torres Strait Islander Social Justice Commissioner. The Commissioners share the resources of the HREOC, including the premises, the conciliators and the legal officers. The Commissioners also share a common objective: 'the promotion of respect for human rights'.

*Functions and powers*

The Commission enjoys a range of functions and powers to enable it to pursue its promotional activities. The investigation and conciliation of complaints has already been noted. The volume of complaints work facing HREOC is evident from Table 1.

**Table 5.1**
**Enquiries and complaints processed by HREOC from 1 July 1993 to 30 June 1994**

| Category | Total | % race |
|---|---|---|
| Enquiries (written, phone, in person) | 34,724 | n.a. |
| Complaints received & within jurisdiction | 1,23 | 8.7% |
| Complaints received & outside jurisdiction | 3,084 | n.a. |
| Complaints closed | 1,052 | 7.3% |
| Referred to tribunal | 67 | 31.3% |

Source: *Annual Report 1993-94*, pp.30-33.

Aside from the complaint handling function of HREOC, other tools include:

1 Examination of legislation and bills to ascertain whether they are contrary to or inconsistent with any human rights (including freedom from racial discrimination) (section 11(1)(e), HREOC Act).

2 Provision of a report to the Minister as to the laws that should be made or other action taken on matters relating to human rights (section 11(1)(j)).

3 Intervention in court proceedings, with leave of the court, where an issue of human rights or race discrimination is raised (section 11(1)(o)).

Finally, HREOC performs a public education function, often in collaboration with non-government agencies. While the HREOC is not empowered to prevent or require the passage of legislation or to dictate the outcome of a court case, its independence from the government of the day does enable it to speak freely on behalf of human rights.

The function of the Aboriginal and Torres Strait Islander Social Justice Commissioner requires special mention. In addition to his community education and promotion role, he prepares an annual 'state of the nation' report on Aboriginal and TSI social justice issues. He has no power to receive individual complaints. The success of the Social Justice Commissioner's annual report in highlighting the continuing deprivation and marginalisation of Australia's indigenous peoples has encouraged the Commission to publish a report in similar style concerning people of non-English speaking backgrounds (NESBs).

## The race jurisdiction

'Racism in Australia' is a vast and complex topic: impossible to quantify; endemic on some levels - that of attitudes to Aborigines, for example; almost non-existent at others - for example, extremist racist groups, while they do exist, have limited political clout and no political representation.

A few comments may give readers in the old world a feel for the situation. Australian was established on the dispossession and genocide of the indigenous peoples. The era of massacres and denial was followed by a long period of enforced segregation, discriminatory criminalisation and the removal of children into Anglo foster or institutional care. Citizenship rights were slowly granted during the 1960s, culminating in a constitutional amendment to include Aborigines as full citizens (1967) and the gradual dismantling of discriminatory legislation (early 1970s). The people of the 1970s, having for so long been taught that Aborigines were inferior and that different treatment was appropriate, naturally continued to perpetrate acts of discrimination. The *Racial Discrimination Act 1975* (RDA) was introduced into this context.

Aboriginal socio-economic indicators, overall, have not improved. While Aboriginal infant mortality rates now paint less of a picture of third world neglect, Aboriginal adult morbidity and mortality seems to have declined. It is certainly still the case that Aborigines are, by far, the sickest, poorest, least serviced, least educated, least employed, most imprisoned people in Australia.

Apart from the RDA, other notable measures introduced to attempt to redress two centuries of marginalisation include the devotion of government funds to purchase land (from 1974) and the possibility for a few of reclaiming traditional lands (*Aboriginal Land Rights (Northern Territory) Act 1976* (Cwth), *Native Title Act 1993* (Cwth)); the establishment of a partially-representative body to distribute federal government funding (the Aboriginal and Torres Strait Islander Commission, 1989); the funding of self-determining Aboriginal organisation (Aboriginal legal and medical services, Aboriginal land councils from the mid 1970s).

As a country of invasion, Australia is also a country of immigration. Prior to the final renunciation of the 'White Australia Policy' (1973), most immigrants were from the U.K. and European countries such as Italy, Greece and Lebanon. Now Australia accepts a large proportion of immigrants from the South-East Asian region and refugees have been accepted from Vietnam, Cambodia and China among others.

While people from non-English speaking backgrounds (NESBs) fare somewhat worse than other Australians on socio-economic indicators, it is recently-arrived immigrants and refugees who are most severely disadvantaged (documented in *State of the Nation*,

1994). Australia's policy of multi-culturalism holds out some hope to these people that they will eventually find security here.

Australia's history, nevertheless, marks it as a racist nation. Those who suggest it is mostly a casual racism on the part of Anglo-Australians - in which we label 'others' but don't usually exclude them - forget the near absolute and very real exclusion of Aboriginal people, the readiness with which visible minorities are excluded in hard times and the pain and alienation caused by words and attitudes, however 'casually' adopted. The Bureau of Immigration, Multicultural and Population Research surveyed overseas students who had studied at Australian universities. Almost three-quarters of them had encountered prejudice and discrimination (Rubenstein, 1995).

Aborigines and Torres Strait Islanders constitute under two per cent of Australia's almost 18 million people. About one-quarter of Australians were born overseas and about one-quarter of those born here have at least one parent born overseas.

## Race discrimination complaints

Australia's *Racial Discrimination Act 1975* (RDA) authorised the executive government to ratify the ICERD which Australia had signed in 1966. Ratification took place in October 1975. Australia has since made a declaration under ICERD article 14 recognising the competence of the Committee for the Elimination of Racial Discrimination to consider communications from people alleging violations of their rights under the Convention.

The RDA makes unlawful discrimination on the grounds of race, colour, descent, national or ethnic origin and status as an immigrant (sections 5 and 9) in all areas of public life as listed in ICERD article 5. Discrimination against the complainant because of the race, etc. of a relative, dependant, household member or associate is also unlawful. Section 9(1) defines those acts which are unlawful (with section 9(1A) making explicit the inclusion of indirect discrimination as described above):

> It is unlawful for a person to do any act involving a distinction, exclusion, restriction or preference based on race, colour, descent or national or ethnic origin which has the purpose or effect of nullifying or impairing the recognition, enjoyment or

94

exercise, on an equal footing, of any human right or
fundamental freedom in the political, economic, social,
cultural or any other field of public life.

*Complaints submission*

Features of the jurisdiction which facilitate the submission of
complaints include:

1 It is an offence to victimise someone because he or she has
  made or proposes to make a complaint of discrimination
  (section 27).

2 A complainant need not wait until the discrimination has
  occurred but may complain of proposed discrimination
  provided there is a firm proposal (*Waters v Rizkalla* ).

3 A complainant who has reacted to intolerance, prejudice,
  harassment and/or discrimination with deteriorating work
  performance, for example, or by lashing out at colleagues, is
  not debarred.  In three cases where the action complained of
  was a response to such conduct on the part of the
  complainant, the reasons have been traced back to the
  original racist treatment and the complainant has succeeded
  (*Kordos, Ardeshirian* ). However, the complainant's response
  must be 'proportionate' to the abuse received (*Tamanivalu* ).

4 An employer may be held vicariously liable for the
  discrimination (or harassment) perpetrated by an employee
  or agent (section 18A).

Features which may discourage potential complainants from
proceeding include:

1 The complaint must be in writing (section 22).  This is
  believed to present a significant hurdle to Aboriginal
  complainants in particular (the complaint need not be in
  English).

2 The requirement for the complainant to be the victim.
  Victims of many of the most intransigent abuses are least

95

likely to appreciate their right to complain, least likely to have the resources to do so, and least likely to put at risk the limited services they do enjoy. Although the Race Discrimination Commissioner is empowered to initiate a complaint on behalf of a victim (section 23), she has never done so. A trade union is empowered to submit a complaint on behalf of a member (section 22). This, too, is rare. And, while representative complaints (analogous to 'class actions') may be accepted, the complainant must be a member of the class who has herself/himself been affected by the action complained of (section 25M).

3   The complaint must be made within 12 months of the act complained of, or the last in a series of acts (section 24). However, the Commissioner has a discretion to waive the limitation period.

4   The written complaint must, on its face, 'raise a question of possible discrimination of a kind which will bring the matter within [the jurisdiction]' (*Nestle Australia* per Vincent J. p.77,844).

5   HREOC is a no-cost jurisdiction so that the parties bear their own costs, unless the circumstances are exceptional (*Siddiqui* ).

6   Unlike State/Territory and other federal legislation, the RDA does not explicitly extend to cases where the discrimination is based on a characteristic appertaining or imputed to people of the complainant's race. The President of the federal tribunal has suggested that treatment based on 'language difficulties' will not necessarily be based on race for the purposes of the RDA (*Cronin*).

7   The federal tribunal may make recommendations only, with the result that it is unable to enforce its own awards (*Brandy*). When a respondent refuses to comply with the order, the complainant must commence proceedings anew in the Federal Court, requiring legal representation and involving a hearing *de novo* of the merits of the complaint (section 25ZCC(7)).

*Proof of discrimination*

Features of the jurisdiction which facilitate the proof of discrimination complaints include:

1   The prohibited ground need only be one reason for the act complained of, and it need no longer be the dominant or even a substantial reason (section 18).

2   While the respondent must have been aware of the complainant's race and taken it into consideration when performing the act complained of, the complainant need not prove that the discrimination was intentional (*Laher*).

3   While the RDA does not extend to religious discrimination,[4] the notions of race and ethnicity are broadly interpreted.  It is generally accepted in Australia that the major religious traditions such as Islam, Judaism and Sikhism would find a place in the concept of ethnicity (*King-Ansell, Mandla v Dowell Lee*).

4   Direct race discrimination cannot be justified on the basis that it is 'reasonable' in all the circumstances (compare indirect discrimination).   The only exception is where the act complained of was a special measure in terms of ICERD article 1.4.   There is no 'genuine occupational qualification' exception in the RDA, in contrast with all other Australian legislation.

Features which may make a complaint more difficult to establish include:

1   The onus of proof of his/her complaint remains throughout upon the complainant.  The following dicta to the contrary have been rejected: 'It seems to me unlikely that Parliament had in mind ... the strict imposition by the Commission of an onus of proof on one party, usually the moving party, as applies in true civil litigation. It seems to me more likely that the Commission's intended task is to try by all reasonable means at its disposal to discover and satisfy itself as to the facts, i.e. to inform itself on the complaint as fully as

possible...' (*Erbs* per Einfeld J p.76,721). In the case of an allegation of direct discrimination, the complainant must prove that a person of a different status would have received more favourable treatment. However, if the respondent relies on an exception or exemption, proof of that lies with her/him rather than the complainant.

2 The evidential problems of establishing all of the elements of indirect discrimination, even though the standard is the lower, civil, standard of proof on the balance of probabilities. However, the absence of a proportionality test greatly increases the accessibility of the RDA over the State Acts. The first successful case of indirect discrimination has recently been decided by the HREOC, a full 20 years after the passage of the RDA (*Siddiqui*). Prior to this only one case of indirect race discrimination (combined with indirect sex discrimination) had proceeded to a tribunal (not HREOC, although as it involved Federal employees it should have been pursued there). This case failed for jurisdictional reasons (*Dao*).

3 Federal tribunals are less prepared to infer a prohibited motivation from the surrounding circumstances than, for example, the Western Australian tribunal (*Slater, Cook v Lancet*). The onus of proof of both the circumstances and inferences lies with the complainant (*Laher*). Nevertheless, the Federal tribunal does seem to have eschewed the Victorian approach of requiring the complainant to establish an 'unavoidable inference' that the act complained of was motivated by the complainant's race (*Arumugam*). Generally the respondent is expected to explain his/her actions.

Table 2 shows that 458 complaints under the RDA were accepted as within jurisdiction in 1993-94, three-quarters of them in just three States - Victoria, South Australia and Western Australia - where the State Commissions process complaints through the investigation and conciliation phases.

The majority of respondents nominated were in the private sector (76.9%), while 56 (12%) were federal government departments or agencies and the remainder (11.9%) State government departments or agencies.

Table 5.2

## Complaints accepted under the RDA
## from 1 July 1993 to 30 June 1994

| By location | | By 'area' | | By ethnicity of complainant | | By sex of complainant | |
|---|---|---|---|---|---|---|---|
| NSW | 59 | Employment | 263 | ATSI | 103 | F | 167 |
| Queensld | 19 | Goods, services, places | 140 | NESB | 158 | M | 235 |
| Victoria* | 190 | Land, housing | 33 | English speaking Background 75 | | Group | 8 |
| WA* | 11 | Education | 10 | Association | 1 | Not recorded | 48 |
| SA* | 139 | Other | 12 | Not recorded | 121 | | |
| NT | 16 | Total | 458 | Total | 458 | Total | 458 |
| Tas | 9 | | | | | | |
| ACT | 15 | | | | | | |

**Total    458**
* Processed by State Equal Opportunity Commissions.
*Source: HREOC Annual Report 1993-94, pp.141-142.*

## Conciliation: powers and process

The RDA requires the Race Discrimination Commissioner or her delegate to attempt to resolve a complaint by 'conciliation' (section 24). However, the Act does not direct her with any degree of specificity as to how conciliation is to be conducted.

It would seem that, in their wisdom, the legislators, recognising the very complex nature of the matters to be conciliated and the subtle and sensitive interpersonal issues involved, considered it advisable to leave the details of the conciliation process to the conciliator, who could take into consideration the particular circumstances of the case (Pentony, 1986, p.5).

As described above, the conciliation conference, if any, is preceded by an investigation and 'mediation' process. While this process relies largely on the co-operation of the parties and the persuasive skills of the conciliator, the Commissioner can call on some statutory powers to assist in reaching a resolution. The two powers of most significance are the power to require production of documents and the power to seek an interim order preserving the status quo.

As can well be imagined, substantiating an allegation of discrimination would be beyond the capacity of a complainant without access to information relating to the reason(s) for the act complained of and to the more favourable treatment of another (whether real or hypothetical). Rarely nowadays will the complainant have direct oral evidence of both matters or have witnesses who volunteer themselves. More commonly, especially in employment discrimination, the relevant evidence is locked into the documents - memos, minutes and reports - generated by the employer. The Commissioner's power to require the production of such documents (section 24B(1)) may be the only chance for the complainant to substantiate the allegation of discrimination.

In order to preserve the status quo between complainant and respondent pending resolution of the discrimination complaint, the Commissioner may apply to the Commission in hearing mode for an interim order (section 24A). The status quo which is preserved may be that which prevailed before the act complained of (*Carson*).

One of the resolution tools available to the Commissioner is to convene a conciliation conference. HREOC conciliators convene conferences in about one-half of cases which proceed that far (Hunter and Leonard, 1995, p.14). Parties can be required to attend (section 24C) upon pain of a penalty in the amount of $1,000 for a natural person or $5,000 in the case of a body corporate (section 27A). Parties attending can be required to produce documents specified by the Commissioner (section 24C).

Neither party is entitled to be legally or otherwise represented, although the conciliator may consent to representation (section 24D(4)). The only statutory requirement for the conduct of conferences is that they be held in private (section 24D(2)).

Pentony, studying the practice adopted by the Commissioner for Community Relations in the 1970s, observed the following features of the conciliation conference (1986, pp.12-13). The conciliator was in charge of the conference at all times rather than being a tool of the parties. The conciliator set the time and place of the conference and its agenda, determined the order of proceeding and established and maintained good order. During the course of the conference, the conciliator would be expected to provide information (e.g. as to the operation of the Act), to suggest new avenues for exploration and to propose possible solutions. While encouraging a spirit of compromise, the conciliator would not 'assign blame or make judgements' (Pentony, 1986, p.14).

These broad features continue to characterise conciliation practice under the RDA today. However, although the RDA itself stipulates that the conference proceedings are to be determined by the conciliator (section 24D(2)), the courts have imposed the basic rules of natural justice. The rationale is that, although no 'decision' results from a conference, nor even a 'finding' as to a party's conduct, an unsuccessful conference 'exposes an individual to the legal hazard of civil proceedings' (*Koppen* per Spender J p.76,670).

One consequence has been increased attention to impartiality on the part of conciliators. In contrast to the position observed by Pentony in the 1970s, when conciliators tended to see themselves as taking the part of complainants (1986, pp.15, 185), conciliators now must be scrupulously free from bias, objective and detached. Western Australian conciliators describe themselves not as advocates for the victims of discrimination but as advocates for equal opportunity principles in an attempt, not always successful (*Investigation and Conciliation*, 1994, pp.50-51), to reassure respondents. The *Koppen Case* itself involved a conciliator whose daughter had been discriminated against by the respondent, a fact she communicated to the parties. This was clearly impermissible. The conciliator must be free from personal involvement in the complaint or with either party.

A conciliation conference is 'privileged'. Evidence of anything said or done during conciliation will not be admissible in any further proceedings relating to the complaint (section 24E(3)). The intention is to free the parties to explore as full a range of possible interpretations of the facts and of possible solutions during conciliation; to admit of maximum flexibility without the need to keep one eye on possible future ramifications; to permit a full without prejudice survey of the parties' positions and interests.

In the period 1993-94, 314 RDA complaints were closed or referred.

Table 3 sets out the outcome categories.

**Table 5.3**
**Outcome of complaints closed from 1 July 1993 to 30 June 1994**

| Outcome | Number | Per cent |
|---|---|---|
| Conciliated | 111 | 35.4 |
| Withdrawn | 45 | 14.3 |
| Conciliation failed - not referred | 6 | 1.9 |
| Complainant lost contact | 40 | 12.7 |
| Complaint declined | 66 | 21.0 |
| Outside jurisdiction | 8 | 2.6 |
| Referred elsewhere | 17 | 5.4 |
| Referred to tribunal | 21 | 6.7 |
| **Total** | **314** | **100.0** |

Source: *HREOC Annual Report 1993-94*, p.142.

*Complaints declined*

The Race Discrimination Commissioner may decline to investigate a complaint which is within the terms of the Act where she finds it to be frivolous, vexatious, misconceived or lacking in substance (section 24(2)(d)). She must outline her reasons in a notice to the complainant. The complainant may seek a review of the decision by the President of the Commission (section 24AA).

*Complaints lapsed or withdrawn*

While a proportion of complaints withdrawn involve complainants satisfied with the respondent's explanation, some undoubtedly involve complainants disheartened by the strength of the respondent's resources or disillusioned by the evidentiary hurdles imposed and so on (Hunter and Leonard, 1995, p.17). Other reasons include private settlement between the parties (Hunter and Leonard, 1995, p.17).

A major reason for lapsed complaints, where the agency loses contact with the complainant, seems to be delay in processing (Hunter and Leonard, 1995, pp.12, 17). Time to finalisation of complaints within HREOC itself is not reported. However, Table 4 provides such information for the State Commissions of New South Wales, Victoria and Western Australia. The Victorian and Western Australian Commissions each process complaints under the RDA.

**Table 5.4**
**Time to finalisation of complaints**

| Time | NSW 1990-91 [a] | Victoria 1990-91 [b] | WA 1991-93 [c] |
|---|---|---|---|
| < 1 month | 27.0% | ? | ? |
| < 3 months | 46.0% | 10.3% | 26.0% |
| < 6 months | 62.0% | 43.5% | 52.0% |
| < 9 months | ? | 74% | ? |
| < 10 months | ? | ? | 74% |
| < 12 months | 77.0% | 88.5% | ? |

Sources: a. NSW Anti-Discrimination Board *Annual Report 1990-91* ; b. Victorian Equal Opportunity Commission *Annual Report 1990-91* ; c. *Investigation and Conciliation*, 1994, p.21.

While the figure for lapsed and withdrawn complaints under the RDA in 1993-94 (Table 3: 27%) compares favourably with the New South Wales figure of 43% in 1990-91 (Anti-Discrimination Board *Annual Report*), it does seem very high, especially if it be accepted that a significant cause relates to the processes of the Commission. The recently appointed Race Discrimination Commissioner, Zita Antonios (mid 1994), made dealing with the backlog of complaints her first priority upon taking office. She reported considerable success in reducing the time to finalisation of RDA complaints for which she is responsible (presentation to Western Australians for Racial Equality, Perth, October 1995).

### Tribunal hearings: powers and process

The Federal tribunal is the HREOC in hearing or inquiry mode, constituted by a single legally-qualified member or by two or more members, one of whom is legally qualified (section 25B). The Commission has provided the following description of the nature of the proceedings:

> An inquiry by the Human Rights and Equal Opportunity Commission is not an adversarial proceeding. It is more properly viewed as an informal proceeding in which the parties do their best to help the Hearing Commissioner discover the true facts and identify where the answer to an issue lies. Experience has shown, however, that inquiries are most successful in achieving these ends when proceedings generally follow the process of examination, cross-examination and re-examination of witnesses (*Practice Note No 1*, December 1994).

Parties may be legally represented by leave of the Commission (section 25G). A Practice Note issued in December 1994 (*No 2*) elaborates the relevant considerations:

> When considering whether to grant leave to a party to be legally represented at the inquiry, the Commission will have regard to whether the opposing party also seeks leave to be represented, whether there is any objection to the party's representation, the size and complexity of the matter, and any other relevant matter.

Legal representation is the rule rather than the exception, with the cost being borne by each party (this being a no-costs jurisdiction). Legal aid is rarely, if ever, available for a discrimination matter (limited funds being reserved principally for defended criminal matters and, moreover, subject to a rigorous means test). In the case of Aboriginal and Torres Strait Islander complainants, however, Aboriginal Legal Services may provide representation free of charge. A few community legal centres will also pursue, at low or no cost, discrimination complaints on behalf of complainants. Finally, the Commission has a discretion to recommend to the Federal Attorney-General that assistance with costs incurred be given to either party (section 27ZB). When such a recommendation is made, the Attorney-General determines the amount to be provided.

Note should be taken at this point of a Western Australian provision which finds no counterpart in federal legislation, namely the obligation imposed upon the Commission in that State to provide legal representation upon request for a complainant pursuing the complaint to the tribunal (*Equal Opportunity Act 1984* (WA), section 93). Typically the representative is the Commission's own legal officer, thus blurring in the minds of some respondents the impartiality of the Commission during conciliation (*Investigation and Conciliation*, 1994, p.63). The WA Commission attempts to address this concern by keeping the two process and their related personnel separate in an administrative sense. A practice which is available to HREOC and which may yield some of the same benefits is that of appointing counsel assisting the Commission (section 25K).

The Commission is not bound by the rules of evidence but may inform itself as it thinks fit (section 25V). The rules of natural justice apply, however. Parties are entitled to give and to call evidence, to examine and cross-examine witnesses and to make submissions (section 25E(1)(b)). While the presiding Hearing Commissioner determines whether or not to admit evidence, that decision 'should be based on whether it is relevant, reliable and logically probative ... and of such a nature that responsible people would rely upon it in serious affairs ...' (CCH, 1995, p.66,454 citing *T A Miller Ltd* p.995 and Flick, 1984, p.72). Thus, 'although rules of evidence, as such, do not bind, every attempt must be made to administer "substantial justice"' (*Ex parte Bott* per Evatt J p. 256) and the rules of evidence are an established guide to achieving that.

Among the material the Commission usually has before it is the Commissioner's report detailing the inquiries she has made (section 24E). This report must not include details of the conciliation proceedings and conference since, as noted above, these proceedings are confidential.

Like the Commissioner, the Commission is empowered to summons a person to appear and give evidence and/or to produce specified documents, and may take sworn evidence (section 25S). It is an offence to refuse or fail to supply information or produce a document without reasonable excuse (section 27. Hearings are, as a rule, open to the public (section 25H). Occasionally a party's name will be suppressed (section 25J), a power usually confined to the protection of victims of sexual harassment.

Table 5 summarises the outcomes of reported tribunal hearings under the RDA to the date of writing (October 1995). A full digest of RDA tribunal and court outcomes can be found at Appendix 1. In perusing this Table and the Appendix, the following should be borne in mind. First cases proceeding to the tribunal are a small proportion (five to ten per cent) of all complaints accepted. Second any complainants have the option of proceeding instead under State legislation. Third the RDA has been amended over time, notably from 1990 no longer to require race to be the dominant reason for the conduct complained of.

**Table 5.5**
**Summary of reported RDA tribunal outcomes**

| Complainant ethnicity | Number% | Successful% | Unsuccessful |
|---|---|---|---|
| Aboriginal | 20 | 55% | 45% |
| NESB | 28 | 25% | 75% |
| Anglo | 5 | 20% | 80% |
| **Totals** | **53** | **19** | **34** |
| **Area of complaint** | | | |
| Employment | 28 | 29% | 71% |
| Accommodation | 3 | 67% | 33% |
| Goods and services | 13 | 69% | 31% |
| Education | 2 | - | 100% |
| Other human rights | 7 | - | 100% |
| **Totals** | **53** | **19** | **34** |

## Racial vilification

Racially-motivated harassment or abuse of a person is treated in Australia as a form of racial discrimination. Racial vilification, or 'incitement to racial hatred', may be a different matter.[5] Article 4(a) of ICERD requires States parties to create the offences of 'dissemination of ideas based on racial superiority or hatred, incitement to racial discrimination, as well as all acts of violence or incitement to such acts ...'. Having failed to secure the passage of the incitement to racial hatred provisions of the, then, *Racial Discrimination Bill*, Australia ratified ICERD with a declaration stating the Government's inability 'at present ... specifically to treat as offences all matters covered by article 4(a)'.[6]

New South Wales (1989), Western Australia (1990), Queensland (1991) and the Australian Capital Territory (1991) have all criminalised select forms of incitement to racial hatred. Western Australia, for example, covers only written or pictorial materials intended to harass or promote hatred of a group (*Criminal Code 1913* (WA), sections 76-80). Intention is not an element of the New South Wales offence, although threatening violence is (*Anti-Discrimination Act 1977* (NSW), section 20D). The New South Wales offence is not confined to published materials but extends to public speech as well. To date only four allegations of racial vilification have been referred to the State Attorney-General for possible prosecution. None of these allegations has been pursued. It is widely accepted that such numbers significantly under state the incidence of serious racial vilification. In the absence of a threat of violence, racial vilification can be the subject of a complaint, as for racial discrimination. In the first five years of operation, 442 complaints were received in New South Wales; about one-half of respondents were media organisations (McNamara, 1995, p.8). It is widely believed that there is a higher incidence of racial vilification which does involve the threat of violence than would be suggested by the comparative figures (*Racist Violence*, 1991, pp.70-72, pp.139-140, pp.181-194). The ACT legislation is based on the New South Wales model with racial vilification a ground of complaint dealt with by conciliation, and serious racial vilification capable of prosecution as a criminal offence.

Following several reports (including Human Rights Commission, 1983, *Racist Violence*, 1991) and a couple of failed attempts, the Federal Parliament considered the *Racial Hatred Bill* in 1995. The model proposed was similar to that in New South Wales and the ACT with a new ground of complaint added to the RDA and three new criminal offences included in the Commonwealth *Crimes Act 1914*.

The criminal provisions were excised in the Senate, the major concern of the Opposition and minor parties being the infringement of freedom of expression. At the federal level, then, we are left with a new ground of complaint in the RDA: an act done, otherwise than in private, because of the race, etc., of the aggrieved person or group and 'reasonably likely' to 'offend, insult, humiliate or intimidate' (section 18C). Exempted acts include artistic works, genuine academic or scientific discussion or debate, and fair reporting or commentary (section 18D). The exemptions seem to be widely drawn. Provided the racist 'acts reasonably and in good faith', he or she may make 'fair comment' on a matter of public interest as an expression of his/her genuine belief. The definition, moreover, creates fine distinctions and a web of technicalities far beyond what has previously been demanded of the Race Discrimination Commissioner (as she herself recently observed with some dismay at a public event: presentation to Western Australians for Racial Equality, Perth, October 1995).

## Evaluation

This brief evaluation is confined to the HREOC's 'enforcement' function through the complaint handling process. The armoury of other tools, outlined above, should not be forgotten in any fuller assessment of the HREOC's potential to achieve its objectives of eliminating racial discrimination and increasing racial understanding, tolerance and harmony (ICERD article 2.1, RDA section 20, HREOC Act section 11). Pre-requisites to the achievement of objectives such as those of the HREOC include clearly stated and well understood objectives, appropriate powers, independence from political influence and adequate resources.

An evaluation of the HREOC's complaint handling process must address a number of levels, bearing in mind the objectives to be achieved:

1. Is conciliation an appropriate model?

2. Is the scope of the Act - e.g. the definitions of discrimination
- adequate?

3. Are the conciliation, inquiry and enforcement powers
sufficient?

*An appropriate model?*

Individual complaint handling primarily 'protects' human rights
by remedying violations. It may also 'promote' human rights
observance more generally in the following ways:
- the threat of a complaint may act as a deterrent to
  discriminatory acts and practices;
- representative actions are possible with outcomes
  affecting a whole class;
- successful indirect discrimination complaints can effect
  systemic change;
- individual complaint settlement can include a
  commitment to reform a policy or practice;
- respondents are informed about the benefits of a non-
  discrimination approach; and
- the wider public is informed through publicity given
  to tribunal decisions.

The Australian conciliation and arbitration model was influenced
by earlier UK and New Zealand schemes. Thornton has described
its rationale as follows:

> While complaint-based legislation embodies a public policy
> determination that discriminatory acts are wrong, it chooses
> not to exert the punitive force of the law, its *raison d'etre* is that
> discriminators should be treated gently, preferably in a
> confidential setting, by means of conciliation and persuasion, as
> their conduct invariably arises out of unconscious racism or
> sexism, rather than from a conscious animus (1990, pp.37-38).

Thornton implies that the assumption of respondent ignorance,
educability and unconsciousness is debatable. It must be said,
however, that Australian governments had other reasons for
preferring the model chosen. One was the ineffectiveness of
criminal legislation. Quite apart from European experience (see

Wilkie, 1989, re Denmark, MacEwen, 1995, re France at pp.124-125, pp.129-130 and re The Netherlands at pp.135-136, p.139), we had our own early experiment. The 1966 South Australian Act made racial discrimination a criminal offence. However, it proved 'virtually unworkable' (Thornton, 1990, p.36). Only four prosecutions were brought in ten years, only one of which was successful.

Australia explained its preference for the conciliation model, as found in the *Racial Discrimination Act 1975*, to the Committee on the Elimination of Racial Discrimination as follows:

> ... it made it possible to confront individuals accused of racially discriminatory action with the true immorality of what they had done and it had a distinctly educational effect on the community; it was informal and readily accessible to those who did not have the financial, education or other means to go through elaborate court processes (CERD, 1979, para.32).

McNamara's comparison of the criminalisation model (based on Ontario's racial hatred laws) and the conciliation model strongly supports the latter. While acknowledging that criminalisation is 'a much stronger statement that racism is being addressed in a serious fashion' (1995, p.15), McNamara points out that the high prosecution threshold and the reluctance of prosecutors to proceed prevent this being a feasible option. A 'clear disadvantage of the conciliation model is that it does place a heavy onus on the aggrieved individual ... to "make the running" in relation to the complaint', possibly fuelling 'the perception that the legal system is ambivalent about the wrongfulness of the alleged act' (McNamara, 1995, p.15). Nevertheless, the conciliation model 'substantially increases the number of complaints handled by the legal system' and 'the focus of proceedings may be more attuned to the needs of complainants' (p.15). Further, it has the potential to acknowledge and highlight the mundanity and the pervasiveness of racism and racial discrimination, whereas the criminal model, by focusing only 'on the "extreme" end of the spectrum' (p.16) offers a false vision of racism as confined to extremists - as 'a manifestation of deviant, aberrant, pathological behaviour' (Jayasuriya, 1989, p.16).

The impact in 1975 of the RDA and the real, if limited, power of the prohibition of racial discrimination should not be denied. Pentony reminds us of its significance. For the first time, the RDA gave people a basis on which 'equality of treatment could be demanded as a right and persons who denied that right could be confronted and exposed' (1986, p.104).

> ... the introduction of the Racial Discrimination Act constituted a major step in the development of relations between the Aboriginal and non-Aboriginal communities. Although the powers conferred by the Act - to call compulsory conferences and to issue certificates to clear the way for court action when conciliation failed [as was then the limit of the powers] - might not seem impressive, they nevertheless constituted a serious threat to anyone seeking to maintain a privileged position by discriminatory practices. The intense hostility and anger often displayed by persons directed to attend compulsory conferences for alleged breaches of the Act is indicative of the potency of that threat (1986, p.70).

However, the limited nature of the complaint process as a tool must also be kept in mind.

> While laws prohibiting discrimination have helped to reduce some of the more blatant and objectionable forms of discrimination, the experience in Australia over a decade of operation of these laws demonstrates that they have not by any means provided a complete solution to problems faced by disadvantaged groups. Strong and enforceable laws against discrimination are very important for the self respect and defence of groups such as Aborigines, women, migrants, gays and people with disabilities. They should not, however, be seen as self implemented, still less as a panacea for social inequality (Kirby, 1993, p.1698).

Another commentator, however, perceives the individual complaint handling process as damaging to the achievement of the broader HREOC objectives. Thornton is reported as saying recently:

> Because HREOC deals with complaints on an individual basis, the underlying problems of discrimination at an institutional level tend not to be addressed. This individualist approach ignores the fact that a complaint is merely one manifestation of a wider problem.
> The process effectively deflects attention away from wider

issues such as the broad societal and institutional oppression of women and minority groups (Matheson, 1995).

The newly appointed Federal Human Rights Commissioner, Chris Sidoti, counters:

> It's impossible to underestimate [sic: reporter's error; he meant 'overestimate'] the extent to which the Commission has made Australians more aware of the centrality of their rights in everyday life (Matheson, 1995).

A second critique of the complaint process draws attention to the inappropriateness of the conciliation model in which victims of discrimination are expected to compromise on their rights in the interests of an 'amicable' settlement; the rights violation being characterised as an interpersonal dispute. 'The legal system does not compel road accident victims or those whose reputations have been damaged to conciliate with the tortfeasors' (Scarff, 1995, p.5).

No Australian jurisdiction has traditionally evaluated complainant satisfaction following a 'successful' conciliation. Did the complainant accept a derisory offer for fear of the publicity of the tribunal process? Or for financial reasons? Or from a desire to finalise a lengthy process? Or from a sense that this was all she was worth? Or because of the conciliator's expectations, real or perceived? The Western Australian Commission is the first to undertake such an evaluation. The first evaluation, published in 1994, sampled and surveyed cases over a two year period. Now every participant is followed up after the file has been closed. Unfortunately the review confined itself to complainant and respondent views about the investigation and conciliation process. Satisfaction with the outcome seems to have been assumed. The review reported significant levels of dissatisfaction with the investigation and conciliation processes among both complainants and respondents surveyed (*Investigation and Conciliation*, 1994, pp.58-62). For example, one-quarter of complainants felt the conciliation process was unreasonable (p.61), while 30% of complainants and fully 49% of respondents expressed dissatisfaction with that process (p.60).

Although they did not survey participants as to their satisfaction with the outcome, Hunter and Leonard (1995) did investigate 'the extent to which the outcomes of conciliation matched what the parties wanted' (p.26) as recorded in the file. Only 11% of complainants received what they had asked for, whereas in 46% of cases the outcome was identical to what the respondent had offered. Another 22% of complainants got 'substantially' what they had sought and another 14% of respondents conceded 'substantially' the same as their original offer. Forty per cent of complainants came away with nothing.

*Adequate scope?*

A feminist critique of the Australian definition of direct discrimination proposed that it would be blind to many discriminatory acts because of its requirement for the complainant to compare himself or herself with a person of a different status (the 'comparator'). The comparator will invariably be an able Anglo male (Thornton, 1990). The comparator's social position, culture and past privileges, however, make him an inapt choice. He doesn't have a large impoverished extended family to whom he is obliged to give shelter upon request. So the Aboriginal public housing tenant evicted for breaching the occupancy limits is readily characterised as having been evicted for that reason and not by reason of race (*Alone*). The comparator is rarely subjected to racist taunts at work or play. When the Sikh student (*Sekhon*) or Samoan footballer (*Tamanivalu*) or Iranian miner (*Ardeshirian*) finally lashes out at his tormentors, the proportionality of his response (on which rests the success or otherwise of his complaint) is assessed by an able Anglo male or female lawyer against the standard of the comparator.

On the other hand, a would-be Aboriginal drinker charged a higher price or refused service by a publican can, if sober and well-behaved, be readily characterised as a victim of racial discrimination (*Tabua*). We all drink in hotels. But what of the Aboriginal drinkers segregated into separate and squalid 'black bars' because they don't meet the saloon's dress standards or they 'feel more comfortable drinking together'? An Aboriginal woman racially abused by a taxi driver is readily characterised as having received discriminatory service (*Chesson v Buxton*). We all travel in taxis. But what of the would-be travellers, marooned kilometres out of town on an Aboriginal reserve with no operative telephone, unable to call a taxi?[8]

The decided cases bear out Thornton's critique in large measure.

113

There is little evidence at the federal level that Hearing Commissioners have appreciated the subtleties and complexity of discriminatory practices. Yet it must be acknowledged that direct discrimination complaints are a very blunt tool with which to attempt the elimination of racial discrimination. Other features which mitigate its usefulness are:

1   that it relies on the victim to identify discrimination, lodge a complaint and pursue it for some months, occasionally for years;

2   that it is ill-adapted to secure changes in practice in the respondent's industry; even the respondent may compensate this complainant but - more cautiously - continue to victimise others;

3   that it addresses individual acts of discrimination but cannot ameliorate underlying inequalities.

With respect to the second point, enforcement agencies have adopted some ingenious measures. The South Australian Equal Opportunity Commission, for example, tried to build into every conciliated employment discrimination settlement a commitment from the employer to institute an EEO program in the workplace (Pentony, 1986, p.140). Following a series of cases in 1991, a HREOC Hearing Commissioner officially informed a liquor licensing authority about the entrenched practices of two licensees of refusing service to Aboriginal customers in the hope that this would be taken into account when licence renewals were sought, and in the hope of educating the licensing authority itself as to the seriousness with which the law treats such practices.

With respect to the third point, some hope is still held out that claims of indirect discrimination will go some way towards addressing systemic discrimination and highlighting the entrenched nature of racial inequality in Australia. As mentioned above, the first successful complaint of indirect discrimination has only this year been decided (*Siddiqui*). Ironically, in light of Thornton's analysis, the complainant was a doctor with Indian and British qualifications. The difficulty with indirect discrimination is the recognition factor. It is astounding, to this author, that senior officers, researchers and scholars whose daily work involves

114

dredging the causes of racial inequalities have no conception of the parameters of indirect discrimination. The under-recognition of situations of indirect discrimination, even by agency conciliation officers has been mentioned above. In this parlous state of public knowledge, it is unlikely that the victims of such discrimination will be able to recognise it as such, beyond a generalised sense of unfairness. The new Race Discrimination Commissioner recognises the potential of indirect discrimination as a cause of action (presentation to Western Australians for Racial Equality, Perth, October 1995) and we can expect more public education on the subject.

*Sufficient powers?*

Before turning finally to the HREOC's inquiry and enforcement power, two matters which have a bearing on the effectiveness of its exercise of its powers and functions require comment: its independence and its resources.

The HREOC is an independent statutory authority answerable to Parliament and the Commissioners hold statutory offices. This independence was very early asserted by the Commissioner for Race Relations in these circumstances. The Queensland Cabinet determined on a policy of refusing to register transfers of land to a federal body established to purchase private land for the use and benefit of Aboriginal communities. The complainants were members of a remote Aboriginal community for whom this body had negotiated to purchase a pastoral lease. Transfer of the lease was refused by the responsible Minister. The Commissioner for Community Relations accepted the complaint and sought legal advice from the Federal Attorney-General's Department. Throughout his attempts at conciliation, the Department recommended against proceeding and provided legal interpretations of the RDA which, if accepted, would have forced the Commissioner to withdraw. Federal-State political sensitivities were clearly implicated. The Commissioner, however, rejected the advice and the complainants were ultimately successful in the High Court of Australia (*Koowarta*).

Apart from the power to appoint and re-appoint Commissioners, the government, of course, holds the purse strings. Commissioners have recently complained, it is reported, of severe funding cuts at a time when complaints work has grown exponentially (Matheson,

1995). Such a claim is difficult to sustain on the data reported in Table 6 which compares the position in 1990-91 with that in 1993-94.

### Table 5.6
### HREOC indicators compared

| Indicator | 1990-91 | 1993-94 |
|---|---|---|
| Complaints received | 2,855 | 2,652 |
| Complaints closed | 1,410 | 1,796 |
| Budget | $10,652,773 | $18,285,170 |
| Staff establishment | 107.4 | 194 |

Sources: HREOC *Annual Report 1990-91* and *1993-94*.

Nevertheless, it is reported that the position worsened significantly in 1994-95, the HREOC sustaining a three per cent funding cut in common with all federal departments and agencies, and a significant increase in complaints lodged (a 20% increase in SDA complaints, a 300% increase in DDA complaints) (Matheson, 1995).

As to the sufficiency of the HREOC's powers it must be said that there is a clear trend away from the notion that discrimination is more than an individual interpersonal dispute. Symptomatic of this trend are:

1 The reluctance of the tribunal to infer an unlawful motive.

2 The insistence of the tribunal on imposing strictly the onus of proof.

3 The highly legalistic procedures adopted by the tribunal.

4 The reluctance to exploit remedies other than damages.

5 The requirement that the complainant commence legal proceedings anew in order to enforce a tribunal award.

Short of criminalising racial discrimination, what can be done to implement a recognition of discrimination 'as an infringement of the community's right to benefit from the talents of all members' and 'a denial of the merit principle which costs us all dearly by diminishing the moral worth of the society' (Scarff, 1995, p.15)?

The following suggestions are offered. First, the Commissioner should be prepared to use, and use aggressively, her complaint initiation powers. Second, the conciliation procedures need tightening: reduction of delay in responding to complaints, provision of accessible information to complainants about the process, keeping parties informed regularly about progress, follow-up of complaints lapsed and withdrawn as well as of those 'successfully' conciliated. One strategy which may assist conciliators to expedite their complaint handling and to interpret complaints accurately is ready access to legal officers. This is rarely done at HREOC but routinely done at the South Australian Commission (Pentony, 1986, p.138).

The HREOC tribunal could, within its existing mandate, adopt a substantially more inquisitorial approach as suggested for the New South Wales tribunal by Judge Mathews in 1986:

> The ultimate responsibility lies with the tribunal rather than the parties, to ensure that so far as possible all relevant material is before it (*Re NSW Corporal Punishment in Schools* p.76,579).

As part of this approach, the tribunal could, as suggested by Justice Einfeld (quoted above), transfer the onus of proof of motive and other matters peculiarly within the respondent's knowledge to the respondent once the complainant's evidentiary onus has been satisfied. Further, the full onus of proof of reasonableness (in indirect discrimination) could be transfered to the respondent (requiring legislative amendment as already foreshadowed for the SDA).

Another procedural amendment recognising the complainant as a representative for a wider situation of inequality would be for HREOC to provide legal representation free of charge to complainants (as occurs under the Western Australian Act) both before the tribunal and in any enforcement proceedings required.

Finally the tribunal needs to be aware of the fact that individual acts of discrimination are typically only part of a larger picture and symptomatic of intolerance, ignorance or racism. Tribunal orders should be tailored both to the individual complainant and to the underlying situation. An order may require the amendment of a discriminatory statement of selection criteria, for example, or the institution of EEO training for senior and middle managers.

The time for a softly softly approach to discriminatory conduct is surely over. It is time for the community to stand firmly behind complainants as our standard bearers for a more tolerant future.

## Cases

*Alone v State Housing Commission* (1992) EOC 92-392.

*Arumugam v Health Commissioner of Victoria* (1987) EOC 92-195.

*Ardeshirian v Robe River Iron* (1990) EOC 92-299.

*Bennett v Everitt* (1988) EOC 92-244.

*Brandy v HREOC* (1995) 127 ALR 1.

*Carson v Minister of Education (Qld)* (1989) EOC 92-261.

*Chesson v Buxton* (1990) EOC 92-295.

*Cook v Lancet* (1989) EOC 92-257.

*Cronin v Department of Social Security* (1992) EOC 92-431.

*Dao v Australian Postal Commission* (1987) EOC 92-193.

*Erbs v Overseas Corporation Pty Ltd* (1986) EOC 92-181.

*King-Ansell v Police* [1979] 2 NZLR 531.

*Koowarta v Bjelke-Petersen* (1982) 153 CLR 168.

*Koppen v Commissioner for Community Relations* (1986) EOC 92-173.

*Kordos v Plumrose (Australia) Ltd* (1989) EOC 92-256.

*Laher v Barry James Mobile Cranes Pty Ltd* (1994) EOC 92-585.

*Mandla v Dowell Lee* [1983] 1 All ER 1069.

*Nestle Australia Ltd v Equal Opportunity Board (Vic)* (1990) EOC 92-281.

*R v War Pensions Entitlement Appeal Tribunal & Anor; ex parte*

119

*Bott* (1933) 50 CLR 228.

*Re New South Wales Corporal Punishment in Schools* (1986) EOC 92-160.

*Sekhon v Ballarat University College* (1993) EOC 92-552.

*Siddiqui v Australian Medical Council* (1995) EOC 92-730.

*Slater v Brookton Farmers' Co-op.* (1990) EOC 92-321.

*T A Miller Ltd v Minister of Housing and Local Government* [1968] 1 WLR 992.

*Tabua v Stemron Pty Ltd* (1991) EOC 92-346.

*Tamanivalu v WA Rugby Union* (1994) EOC 92-636.

*Teoh v Minister for Immigration* (1995) 128 ALR 353.

*Waters v Rizkalla* (1990) EOC 92-282.

# Appendix 1

## Digest of reported tribunal and court outcomes: RDA matters

| Year Case # | Complaint | Outcome |
|---|---|---|
| 1982 | Aboriginal community objected to State policy of refusing to register transfers of land | State policy discriminatory and unlawful |
| 1984 106 | Anglo complainant (naturalised) denied freedom of residence based on race (i.e. not born in area of chosen residence) | Unsuccessful, birth location the reason; no race nexus |
| 1985 123 | Aboriginal complainant objected to permit requirement to enter land belonging to an Aboriginal community of which he was not a member | Unsuccessful, permit requirement was a special measure of protection |
| 1987 199 | Refusal of hotel service, Aboriginal complainant | $5,000 for embarrassment and personal affront (not enforced by Federal Court - new evidence established no discrimination) |
| 1988 297 | State legislation cancelling native title, Aboriginal complainants | Legislation of no effect |
| 1988 219 | Allegation that Australian tax laws discrimination against newly arrived immigrants, NESB complainant | Unsuccessful, no race nexus |
| 1989 256 | Discrimination and harassment in employment, NESB complainant | $23,800 economic loss + loss of personal dignity ($7,000) |
| 1989 283 | Discrimination during employment training and denial or permanent employment, Aboriginal complainant | Unsuccessful, poor performance the reason |
| 1989 252 | Refusal by trade union to reinstate membership, NESB complainant | Unsuccessful, no evidence that dominant reason (then required) was race |
| 1990 299 | Discrimination and harassment in employment, NESB complainant | $10,000 lost wages, hurt and humiliation |
| 1990 303 | Refusal of hotel service, Aboriginal complainants | $2,000 + $1,000 respectively for embarrassment and humiliation; written and public apology |
| 1990 306 | Discrimination against NESB lecturer during employment and in termination of employment | Unsuccessful, reason was English language difficulties |
| 1990 327 | Discrimination in employment training and denial of permanent employment, Aboriginal complainant | Unsuccessful, no race motivation |
| 1990 355 | Discrimination in terms and conditions of employment, NESB complainant | Unsuccessful, cause was his performance |
| 1991 345 | Refusal of hotel service, Aboriginal complainants | $1,000 each for humiliation and embarrassment; written and public apology |

| | | |
|---|---|---|
| 1991 346 | Refusal of hotel service, Aboriginal complainant | $1,200 for injury to feelings; written and public apology |
| 1991 347, 348 | Refusal of hotel service, Aboriginal complainants | $1,000 each for embarrassment; written and public apologies |
| 1991 349, 350 | Refusal of hotel service, Aboriginal complainants | $1,000 each for humiliation and embarrassment; written and public apologies |
| 1991 378 | Refusal of hotel service, Aboriginal complainants | $1,200 each for humiliation and embarrassment |
| 1991 387 | Discrimination in employment terms and conditions, NESB complainant | Unsuccessful, insufficient evidence of some acts; no race nexus established re others |
| 1991 359 | Discrimination in employment terms and conditions, NESB complainant | Unsuccessful, reason was performance and a communication breakdown |
| 1991 372 | Cancellation of reception centre booking, Aboriginal complainant | Unsuccessful, reason was that booking could not be confirmed |
| 1991 409 | Denial of permanent employment, NESB complainant | Unsuccessful, discrimination established but not that race was a factor |
| 1991 427 | Football league discipline more severe, Aboriginal complainant | Unsuccessful, discipline more severe but race not the dominant reason (as then required) |
| 1992 453 | Denial of tenancy, Aboriginal complainant | Unsuccessful, tenancy reserved for another |
| 1992 415 | Closure of Aboriginal school | Unsuccessful, race nexus proved but students not disadvantaged |
| 1992 431 | Discrimination during employment, NESB complainant | Unsuccessful, no race nexus, her temperament the cause |
| 1992 411 | Discriminatory conditions of employment and refusal of promotion, NESB complainant | Unsuccessful, race not a factor |
| 1992 463 | Refusal of booked bus seat, Aboriginal complainant | Unsuccessful, booking error |
| 1992 462(3) | US born, naturalised Australian basketball player objected to 3 year domicile requirement in Australian league | Unsuccessful, residency requirement not based on race |
| 1992 470 | Discriminatory treatment in employment, NESB complainant | Unsuccessful, treatment he received was the norm |
| 1992 479 | Discriminatory service provision by doctor who used racist words, NESB complainant | Unsuccessful, when the words were spoken no service was being sought or provided |
| 1993 518 | Refusal of accommodation, Aboriginal complainant | $700 for lost rental + $20,000 for pain, humiliation, distress and loss of personal dignity |

| | | |
|---|---|---|
| 1993 552 | Racist abuse by fellow students at a tertiary institution and discriminatory exclusion from the institution, NESB complainant | Unsuccessful, abuse established but institution had acted appropriately; exclusion was based on unsatisfactory progress |
| 1993 545 | Failure to obtain promotion due to stereotyped assessment of literacy, Aboriginal complainant | Unsuccessful, no inference of a racist motivation possible |
| 1993 519 | NESB senior managers found surplus to requirements were offered a resignation package rather than a superior redundancy package | Unsuccessful, no material on which to find Anglo senior managers would have been treated more favourably |
| 1993 493(5) | Complainant and NESB associates denied entry to a club | Unsuccessful, reason was inflexible application of club's identification rules |
| 1993 547 | NESB prisoner denied access to rehabilitation programs in prison | Unsuccessful, disadvantage established but all federal prisoners liable to deportation were treated similarly |
| 1993 537 | Grant of land to an organisation not representative of traditional owners, complainants, was discriminatory because it had the effect of extinguishing their native title | Unsuccessful, the grant did not have that effect; moreover it was for their benefit as a special measure |
| 1993 653 | Private vendors withdrew house from the market rather than sell to Aboriginal housing association complainant for Aboriginal occupancy | Declaration that respondent should not repeat the unlawful conduct; local publication of an apology |
| 1993 562 | Anglo complainant challenged Australian Government's complicity in racist policies in Fiji by accepting Fijian standards in awarding scholarships to Fijian students | Unsuccessful, complainant not a person aggrieved |
| 1994 565 | Racist of abuse of non-Aboriginal employee by Aboriginal co-worker | $12,000; apology |
| 1994 585 | Racist slogans at work and discriminatory termination, NESB complainant | $1,000 for injury to feelings, but termination based on conduct not race |
| 1994 643 | Race and sex discrimination in employment termination, NESB complainant | $22,000 for loss of employment, pain and suffering, and humiliation |
| 1994 587(2) | Non-Aboriginal employee harassed by Aboriginal employer | Conflict between the two not racially motivated |
| 1994 639 | Aboriginal job applicant not employed | Unsuccessful, no racist considerations proved |
| 1994 594 | NESB (Muslim) job applicant not employed | Unsuccessful, reason was his limited qualifications and knowledge |
| 1994 649 | NESB job applicant not employed | Unsuccessful, reason was lack of merit |

| | | |
|---|---|---|
| 1994<br>585 | NESB worker abused at work and summarily dismissed | $1,000 for the racist abuse; discriminatory termination not proven |
| 1994<br>580 | NESB complainant became a police suspect because of his ethnicity | Unsuccessful, reason was a misunderstanding of his conduct |
| 1994<br>636 | Suspension of a NESB rugby union player following his involvement in violent incidents | Unsuccessful, complainant's violence was in response to racist taunts but was disproportionate |
| 1995<br>728 | NESB complainant abused at work and dismissed | $1,000 for injury to feelings; but dismissal was based on poor performance |
| 1995<br>710 | NESB complainant abused at work and dismissed following a performance report motivated by racism | $7,500 for past economic loss, pain and suffering |
| 1995<br>670 | NESB school teachers retrenched | Unsuccessful, reason was their subject matter not their race |
| 1995<br>730 | NESB overseas-trained doctor objected to quotas imposed on such practitioners wishing to practice in Australia | Quota impaired the exercise on an equal footing by persons of a national origin other than Australia or New Zealand of the human right to work; $10,000 for injury to feelings and humiliation; $15,000 for loss of economic opportunities; $15,000 for legal expenses |
| 1995<br>687 | State Government challenged the Federal *Native Title Act* as providing more favourable treatment to Aborigines | Unsuccessful, the *Act* protects Aboriginal land title from discriminatory extinguishment |

Note that prior to 1984 only 'landmark cases' were reported.

124

[1] Another significant class of people excluded from State legislative access are workers employed under a federal industrial award who are complaining about employer discrimination.

[2] This doctrine is currently under some strain. Most recently the High Court held that a treaty which has not been incorporated should nevertheless be taken into account by administrative decision-makers where citizens' expectations have been raised by the fact of ratification of the treaty (*Teoh*). The Federal Parliament is considering a Bill to nullify the effects of that decision.

[3] Declaration of the Rights of the Child, Declaration on the Rights of Mentally Retarded Persons, Declaration on the Rights of Disabled Persons.

[4] Three States and both Territories make discrimination on the ground of religion or religious conviction unlawful: Victoria, Queensland, Western Australia, the Northern Territory and the Australian Capital Territory.

[5] The distinction is not always clear. An example is the display in the public area of a police station of a poster indicating the station housed the local branch of the Ku Klux Klan. While arguably inciting racial hatred in non-Aboriginal visitors, the poster may also amount to discrimination against Aboriginal visitors.

[6] Some years later, Australia ratified the ICCPR with a reservation concerning article 20.

[7] The facts of *Alone* are somewhat different. She was evicted after a period in hiding from her violent spouse. Since she was not residing in the house, the authority determined that she had vacated without notice and leaving the house inadequately secured.

[8] Actually, the more common observation is that taxis make a roaring trade from such communities because no cheaper form of public transport is provided between the town and the reserve to transport the weekly shopping, etc.

# 6 Anti-discrimination law: a Canadian perspective

*John Hucker*[1]

## Introduction

Although it is not intended to recount at length the details of the Canadian Human Rights Commission's operations, it is worth saying that it falls within the standard model of an anti-discrimination agency. The Commission accepts complaints from individuals who believe they have been the victims of discrimination in employment or in the provision of services. There are some ten proscribed grounds under the Canadian Human Rights Act (C.H.R.A.), including race, sex, disability, age, family or marital status and sexual orientation.[2] Complaints may be brought against government departments or agencies or against corporations which are under federal jurisdiction. The latter include many of the larger interprovincial enterprises such as banks, airlines, broadcast companies, and the Post Office.

Complaints are investigated by Commission staff and the findings summarized in a written report which is then disclosed to the complainant and the respondent, each of whom is provided with an opportunity to make written submissions. The report, together with any submissions received, is then presented to the Commissioners for decision. They may decide to dismiss the complaint if they are not satisfied that evidence of discrimination has been established. Where there is evidence of discrimination, the case will usually be sent to conciliation, so that an effort can be made to find common ground between the parties.

Conciliation is usually undertaken by CHRC staff, although on occasion the Commission has retained the services of outside specialists. The process involves discussions, in person or by telephone, with each party, during which the conciliator ascertains the nature of the remedy being sought by the complainant and conveys this information to the respondent. It will commonly be necessary to persuade complainants to temper their demands and respondents to table more realistic proposals for settlement. Offers and counter-offers are communicated to the parties by the conciliator until such time as a settlement is reached or it becomes clear that non is possible.

During the conciliation exercise, the conciliator will be guided by current jurisprudence, which has developed *de facto* benchmarks for the compensation to be awarded for particular kinds of discrimination. In addition, when deciding to send a case to conciliation Commissioners will sometimes indicate what they view as an appropriate remedy. Thus, if an employee has been the victim of harassment stemming from remarks made by her colleagues at work and has subsequently quit her job for reasons not clearly related to the harassment, the Commissioners may suggest that the objectives should be limited to obtaining an apology and a modest payment of damages and should not extend to the complainant's reinstatement or the payment of compensation for lost earnings.

Commissioners must approve the terms of all settlements. If they are not satisfied that a complainant has been fairly compensated or that an employer has agreed on the steps necessary to eliminate discriminatory practices, they may refer the matter back for further conciliation. Conversely, where conciliation has not succeeded, complaints are returned to the commissioners, who must decide whether to send the matter forward for a hearing before a human rights tribunal or to take no further proceedings. The latter outcome can ensue when the Commission is of the view that the complainant's demands are unreasonable in the face of an offer by the respondent to settle matters or where the evidence of discrimination is weak and unlikely to be sustained at a hearing. Canadian courts have made it clear that the Commission enjoys a broad discretion when deciding whether or not to ask for the appointment of a tribunal.

Federal human rights tribunals operate independently of the Commission. With the exception of the Tribunal President, their membership is drawn from a panel of part-time appointees which includes lawyers and non-lawyers. The decisions of human rights tribunals are binding. They commonly involve the award of damages to compensate the complainant for the losses attributable to the discrimination, including lost earnings, and may include an amount of up to $5,000 for hurt feelings.[3] Tribunals may also require a respondent to take corrective action, for example, by changing a discriminatory policy or, in a case of workplace harassment, arranging for the delivery of appropriate training to its staff.

Human rights commissions are today an established feature of the Canadian legal landscape where, in addition to the federal commission, similar agencies exist in each of the 10 provinces. While the commissions enjoy broad public support, they have been subject to criticism in recent years for the slowness of their procedures and for sometimes venturing further afield than would appear to be justified by their mandate. This chapter will return later to the performance of human rights institutions in Canada but first it will address some issues of a broader nature concerning work of anti-discrimination agencies.

*Anti-discrimination laws as marginal in their impact*

It is difficult to dispute the contention that anti-discrimination laws in themselves can not be expected to bring about fundamental change to the lives of racial or other minorities. There are, of course, many more factors which contribute to the well-being of different groups in society. From a Canadian perspective where the Ontario provincial government is cutting welfare payments by more than twenty percent and reducing government services in general, to pave the way for a promised thirty percent reduction in income tax rates for the more affluent among us, it would be unrealistic to suggest that the continued existence of human rights laws will do much to soften the blow for minority group members - especially the disabled and Aboriginal Canadians - who are over-represented among those dependent upon state support.

And yet, this is not to gainsay the impact that anti-discrimination norms can have at a given point in time. Perhaps the most telling instance where a judicial call for equality galvanized governments into action was the memorable 1954 decision of the United States Supreme Court in *Brown v. Board of Education*.[4] After Brown, it was no longer possible to argue that separate educational facilities for black students could be regarded as equal to those available to

128

their white counterparts. More than a generation later, the impact of this landmark decision continues to reverberate in the U.S. school system, where ambitious programs intended to achieve racial balance have altered the make-up of schools in many of that country's urban centres.

But *Brown* arose from a constitutional guarantee of equal treatment which was given force by the highest court in the land, while anti-discrimination laws operate at a lower level in the legislative hierarchy. It would certainly be quixotic to suggest that administrative bodies such as human rights commissions can singlehandedly bring about social change. Such was never intended to be their role. They can, however, provide redress for victims of unequal treatment and increase public awareness of the many and pervasive forms taken by discrimination. If the public does not wish to hear this message, there is admittedly not a great deal the agency can do, and in that sense anti-discrimination laws will usually remain on the periphery of public debate. They may, nonetheless, be a factor in the development of public policy. For example, commencing in the late 1980s the Canadian Human Rights Commission (CHRC), in a series of annual reports which received considerable media coverage, identified the plight of Aboriginal Canadians as the major human rights challenge facing the country. Partly as a result of the CHRC's stance, the Canadian government in 1991 appointed a Royal Commission with a mandate to examine and make recommendations for change on a broad range of social and legal issues affecting the governance of Aboriginal Peoples. Other agencies such as the Commission on Racial Equality in Britain have also spoken out forcefully on government policies where they see these as having adverse consequences for race relations.

*Single or multiple grounds*

In Canada there is a tendency to view human rights laws as a progression, starting with efforts in the 1940s and 1950s to counter racial prejudice in the field of employment through the passage of fair employment laws.[5] These initiatives were subsequently expanded to prohibit discrimination or other grounds, notably, sex, disability and age. Today, anti-discrimination statutes in most provinces feature a comprehensive array of prohibited grounds including family or marital status and, most recently, sexual

129

orientation.[6]    The flowering of substantive anti-discrimination statutes has been accompanied by the establishment of human rights commissions which are empowered to deal with discrimination in its varied manifestations. To suggest, therefore, to a Canadian audience that individual categories of discrimination, such as race, sex or disability, should be tackled through distinct legal regimes, each with its own administrative apparatus, would be to generate responses ranging from surprise to puzzlement.   Indeed the tenor of the times in Canada today is to seek further consolidation, by combining human rights commissions with analogous bodies such as ombudsmen.

But on this side of the Atlantic the denizens of the Commission on Racial Equality and the Equal Opportunities Commission do not seem at all keen to join forces in a common battle against prejudice. An outsider might be pardoned for attributing this standoffishness at least in part to institutional resistance to change - a virus to which presumably not even anti-discrimination bodies are entirely immune.   But, there is clearly a degree of support that this institutional separation enjoys among academic observers. Arguably an omnibus commission risks some dilution in its expertise on the particular issues involved in, say, race or sex discrimination.   There are, however, common patterns to discrimination when particular groups - be they racial or sexual minorities or disabled persons - are denied jobs or services.  If an objective is to move society away from negative stereotyping, no matter which group is the target, it is reasonable to suppose that the additional authority (and resources) available to broadly mandated human rights commission will in general facilitate the task.

The suggestion that particular groups need their own agency because the objective of these bodies is to take positive action on behalf of the group in question and not merely to seek a notional 'equality', is in the author's view, unpersuasive. A single issue agency is arguably best placed to advocate in support of the special needs of its 'client group'. But there is a downside to this, since the agency inevitably risks some loss of credibility and a consequent reduction in its capacity to influence events if it is seen as a captive of a particular segment of society.  The problem is compounded if the agency must also, at other times, exercise an adjudicative, and therefore non-partisan, role with respect to complaints of discrimination that are brought before it.

Another element to be considered is the spill-over effect which

130

will allow one minority to benefit from legal advances which are a result of complaints brought by those belonging to a different group. As an example there is a duty which exists under Canadian law to accommodate individual needs in employment. This principle may require work schedules to be adjusted so that, for example, a Jewish or Muslim person will not be forced to work on a religious holiday. It can equally be seen to call for reasonable accommodation of the needs of a disabled employee who seeks a minor modification of the work-site to enable him or her to function to their full capacity. While broader principles can emerge in anti-discrimination jurisprudence irrespective of any particular agency structure which is in place, it is reasonable to assume that the effectiveness of such laws will be enhanced by an integrated approach to their administration. In the final analysis economics rather than ideology will almost certainly carry the day, and it can be predicted that over time some degree of amalgamation of agencies will occur in order to realise the financial savings that can be expected to accrue from the elimination of administrative duplication.

*The involvement of agencies in conciliation or mediation*

The CHRC has, since its inception in 1978, employed conciliation as a practical way to resolve many human rights complaints. This effort to find common ground between the parties is successful in nearly fifty per cent of the cases referred. Search for compromise does not mean that a transgressor will be able to wriggle off the hook or that the complainant will have to accept less than his due. As noted earlier, conciliation can operate to reduce expectations on the part of complainants who may assume, incorrectly, that a decision by the agency to pursue their case signals that every element of the complaint has been upheld. It can also serve to convince a respondent, who does not believe he has done anything wrong, that indeed the law requires him to change his practices and provide a measure of compensation to the complainant. Endeavouring to resolve complaints informally need result in no derogation from human rights principles, provided that the conciliator is alert to the power disparity which often exists between the parties, particularly where the respondent is a corporation or government department.

The question, it is suggested, is not whether conciliation should be attempted in advance of having recourse to more formal proceedings but whether, if conciliation fails and the complainant wishes to pursue matters, he should have the right to a full hearing. In Canada this is generally not the case. The CHRC and its provincial counterparts generally decide whether to refer a complaint for a hearing. Where there is no settlement between the parties, the CHRC not infrequently concludes that matters should end at the conciliation stage, even though the initial investigation has found some evidence of discrimination. This result is one which, to put it mildly, complainants do not always understand. It also leads to not infrequent attempts to challenge the Commission's decision by way of judicial review. Even if the agency is not convinced that it would be an appropriate use of its resources to pursue a particular case to the tribunal level, there are valid arguments in favour of permitting the complainant to do so if he is prepared to have carriage of his own case. This is what occurs in other jurisdictions under anti-discrimination laws, and it reflects an approach which is more consistent with a respect for individual choice.

*The relationship between anti-discrimination agencies and governments*

This area is of some delicacy and doubtless contains fodder for graduate student theses. A cynic might argue that the establishment of human rights commission or similar bodies is an easy way for a government to be credited with a commitment to human rights principles which may not in fact run very deep. The issue of an agency's independence is not easily pinned down. The Canadian Human Rights Commission certainly sees itself as independent of the government of the day. Given that more than half of the complaints investigated are against government departments or agencies and that a good part of the agency's time is spent arguing against government lawyers in the Courts or before human rights tribunals, the Canadian government no doubt views the agency in a similar light. By way of illustration, one continuing dispute between the CHRC and the government involves a far-ranging complaint filed by public service unions several years ago, alleging that many female employees are paid at a rate lower than that applied to work of equal value performed largely by males. After lengthy but unsuccessful attempts to resolve the matter, the government announced in 1990 that it was making a one-time

132

payment of more than $300 million in settlement of the complaint. The CHRC examined the figures, concluded that this impressive amount was not sufficient to bridge the wage gap which existed and sent the case forward for a hearing before a tribunal, where litigation continues to the present day.[7]

Consequently the CHRC sees itself as an agency that maintains its distance from government. And yet, it is paid by the government, its commissioners are appointed by the government and, if it wished, the government could pass legislation next month terminating the agency's existence - a fate which befell one provincial Human Rights Commission in the early 1980s.[8] Independence, then, is a matter of degree and is influenced by such factors as an agency's formal line of accountability (does it report to Parliament or to a government Minister?), the degree of control it exercises over staff (does it employ its own investigators or must it rely upon personnel assigned to it by a government department?), and the willingness of a Chief Commissioner to accept certain career risks by pursuing issues which are clearly uncongenial to government or powerful interests within the private sector.

## Current challenges facing human rights agencies in Canada

### Complaints and their limitations

The assumption behind the creation of a human rights commission is that it will, through the use of relatively informal procedures, ensure the availability of a prompt and inexpensive remedy for victims of discrimination. In particular, commissions are expected to be more accessible than the courts, whose formalism and cost can deter all but the most intrepid (or affluent) from initiating proceedings. Unfortunately, some tarnish has appeared on the human rights model in recent years.

A high dismissal rate for complaints, particularly those involving race, has prompted criticism of commissions as being insufficiently sensitive to the more subtle forms of discrimination which continue to confront minorities in Canada. The legal burden of proof placed upon a complainant would not appear overly onerous: he or she has to meet the civil rather than criminal standard of proof, and Canadian courts have affirmed that race (or any other prohibited ground) need be only one among several elements contributing to an individual's difficulties in order for a complaint to succeed. Nonetheless, complainants will sometimes be at a disadvantage in seeking to show that discrimination has in fact occurred. If refused a job or promotion, their recollection of what happened will often be countered by an employer able to produce written records supporting its side of the story. Senior government or corporate officials are also generally more at ease with the investigative process than is a complainant, for whom this might well be an initiation into the mysteries of the legal system. In addition, witnesses to racial slights may not exist or may be reluctant to support the complainant's version of events for fear they will be seen as criticizing an employer on whom they are dependent for future work or advancement. All of this can be a frustrating experience for a complainant and can, when multiplied, contribute to an impression among minority groups that a human rights commission is unable or unwilling to come to their assistance in situations where, to their mind, discrimination certainly exists.

A more generalized problem arises from the delays which have become endemic for many commissions in Canada. Growing workloads, together with financing which has failed to keep pace with this growth, have contributed to backlogs in complaints investigation. Perhaps ironically, expanding notions of due process have also contributed to a general slow-down in the pace of human rights machinery, It is axiomatic that a party has the right to know the nature of the case he has to answer. Accordingly, the CHRC and most other commissions in Canada routinely disclose investigation reports to the complainant and respondent. The parties are then given an opportunity to submit written comments which will be taken into account by the Commissioners when they make their decision. The courts have recently said that this may not be sufficient. In *Mercier v. Correctional Services Canada*[9], a complaint of job discrimination based on sex and disability was dismissed by the CHRC. The complainant proceeded to challenge this decision by way of judicial review, arguing that the Commission had acted contrary to the rules of procedural fairness because she was not afforded the opportunity to see and make additional comments on the respondent's submission. The Court agreed with her, ruling that such submissions should be cross-disclosed when they contain new evidence or include challenges to the other party's credibility.[10]

On occasion dissatisfied parties to a complaint seek to delve behind the investigation report itself and obtain witness statements or notes compiled by an investigator, although none of these materials are before the Commissioners when they decide a case. To date the courts have declined to support these fishing expeditions[11], but the growing propensity of complainants and respondents to apply for judicial review if they are not happy with the direction a complaint is taking has undoubtedly contributed to caution on the part of commissions in how they go about their business, thereby further slowing the pace of investigation. Fact-finding also becomes harder as witnesses move away and recollections fade. In turn, settlements are more difficult to achieve as parties' positions harden with the passage of time.

## Beyond equal treatment

It was indicated earlier that Canadian law recognizes that equal opportunity may require more than equal treatment under the law, if this results in adverse consequences for certain categories of people. Hence, the concept of 'reasonable accommodation' requires employers to make adjustments to the workplace or to employment practices in order to accommodate an individual's needs. The leading case, *Alberta Human Rights Commission v. Central Alberta Dairy Pool*[12], involved a complaint to the Alberta Human Rights Commission brought by an individual who had asked for a change in his shifts so that he would not have to work on days which conflicted with his religious sabbath. The Dairy Pool refused to accede to his request, and matters came to a head when he was told he had to work one Easter Monday, failed to show up on the day in question and was fired. A provincial board of inquiry upheld his complaint that this amounted to discrimination on the ground of religious belief, finding that the employer had a duty to accommodate the complainant unless it could establish that this would involve undue hardship, a burden it had not discharged. In affirming the board's decision, the Supreme Court of Canada enumerated some factors which would be relevant in deciding whether undue hardship had been established. These included financial cost, the impact of such adjustments on the morale of other employees and the size of the employer's operation.[13]

Canadian human rights laws make clear that the implementation of special programs aimed at assisting historically disadvantaged groups need not amount to discrimination.[14] The term 'affirmative action', commonly used in the United States, is largely eschewed, but Canadian courts and legislatures have recognized that if certain chronically underprivileged groups are to be provided with a genuine opportunity to advance economically, there is a need for more far-reaching remedies than those traditionally available through the processing of individual complaints. In the most notable case, the Supreme Court of Canada in *Action Travail des Femmes (ATF) v. Canadian National Railway*[15] upheld the order of a human rights tribunal directing the railway to implement a special program for the recruitment of women into blue-collar jobs. The tribunal found that the complainants had been the victims of sexual discrimination resulting from long-standing recruitment practices at CN that placed undue reliance on strength tests and other physical requirements. At the time of the complaint, women comprised less than one per cent of the railway's workforce, compared to a national level of thirteen percent representation in similar employment. CN was ordered to hire women for at least one in every four blue-collar jobs it staffed until such time as their representation reached the thirteen per cent level. The ATF case remains the high watermark of judicial endorsement of a broad remedial approach aimed at eliminating the effects of past discriminatory practices.

*Employment Equity*

In the early 1980's, a Royal Commission on Employment[16] chaired by Judge Rosalie Abella concluded that existing anti-discriminatory legislation and voluntary affirmative action measures had not proven successful at removing the systemic barriers to employment which confronted women and other groups. The Abella Report, which had a major impact on the thinking of government and community groups, recommended the introduction of legislation which would place a duty on employers to identify and eliminate discriminatory barriers in the work place.

Largely as a response to Abella, Parliament enacted the 1986 *Employment Equity Act.*[17] The legislation, the first of its kind in Canada, required all federally regulated employers with more than 100 employees to file an annual report on the representation levels in their workforce of each of the so-called designated groups - women, Aboriginal peoples, visible minorities and the disabled - and their distribution by occupational category and salary range. A similar breakdown was to be provided on the number of employees hired, promoted and terminated. Employers were also required by the new law to prepare annual plans indicating how they intended to achieve employment equity.[18]

Apart from a potential fine of up to $50,000 for failing to file an annual report, the *Employment Equity Act* included no sanctions for failing to achieve a representative workforce. However, as a partial response to criticism of the legislation's weakness, a provision was inserted prior to its passage directing that copies of the annual reports from employers were to be made available to the Canadian Human Rights Commission.[19] Ministerial statements at the time suggested that the CHRC would thereby be in a position to monitor progress under the Act, although it was given no additional powers to do this.

The 1986 Act was not generally viewed as a success. Initial opposition from employers eventually subsided into a somewhat grudging acceptance, tinged with continuing disquiet at the idea of any outside agency having access to details concerning their internal management practices. For their part, the designated groups were far from satisfied with the legislation, which they viewed as essentially toothless.

The Liberal Government which came to power in Ottawa in late 1993 had committed to strengthening employment equity and in late 1994 it introduced a comprehensive series of amendments to the Act which received Parliamentary approval in December 1995.[20] The 1995 Employment Equity Act extends coverage of the law to the federal public service, unlike its 1986 predecessor which, for reasons that remain unclear, applied only to the private sector. The new law empowers the CHRC to undertake compliance audits of employers and where necessary to direct an employer on the establishment of short-term hiring goals. Consistent with the affirmative action model, the law is not concerned with establishing whether or not past discrimination exists but rather with achieving structural change in companies or government departments whose workforce profile departs markedly from what might be expected when the availability of designated group members is taken into account.

## Conclusions

Canada today is in a period of sometimes uneasy transition as it moves beyond the individual and his or her difficulties into a new stage in the human rights progression, where anti-discrimination agencies endeavour to come to grips with 'systemic' discrimination. Here the situations the law confronts are not aberrational in the sense of being a departure from the norm, but are continuing features of everyday life. The focus is not on the businessman who refuses someone a job because he does not like their colour or ethnic origin. Nor is it on the restaurateur who sexually harasses his waitresses. Instead, the challenges are those posed by such realities as women in full-time employment in Canada earning on average only 72 per cent of the wages paid to men, and disabled persons and Aboriginal Canadians remaining woefully underemployed in our society.

Resistance to affirmative action comes primarily but not exclusively from the political right. In Canada, the 1995 Ontario election saw the ascent to power of a Conservative Party committed to repealing a recently introduced provincial Employment Equity Act.[21] The change in provincial government and the demise of the 1994 law seemed to embolden the critics of employment equity who were eager to produce anecdotal evidence of highly qualified white males being denied positions in favour of less qualified women or minority group representatives. Those who continue to favour affirmative measures are for the moment less vocal, faced as they are with the admittedly more complex task of convincing a sceptical audience that without some type of intervention, historic patterns of employment are unlikely to change very quickly and that the losers will be not only the disabled and Aboriginal Canadians who are unable to find work but society at large.

Challenges undoubtedly lie ahead for anti-discrimination agencies, particularly as their reach extends into more deep-seated patterns of inequality. The shift in focus in recent years from equal treatment to the more contentious concept of equal opportunity has caused disquiet and has served to politicize the human rights arena. In today's climate of economic uncertainty there is undoubtedly a vein of resentment to be tapped by those who inveigh against 'special rights' for women, racial minorities or homosexuals, and we can probably look forward to continuing public debate over the legitimacy of programs aimed at securing equal opportunity for all groups within Canada.

[1] The author is Secretary General, Canadian Human Rights Commission. The views expressed in this paper are those of the author and do not necessarily represent those of the Commission.

[2] *Canadian Human Rights Act*, R.S.C. 1985, c. H-6, s.3. The *C.H.R.A* does not, as enacted, include sexual orientation as a prohibited ground of discrimination, but in *Haig v Canada* (1991) 94 D.L.R. (4th) 1, the Ontario Court of Appeal upheld a challenge to s.3 of the *CHRA* brought under s.15(1) of the *Canadian Charter of Rights and Freedoms*, in which the applicants argued that the failure to include sexual orientation amounted to a denial of equality to homosexual persons. The Court ordered that sexual orientation be read into s.3 of the *CHRA* The Government of Canada decided not to appeal this decision to the Supreme Court of Canada and since the *Haig* decision, the CHRC has accepted complaints based upon sexual orientation.

[3] *Ibid*, s.53(3)

[4] 347 U.S. 483 (1954).

[5] See Tarnopolsky and Pentney, *Discrimination and the Law* (Toronto, Carswell Publisher), 1994 Rev. Ed., Chapter II, The Rise and Spread of Anti-Discrimination Legislation.

[6] For a summary of current Canadian anti-discrimination laws, see Tarnopolsky and Pentney *(supra)* at pp. 2-9 to 2-29. I have examined aspects of anti-discrimination laws in Canada in two recent articles. See Hucker, *Moving Towards the Elusive Goal of Equality: Reflections on Canada's System of Human Rights Enforcement* (1994) 25 Cambrian L.R. 33; and Hucker, *Towards Equal Opportunity in Canada: New Approaches, Mixed Results* (1995) 26 St. Mary's L.J. 841.

[7] See Canadian Human Rights Commission Annual Report 1990, at pp. 49-50.

[8] For an account of the abolition of the British Columbia Human Rights Commission in 1983, see Black, Human Rights in British Columbia: Equality Postponed (Canadian Human Rights Yearbook 1984-85, p. 219).

[9] [1994] 3 F.C.3 (Federal Court of Appeal.

[10] *Ibid* at p. 14, per D'cary, S.A.: 'I am not saying that the rules of procedural fairness require that the Commission systematically disclose to one party the comments it receives from the other; I am saying that they require this when those comments contain facts that differ from the facts set out in the investigation report. . . It would seem to me that it would be in the Commission's interest, if only to protect itself in advance from any criticism, to require that the parties exchange their respective comments.'

[11] See, for example, *Canadian Human Rights Commission and Patlak* and *Royal Bank of Canada* (Federal Court of Appeal decision, April 11, 1995).

[12] [1990] 2 S.C.R. 489.

[13] *Ibid*, at 521, per Wilson, J.

[14] See, for example, Canadian Human Rights Act, S. 16(1): 'It is not a discriminatory practice for a person to adopt or carry out a special program, plan or arrangement designed to prevent disadvantages that are likely to be suffered by, or to eliminate or reduce disadvantages that are suffered by, any group of individuals when those disadvantages would be or are based on or related to the race, national or ethnic origin, colour, religion, age, sex, marital status, family status or disability of members of that group, by improving opportunities respecting goods, services, facilities, accommodation or employment in relation to that group'.

[15] 40 D.L.R. (4th) 193 (S.C.C.).

[16] R.S. Abella, Report of the Commission on Equality in Employment (1984).

[17] *An Act Respecting Employment Equity*, 1986 S.C., c.31.

[18] *Ibid*, s. 5.

[19] *Ibid*, s. 8.

[20] *Employment Equity Act, 1995* S.C. c.44. The law received Royal Assent on December 15, 1995.

[21] *An Act to Provide for Employment Equity for Aboriginal People, People with Disabilities, Members of Racial Minorities and Women*, 1993, S.O., c.35. The Act came into effect on September 1, 1994. It was repealed on December 13, 1995, by the new government: Bill 8, *An Act to Repeal Job Quotas and to Resolve Merit- Based Employment Practices*. See 'Quashing of "Quota Law" a Defining Moment', *Toronto Star*, December 16, 1995, page E-1.

# 7 Enforcement of equal treatment: the role of the Equal Treatment Commission in the Netherlands

*Jenny E. Goldschmidt*[1]
*Lilian Goncalves Ho Kang You*[2]

## Introduction

To be able to evaluate the merits of any enforcement agency or policy, it seems useful to consider the conditions and demands for effective anti-discrimination law.[3] Consequently attention is drawn to these general aspects before explaining the Dutch experience.

## Conditions for effective anti-discrimination law

The effectiveness of equal rights law or anti-discrimination law depends both on the content of the relevant law and on the way for which its enforcement has been provided.

### The content of the law

As to the content of the law itself, one of the most important preconditions is that the relevant provisions are open enough to permit the incorporation of different perspectives and, at the same time, that the norms are sufficiently strict to prevent the incorporation of discriminatory propensities in their interpretation. It is extremely important to realise that power and dominance are sources of discrimination, and that dominance has an inherent tendency to reproduce itself. In essence, law results from a specific balance of power, and thus necessarily reflects a dominant point of view. Dominant perspectives tend to be presented as objective reality.[4] Other realities are not easily incorporated in such a legal context.

An example of making a norm sufficiently open to other perspectives is the incorporation of indirect discrimination in the concept of discrimination. The concept of indirect discrimination can help us to identify apparently neutral practices as discriminatory. For a fruitful development of the concept it is important that, both in the determination of the disparate effect and in the consideration of the possible objective justification, the specific backgrounds of discrimination are taken into account. However, although open norms are important to enable fundamental changes, the anti-discrimination law itself must also be strict to prevent exceptions being easily accepted. The same power structure that excludes other perspectives will eagerly look for arguments to reason that specific forms of unequal treatment do not amount to discrimination, and thus the scope of anti-discrimination law risks being narrowed down to undisputed flagrant cases of discrimination.

## Enforcement

As anti-discrimination law purports to modify an unequal division of power in society, it has to be taken into account that those who have to adapt their behaviour to the law are not very willing to do that. The law has to be applied in trade unions and other organisations, where dominant groups will resist changes that threaten their positions. Moreover, application and interpretation of non-discrimination law demand a thorough knowledge of the background, problems and dilemmas of equality law.

This means that special law enforcement agencies are important, provided that they have sufficient investigation powers and sanctions and that they are easily accessible to the discriminated. As to the latter, they are often in a rather vulnerable position, which

142

means that the enforcement of anti-discrimination laws should not depend merely on individual complainants. The admissibility of organisations to anti-discrimination proceedings is therefore very important. Needless to say, such proceedings should be free or at very low cost.

Taking into account these general conditions for effective enforcement of anti-discrimination law, the position and practices of the Equal Treatment Commission in the Netherlands is now considered.

## The Equal Treatment Commission in the Netherlands

### Introduction

Although the Equal Treatment Commission celebrated its first anniversary in September 1995, it has a pre-history of twenty years. Implementing the EU directives on equal treatment of men and women, special commissions to interpret the law and to promote its enforcement were set up in the seventies. In 1994 the Equal Treatment Act was passed and a new Commission was established (see also the contribution of Rodrigues, chapter 3), which also took over the tasks of the previously existing Commission on Equal Treatment of Men and Women.

The Equal Treatment Commission considers complaints with regard to unequal treatment based on the following grounds:

- religion
- personal conviction and views
- political orientation
- race
- gender
- nationality
- sexual preference
- marital status

It is forbidden to treat people differently on these grounds of discrimination in the following situations:

- *In working relationships.* Unequal treatment is forbidden in any area that is related to work, from job advertisements to actual employment. It is also forbidden in the following areas: salary, holidays, promotions and opportunities to follow courses. These regulations also apply to people in the liberal professions, such as barristers, solicitors and doctors.

- *In offering goods or services.* Unequal treatment is unlawful in concluding, implementing or terminating agreements on the subject.
- *In providing advice about educational or career opportunities.*

## Status and composition

The Commission is an independent body. It is made up of nine members and nine deputy members who are appointed for a period of six years (and can be reappointed immediately) by the Minister of Justice in consultation with four other Ministers. They can only be dismissed after a procedure similar to that followed in the Judiciary. The chair and co-chairs must fulfil the same requirements for appointment as a district court judge and are appointed on a full time bases. The six members are appointed on a fifty percent bases. All are selected because of their expertise and knowledge in the field of equality policies and anti-discrimination law. The Commission is supported by a 16-staff office. Moreover, the Commission may call on the assistance of civil servants designated by the competent Ministers. Thus, the Commission frequently calls in the expertise of job evaluation experts.

The Commission is subdivided into three Chambers. Chamber I deals with complaints of gender-based discrimination, Chamber II deals with complaints of discrimination on the grounds of race and/or nationality and Chamber III deals with complaints on all other grounds. The chambers can take over cases from each other in case of an overflow in one chamber.

## The Commission's objective and functions

The Equal Treatment Act mentions certain specific tasks assigned to the Commission. The more general objective can be deduced from the history of the Equal Treatment Act, especially the Explanatory Memorandum, and can be described as follows:

The objective of the Commission is to interpret and promote optimum enforcement of equal treatment legislation within the judicial framework of this legislation. The tasks of the Commission

144

which are specified in the Act can be summarised as follows:

- investigation of complaints on request in order to give
- rulings,
- investigation on its own initiative in order to give rulings,
- recommendations in addition to its rulings,
- bringing cases to court.

These various tasks result in a Commission which has two faces: First, the Commission is the independent semi-judicial body in charge of making independent rulings but the Commission can also be seen in its position of independent prosecutor. This double face makes for certain tensions and dilemmas in pursuing the Commission's objective.

In enforcing the objective of the Commission one should take into account that the Equal Treatment Law is not a 'neutral' law as it deals with bringing about social change. As mentioned earlier, the enforcement of equal treatment laws implies recognition of an unequal division of power in society. The Commission therefore cannot be a 'neutral' Commission. Not being neutral does not imply being prejudiced or partial. It does imply that the Commission's task is to contribute to the removal of inequality. It is crucial to understand this non-neutral character.

*The work of the Commission*

a. The essence of the Commission's business is to consider complaints. Complaints can be filed by individuals who believe they are suffering discrimination under the relevant laws, by a natural or legal person or agencies who wish to know whether they are guilty of discrimination under those laws, by persons deciding cases, or disputes concerning discrimination, by specific works councils or civil servants' committees, and by legal persons or incorporated associations which promote the interests of those whose protection is the objective of the anti-discrimination legislation.

In this context it is noteworthy that Dutch law [5] provides for class actions, a provision which is unique in the European Union. This entails that the legal persons and other entities mentioned above may also bring cases to court in order to enforce compliance with the relevant equal treatment laws (see the contribution of

Rodrigues, chapter 3)

This prospect of group action offers considerable advantages to individuals who suffer discrimination, especially in situations where they are dependent on those who discriminate against them and thus unwilling to bring their case to the Commission. A group action, to be distinguished from an action brought on behalf of complainants by an organisation, can restore the balance between the complainants and the other party. In general it could be said that group action is a more obvious way than individual action to ensure enforcement of equal treatment laws.

The Commission plays an active role in the investigation of complaints. This entails that the Commission asks for information both from the parties involved and from others. The Commission also visits parties to conduct investigations on their premises. Especially in job evaluation cases the Commission calls on the assistance of job-evaluation experts. These experts incorporate the relevant questions of the Commission in their research. As they are independent experts their findings are more easily accepted.

The Commission also consults other experts and hears witnesses.

b.   The Commission does not have to wait for complaints. The investigative powers of the Commission are not limited to (individual) complaints upon request. The Commission may also conduct an investigation on its own initiative in order to give a ruling. This power however, is limited to those cases of persistent discrimination under the relevant laws which take place either in the public service or in one or more sectors of society. By reason of the Memorandum of Reply to the Act, such investigation may not be conducted in one particular company or institution but should comprise one or more sectors of society, without identifying a specific complainant. An investigation may also cover various sectors, when related to a certain subject such as 'home-work contracts'.[6]

c.   The Commission may also take legal action in order to obtain a court ruling that conduct contrary to the relevant equal treatment regulations is unlawful, that it should be prohibited or that the consequences of such conduct should be rectified. This power has been one of the most disputed subjects of the Equal Treatment Act. The reason for giving this power to the Commission was to provide some comfort for the absence of enforceability of the

146

Commission's rulings.

The Commission has not yet taken any case to court. There are certainly some advantages of the use of this instrument in cases of serious discrimination, in order to establish a precedent. A court action could also be instrumental where certain individuals or groups would not have appropriate opportunities to challenge certain forms of inherent discrimination. A successful case might in general enhance the status of the Commission's rulings, which is important in the absence of enforceability. The disadvantages are also evident. An unsuccessful party might feel betrayed, when he has cooperated in the investigation by the Commission and the information is used against him in court. Here the two different positions of the Commission might collide. It needs no explanation that an unsuccessful action would damage the Commission's image. Moreover, one of the purposes of establishing the Commission is to prevent cases being taken to Court.

So far the Commission has concentrated its efforts on investigating individual complaints in order to gather expertise, especially with regard to the new grounds of discrimination.

d. To its rulings the Commission may add recommendations in a specific case. Recommendations may be useful to clarify how the rulings of the Commission can be implemented in daily practice. This is especially important in cases where it is not evident how equality can be put into practice in a concrete situation and might demand from time to time some creativity from the Commission's side. Good recommendations may widen the impact of the Commission's conclusions and contribute to compliance with the applicable equal treatment regulations.

*Mediation*

The Equal Treatment Act does not specifically mention mediation as a function of the Commission, but it does not exclude it either. Mediation can be an instrument to enforce the law. The predecessor of this Commission did not mediate. The advantage of mediation is that a problem can be solved (in conformity with equal treatment legislation) before it escalates. However, there can also be some disadvantages. Mediation prevents establishing case law, which is especially important for a new Commission. Mediation requires not only knowledge of all the facts and circumstances, but also of all applicable law, which could be beyond the scope of the Commission. Furthermore the parties could get the impression that equal treatment is negotiable.

Although the first cases of mediation have reaffirmed the difficulties of mediating equal treatment issues, the first impressions are that it is worth trying.

**Fulfilment of preconditions for effective anti-discrimination law where the Commission is concerned.**

*Open ends in a closed legal context*

The importance of open norms and strict legal provisions as conditions for effective non-discrimination law have already been emphasised. The Dutch equal treatment legislation indeed has a rather strict system, allowing only a limited number of exceptions.

However, although in the debate on the bill for the Equal Treatment Act, attention was paid to the relevance of several other (international) provisions of non-discrimination, the powers of the Commission are limited to the specific equal treatment laws. Of course, by means of treaty-consistent interpretation the Commission can incorporate elements of other legal provisions in the equal treatment laws. However, this possibility is limited to cases where the equal treatment laws themselves are applicable. Cases which fall outside the scope of these laws cannot be dealt with by the Commission. As physical or mental disabilities and age, for example, are not included as forbidden grounds of discrimination, the Commission does not have the power to hear cases on discrimination of disabled or elderly people. Also, the scope of the laws being limited to specific conduct in specific areas, it is difficult to bring other discriminatory acts under the law and thereby within the powers of the Commission. Thus, the use of abusive language or racist remarks in working relations can only be dealt with if such practise can be considered unlawful discrimination with regard to terms and conditions of employment. Nor can discrimination in the use of specific public powers, such as the issue of permits, be dealt with.

Furthermore the limited number of exceptions may cause problems because it seems to exclude the possibility of weighing whether or not certain cases fall within the scope of the exceptions based on reasonableness. Also strict norms can be difficult to apply in such a way that they can be accepted as just. Take for example the employer who refuses to enter into a contract with a pregnant woman for a job for six-month's. (Pregnancy is a form of direct discrimination which cannot be justified.)

With regard to indirect discrimination, EC case law is unclear as to the way disparate impact should be measured. The Commission is analysing how to address various issues such as: how to deal with numbers (absolute/relative); importance of relative numbers, disadvantages or detriment in case of job segregation; terms of reference: how general or specific? How much difference is required to presume 'disparate impact'? There are several cases pending on these questions in the EC Court.

There are undoubtedly limits to the concept of indirect discrimination. In general there is a lack of understanding that indirect discrimination is discrimination. It is therefore important that supporting legislation will be enacted such as equal treatment of part-time workers.

A bill, which prohibits unequal treatment on account of hours of employment, was recently passed.

*Enforcement*

With regard to the enforcement of anti-discrimination law, the importance of sufficient investigative powers and sanctions as well as the accessibility of enforcement agencies to the discriminated need to be emphasised.

*a. Investigative powers.* The bases for the investigative powers of the Commission lies in the Equal Treatment Act. Article 19 provides that it is compulsory for everyone to give the Commission the information it requests and that refusal to do so constitutes a criminal offence.[7]

In practise it is generally sufficient to ask for cooperation. If necessary just mentioning the risk of criminal sanctions is sufficient to receive the required information. But times seem to be changing. This may be caused by the fact that more and more cases of unequal treatment are brought before the Commission in areas where equality is not an issue as yet. In those cases when parties are not willing to cooperate, the Commission may of course invoke criminal sanctions, but it does not want this to become regular practise. The question is whether the Commission should pursue its request for information by all means, or it has to accept that in specific cases equality might be a bridge too far to be reached by equal treatment legislation. Do we see the limits of the law there? It may be true that the power of the law is limited. However by testing the effectiveness of the law through criminal enforcement proceedings in those specific cases, on the long run equality may be improved.

*b. The burden of proof.* The Commission faces the problem that many complaints, especially with regard to the new grounds such as racial discrimination, are vague or do not fall within the scope of the equal treatment legislation. The latter will change when people get more acquainted with the law. The problem of proof with regard to discrimination is not easy to overcome. As mentioned before, the Commission has a dual position. In its position of prosecutor it is the Commission's task to investigate and search for proof. At the same time it is the Commission's task to establish whether there is proof of unlawful discrimination and to establish which party has the burden of proof as well as the conditions for a shift of burden of proof.

In civil law procedures judges are bound to apply the general regulations with regard to proof as laid down in the Code of Civil Law Procedure. These regulations are not imperative for the Commission. Although the Commission does not completely shift the burden of proof, the Commission demands that those charged with unequal treatment sufficiently clarify that their acts or reasoning were based on facts or circumstances, which were not related to unequal treatment.

*c. Sanctions.* As stated before, the rulings of the Commission are not enforceable at law.  In this respect, the position of the Commission is - to some extent - similar to that of the Ombudsman. The Ombudsman however has to deal with only one 'offender', the Government, which in general is a cooperative party.

In the absence of enforceability, the impact of the Commission's rulings therefore depends on their quality, the authority of the Commission and the active investigation of the Commission itself. In the parliamentary debate on the Equal Treatment Act it was suggested to give the rulings of the Commission some binding

150

force, by giving them the status of an expert opinion which the courts cannot overrule without giving well-founded reasons. This suggestion was rejected by the Government. Instead, the Commission has been given power to bring a case to court to obtain an injunction prohibiting conduct contrary to the relevant anti-discrimination laws or to obtain an order that the consequences of such conduct be remedied.[8]

To enforce its rulings the Commission may publish its conclusions. Also, an active follow-up of cases may add weight to the rulings. For example in case of unlawful discrimination in a certain branch, the Commission informs the umbrella-organisation and requests cooperation in order to remedy such unlawful behaviour.

*d. Impact of rulings.* In order to evaluate the impact of the Commission's rulings it is of interest to analyse if and to what extent judges take them into account and whether parties observe the rulings.

The Supreme Court ruled (judgment of 13 November 1987) that 'taking into account the specific expertise of the Commission and the weight that the law attaches to its advice, a judgment contrary to the Commission's rulings can only be given on well-founded reasons.'

However, the Supreme Court in its judgment of 24 April 1992, did not pay attention to the fact that the Commission's ruling had been put aside by the lower courts without giving well-founded reasons. In both cases the Supreme Court declared the judgment of the lower courts, which were contrary to the Commission's rulings, null and void.

It is not clear yet what weight the Supreme Court will attach to the Commission's rulings under the new legislation.

The extent to which the lower courts take account of the Commission's rulings varies greatly.[9] This may be caused by the different terms of reference; the Commission considers only those aspects of the case which are relevant under the Equal Treatment Laws.

It is of course also of vital interest to evaluate whether the parties involved observe the Commission's rulings. The first impressions of the Commission are on balance positive. Most rulings are seriously taken into account and several have caused changes in discriminatory practices and regulations. Following are a few examples.

Certain municipal credit banks refused to give credit to people based on the fact that they did not have a permanent residence permit. The complaint was that this lead to discrimination on bases of race or nationality. The Commission ruled that it was acceptable for credit banks that conditions to prevent financial risks were established. These conditions however were too general and therefore people who did not represent an increased risk were excluded. The credit banks informed the Commission that they will review their procedures taking into account the Commission's rulings.

An insurance company refused to pay an allowance on account of disability-insurance in case of pregnancy and delivery. The relevant insurance-policy conditions excluded payment in such a case. The Commission ruled that such conditions are against the law. The company informed the Commission that it is willing to alter these conditions to a certain extent.

*e. Accessibility.* Although the proceedings of the Commission are free and easy accessible, fact is that for quite a few complainants, especially from minority groups, filing a complaint in writing is not an easy task. Moreover, the principles of fair trial impose certain formalities and procedures, which may not be readily understood by complainants. The Commission does not have consulting hours. Information can be obtained only by telephone or in writing. The Commission therefore is now experimenting with in house interviews with complainants who have difficulties in filing a complaint in writing. Furthermore the Commission is analysing what other methods might increase the accessibility of the Commission.


**Conclusion**

The Commission took up its duties in its current form as recently as September 1994, and has therefore been operational now for a relatively short time.

As of 1 September 1994 until 31 December 1995 the workload of cases amounted to 339, of which 213 were concluded in this period. This included 100 cases in which the Commission gave a ruling.

Of the total amount of cases concluded, 122 complaints were based on gender, 44 on race and/or nationality, 18 on marital status and 8 on religion and personal conviction.

In the next year or two the Commission will focus on conducting the first investigations on its own initiative in a sector of society, where persistent discrimination is taking place.

As stated before, new legislation that prohibits unequal treatment on account of working hours has been passed. This legislation will enlarge the scope of grounds of unequal treatment that can be considered by the Commission.

A body like the Commission, relatively easy accessible, with rather informal procedures, actively involved in collecting proof, with investigative powers and admissibility of class actions seems in accordance with requirements for effective anti-discrimination law enforcement. However, more time and experience is needed to establish its possible shortcomings and strength.

[1] Prof. Jenny E. Goldschmidt is Chair of the Equal Treatment  Commission in the Netherlands.

[2] Lilian Goncalves - Ho Kang You is Co-Chair of the Equal Treatment Commission in the Netherlands.

[3] These conditions can be derived from various research and literature such as:
John Griffiths, De sociale werking van rechtsregels en het emancipatoire potentieel van wetgeving, in: T. Havinga en B. Sloot (redactie), Recht, Bondgenoot of barriere bij emancipatie, Den Haag 1990, pp. 27-46;
P.F. van der Heijden, De verovering van het gelijk, in:
J.E.Goldschmidt, A,W. Heringa en F. van Vliet (redactie), De Zijkant van het gelijk, Zwolle
1991, pp. 115-127;
Sylvia A. Law, 'Girls can't be plumbers'- Affirmative action for Women in Construction: Beyond Goals and Quotas, in: Harvard Civil Rights-Civil Liberties Law Review, Vol. 24 (1989), pp. 45-77.

[4] A.C. Scales, The emergence of feminist jurisprudence: an  essay, in: Yale Law Journal 95 (1986), pp. 1373-1403, p. 1378.

[5] Civil Code section 3:305a and 3:305b

[6] Memorandum of Reply to the Equal Treatment Act page 25-26.

[7] Section 184 of the Netherlands Penal Code.

[8] Section 15 of the ETA

[9] J.A.H. Blom, De effectiviteit van de Wet gelijke behandeling m/v,  Eerste deelonderzoek, Den Haag 1994 pp 21-29.

# 8 The British Commission for Racial Equality as an enforcement agency

*Chris Boothman and Martin MacEwen*

## Historical background

The Commission for Racial Equality shares common ground with that of the Equal Opportunities Commission in that the Acts by which they were established, those of 1976 and 1975 respectively, provided similar powers and duties and similar roles regarding enforcement.

However, prior to the Race Relations Act of 1976, the twin roles of enforcement and promotion had been divided between the Race Relations Board and the Community Relations Commission respectively. The first race legislation in the UK was introduced over thirty years ago in the form of the Race Relations Act 1965 which established the Board and an embryonic enforcement machinery.[1]

This machinery, based on a process of conciliation, was borrowed from the USA and emphasised a preference for remedial rather than punitive sanctions which had been part of the original Bill considered by parliament. Excepting incitement to racial hatred which became a criminal offence, the limited acts of direct discrimination covered by 1965 Act constituted civil offences but were generally only enforceable by the Board. The Board through its local conciliation committees would receive complaints, investigate

155

them through a conciliation officer and form an opinion as to whether or not unlawful discrimination had occurred. Because such unlawful acts were restricted to places of public resort (including service in a public hotel, restaurant, theatre or bar for example) it was soon recognised by the Labour Government that the provisions required to be strengthened.

However the general approach to enforcement found in the 1965 Act was replicated in the 1968 Act. This was informed by the Street Report of 1967 which examined provisions in the USA (chapter 5) and in Canada (chapter 7), in particular, and made a number of recommendations for broadening the scope of the legislation.[2]

Taking on board the extent of discrimination verified by the PEP report of 1967[3], the fact that the UK government had become a signatory to the UN Convention on the Elimination of Racial Discrimination[4] and the opinions of a number of influential lobby groups[5] the Race Relations Act 1968 while keeping with the conciliation model, widened the area of unlawful discrimination considerably. Thus it became unlawful to discriminate on racial grounds in respect of employment, education and housing in both the public and private spheres as well as the generic 'provision of goods, facilities and services to the public or a section of the public'. The Race Relations Board was also empowered to conduct formal investigations on its own initiative where there were grounds for suspecting an offence may have been committed against an individual (section 17).[6]

To an extent the strengthening of the substantive provisions of the legislation put strain on the credibility of the conciliation process which retained the two tier structure of Board and conciliation committees. A further complication was that for employment complaints it was necessary to exhaust the industrial machinery by referral through the Department of Employment, a woolly compromise cooked up by unions and employers, before the Board might investigate. Many complainants felt aggrieved when the local conciliation committee formed an opinion of unlawful discrimination but was unable to negotiate a settlement or obtain an undertaking against repetition of the unlawful act.

To make matters worse, the Race Relations Board, understandably applying a more onerous burden of proof than that required for an 'opinion', would often decide that it would be imprudent to pursue the case to the designated county court or, in Scotland, the Sheriff Court.

156

The low number of complaints between 1968 and 1976, averaging less than one thousand per annum[7], is indicative of a degree of dissatisfaction. Reasons for the enforcement process failing are said to include, a lack of knowledge of the Board and its powers, a reluctance to complain, particularly in respect of employment cases, the exclusion of indirect discrimination, the paltry settlements which were offered, the strain associated with the complaints process and the low prospects of success.

At a strategic level, the 1968 Act had further faults. The Race Relations Board was clearly reactive to complaints rather than proactive to tackling areas of discrimination. This was reflective of the individual complaint based process (there were no powers of class or group action), the lack of research or strategic planning required by the legislation, the failure of the terms of section 17 to permit strategic investigations and the unhelpful interpretation of the courts of the relatively few cases which they had to consider.[8] In addition while the Board was involved in promotional activity this was seen to overlap with the responsibilities of the Community Relations Commission set up by the 1968 Act.

Proposals for legislative change were intimated in the White Paper of 1975 'Racial Discrimination'(Home Office Cmnd. 6234, HMSO). '...it is essential...', the paper observed at paragraph 81, 'that the law should be capable of providing adequate redress for the victim...as well as eliminating discriminatory practices which are against the public interest.' In adopting what the government described as the new and radical approach of the provisions of the Sex Discrimination Bill, then before Parliament, the new enforcement body was expected to combine 'the rights of individual access to legal remedies with the strategic functions of a powerful....commission responsible for enforcing the law on behalf of the whole community'.

Accordingly the most radical change in process was the right of complainants to seek remedies directly from the courts or, in the case of employment matters, the industrial tribunals rather than going through the Board. Industrial tribunals were said to have the advantages which the Franks Report had identified in 1957: in comparison to courts they are accessible, informal, endowed with appropriate expertise and, perhaps above all cheap.[9] The new CRE, however, had exclusive power to bring proceedings with regard to discriminatory practices, advertisements, instructions and pressure as well as persistent discrimination.

157

The CRE combined the functions of the Board and the Community Relations Commission and inherited, as a result, the network of community relations councils which had been built up and partially resourced by the old commission.

In terms of substantive law, the inclusion of indirect discrimination as being unlawful unless justified on non-racial grounds, the more extensive powers of investigation given to the CRE and the tightening up of some of the previous loopholes, such as the exclusion of so-called private clubs, provided a more convincing array of protection against discrimination than was offered by the 1968 Act.

## The new Commission and its enforcement performance

The new Commission and the workings of the Race Relations Act 1976 did not have to wait too long to incur governmental criticism, albeit at the hands of a more sceptical Tory administration. The Home Affairs Committee's first report for session 1981-82 was on the Commission for Racial Equality (HMSO, HC46-1). The Committee said that the CRE should do the following:

1. Confine its promotional work to the eradication of discrimination to emphasise the linkage with enforcement.
2. Get rid of the lamentable backlog of formal investigations: the CRE had taken on more than it could handle.
3. Restrict intervention in partisan debate: while this was not a complete gagging order, the Committee were annoyed by the Commission's support for the ILEA and suggested that there was no need to voice opinion adequately expressed by ethnic minority groups.
4. There should be a review of management and staffing and the essentially non-executive and supervisory functions of the commissioners should be emphasised. The Committee wanted more lawyers, more regional staff, better clerical support and better training to counterbalance the criticism that the CRE staff were discourteous and lacked discretion in dealing with the public.

A number of significant reviews of the work of the CRE took place in the 1980s, and early 1990s including the PEP report 'Racial discrimination: Seventeen Years After the Act' (Brown and Gay, 1986), the PSI study 'Racial Justice at Work', McCrudden et al (1991), the study of other jurisdictions as a basis of comparison (MacEwen, 1994[10] ) and the CRE's own reviews of 1985 and 1992.

While it is not possible to distill their observations and recommendations on enforcement, it is generally accepted that the individual complaint based model found in the 1976 Act has a number of difficulties, particularly in its failure to take on board the systemic nature of discrimination. Discrimination is characterised by this model as an individual aberration rather a process which has been insidiously absorbed into the dominant norms to such an extent that it is not readily recognised. Thus the 'sons and daughters' council housing policy of Tower Hamlets by which preference in housing allocations is given to established communities over relative new comers- and therefore clearly constitutes indirect discrimination- is judged to be 'fair' without reference to the objective housing needs of the whole community including those from Bangladesh.

Conversely, there is little acceptance of alternative models, particularly those which focus on group remedies the aim of which is to look for tangible improvement in outcomes for disadvantaged ethnic minority groups. In the USA the group approach has been challenged by court decisions following *The University of California Regents v. Bakke* (1978) 438 US 265. and there is little scope for such positive action in the provisions of the current legislation in Britain. Accordingly for the present it is only fair to judge the performance of the CRE against the existing law. The following describes what the CRE now aims to achieve.

### The CRE today

Commission for Racial Equality now sees its law enforcement role in the context of its greater role including its promotional functions. It is not simply spending money on expensive lawyers to go to court. One has to look at what the Commission is trying to achieve, whether it is being effective and whether there are other ways of achieving what is wanted. The statute talks of the CRE working towards the elimination of discrimination, promoting equality of opportunity, promoting good relations between people of different racial groups and keeping the working of the Race Relations Act under review. Those statutory duties have been there since 1976 but different Commissions have chosen to interpret those duties in different ways.

The complexion, the direction, and the role of the Commission can often be identified with the people who are leading the Commission at any particular point in time. The Commission is made up of a number of individuals who are appointed to the Commission for Racial Equality by the Home Secretary - fifteen individuals, one of whom is appointed as chairman. The chairman is appointed for a period of five years, the other so-called ordinary commissioners are appointed for periods of two years and which can sometimes be extended. It is fair to say that the lifetime of the Commission had been a succession of five year cycles and in a sense the strengths and weaknesses of the chairman at the time have dictated what the organisation did, what it was viewed as, what its aims and objectives are.

### Creating a new vision

A new chairman was appointed years ago in 1993 and, for the first time, the chair was a member of an ethnic minority community. Many have said that he came in with a very clear vision of what the Commission should be doing. One of the first things that he did, in consultation with another group of new commissioners who were appointed, was to set a new vision for the Commission for Race Equality. Something that concerned him was that there was confusion about the Commission's role and for what it stood. It was felt that there was a need to try and formulate a message which could be accepted by the whole nation and which would go some way to making the organisation have some kind of common ownership, not just amongst ethnic minorities; so what was formulated was a new aim for the Commission:

> The Commission for Racial Equality is working for a just society which gives everyone an equal chance to work, learn and live, free from discrimination and prejudice and from the fear of racial harassment and violence.

Now that new aim was designed to try to get away from the idea that the Commission for Racial Equality is only there to protect the

160

rights of minorities. It was felt that that perception, of the role that had been ascribed to the Commission was not one that should be carried forward into the future. It was felt to be holding the work of the CRE back, and it was not ensuring that it was getting the right kind of networks and partnerships together to achieve racial equality.

## Partnerships and networking

The commissioners recognised at a very early stage that the CRE, on its own, was not able to achieve racial equality. The CRE now has a budget of some £15m - it is twice as much as the Equal Opportunities Commission has but it still, nevertheless, is not a lot of money and it does not necessarily go very far if strategy for racial equality is just founded on the organisation. So early after the formulation of the aim, it was decided that another priority should be to send out a very clear message that the Commission was in business to achieve racial equality through others, through partnerships and through networks in society.

Networks and partnerships are therefore regarded by Commissioners as a very important part of its work. The work of racial equality is a massive endeavour and the resources that the CRE has are not sufficient to do that work. Just to give an example, the Commission aims to ensure that every victim of discrimination with a winnable case, has representation in a tribunal or court. Clearly the CRE is not in a position to do that alone, but what it does is to try to ensure that there are other agencies that can provide representation, some funded directly and others whom the CRE feels have a responsibility to provide a service and on whom the CRE puts pressure to do so. This building of networks and building of alliances is seen as a major part of todays work and, consequently, it means that it becomes problematical to get into conflict situations with those concerned at the same time. There is a difficult game that the Commission has to play with service providers and employers on the one hand trying to cajole them, consulting with them, working with them but also quite often funding cases against them or taking direct Commission action against them

Consequently the Commission decided to formulate a number of campaigns as part of its public awareness focus. Along with that it was decided that there should be new priorities. The

Commissioners decided that the work of the Commission had been spread far too thin and they decided to introduce a new focus by setting up priorities.

## Setting priorities and restructuring

The first priority became assistance to victims of discrimination, the second priority tackling institutional discrimination, the third priority dealing with racial harassment and violence, the fourth prioritising youth and the last building a public awareness programme. Those were the new priorities that the new Commission, in 1993, decided to embark upon in its first year.

Following on that, it also decided to restructure the Commission to provide a service essentially through regional teams. The CRE has set up a regional team for London and the south which operates mainly out of its London office where the majority of staff are presently based. It has an area team covering middle England, for want of a better phrase, which is the Midlands and Wales and there are offices in Birmingham and Leicester. There is a recently opened office in Cardiff and a team for the north which covers the north of England and Scotland with offices in Edinburgh, Manchester and Leeds. The new Commissioners decided that the CRE should try to move away from locating all the staff in the centre in London and push more staff out to the regions where it felt that the work should be done.

The CRE employs approximately 200 staff directly and under its grant aid powers, it funds or part-fund 86 Race Equality Councils round the country. This is a network of individual organisations whose objectives are similar to the Commission but who are independent voluntary organisations part-funded both by the Commission and relevant local authorities. Those 86 Race Equality Councils contribute beyond two hundred staff to racial equality work over and above those directly employed by the CRE.

The CRE has a budget of £15m of which about £5m goes on grants mainly to fund the Race Equality Council movement, £8m on salaries, travel and general expenditure, £1m is spent directly on funding case work and another £1m is split among things like publications, conferences and new technology.

The £1m spent on case work is not the entire law enforcement picture because approximately £1m is spent on indirect work

162

through race equality councils, other specialist complaint organisations and other forms of advice and assistance. In summary, the Commission spends approximately £3m directly and indirectly on assistance to victims of discrimination.

## Charter standards

Another part of what the Commissioners wanted to do in designing the new Commission was to set out Charter Standards. It is said that some of the failings of law enforcement agencies include being slow, cumbersome, inefficient, and unresponsive. The Commissioners decided they weren't prepared to tolerate an organisation that had all these kind of negative connotations and so they decided to adopt the government's Charter Standards and the CRE has developed a client-centred approach to the work it does. It has standards, for instance, in answering the telephone and responding to letters.

The Commission has a number of documents which set out the service that it offers to different sections of the community. It has a service offered for victims of discrimination, it has a service for employers and service providers. Indeed the CRE even goes so far as to say to respondents what they can expect of the Commission when it either threatens or ends up taking legal action. This is all part of a more explicit ethos of trying to project with clarity what the Commission is, what it can offer and how it will operate.

## Complainant aid and investigations

In terms of complainant aid, the duty is to consider every application for assistance. The CRE is not in the fortunate position of the Equal Opportunities Commission; it does not have the Treaty of Rome to fall back on. The CRE does not have the ability to go beyond the English or Scottish Courts and its experienced of the English courts is such that it not have unqualified confidence in securing justice in the judicial system. That, as well as the kind of demands that have been placed on the Commission by the ethnic minority communities, has meant that the approach to case work is now more focused on individuals.

In the past the CRE has spent large amounts of money pursuing so called strategic or landmark cases but it had a number of fairly painful experiences in the early 1990s when in two cases alone which it lost it ended up paying out somewhere in the region of £2-300,000, a third of its direct budget on cases and at that time that really focused its attention on the effectiveness, the efficacy and efficiency of funding major cases. Although it clearly keeps a look-out for cases that will change the law in a radical way and will have an impact on discrimination across the board, it is not something it rushes to do. Instead its focus is on ensuring that individuals get justice. In terms of the statistics last year, it received somewhere in the region of 1700-1800 applications for assistance. Out of these applications, it gave direct assistance to somewhere in the region of 230, it arranged for representation for about another 112 cases and in the majority of the rest of the cases it provided advice and assistance.

In terms of making complainant aid a reality, it has tried to establish a complainant aid network. Because it cannot undertake all the enforcement work itself, it recognises that there are others who have a role to play. It has funded a number of specialist organisations in different parts of the country to do specialist complainant aid work. They are essentially organisations which are set up to do representation. It has also decided that its funded race equality councils should do a certain amount of case-work themselves and it has made part of their terms of reference the provision of complainant aid services.

The CRE has insisted that trade unions do case work on behalf of their membership. In an effort to make that a reality it had to go to the extreme in one case of actually embarking upon a formal investigation against a major union, RMT, where it had a complaint that the union was not representing its ethnic minority members in race cases. The CRE then embarked upon a formal investigation to force the union to provide representation.

On the back of that example of forcing a trade union to provide representation, the CRE launched a major initiative to persuade the whole of the trade union movement to be provide effective representation for their members. By doing that it has been able to divert a large number of cases from Commission assistance to trade unions. What it has had to do to reinforce that initiative is provide training and back-up to trade union officials and other lawyers who are acting on behalf of complainants. The CRE also expects Citizen Advice Bureaux, Advice Centres and Law Centres to provide a service to victims of discrimination and in future it will be making demands on them and setting standards as to how it thinks that work should be done.

It will becoming apparent that Commissioners, as individuals, have now imposed themselves on the organisation fairly forcefully and indeed they have a much greater input into the work of the Commission. It has established regional committees in which certain Commissioners are given regional briefs. Consequently, they are more directional in the work that goes on in the region but that in itself has created some problems in terms of managing the organisation. Sometimes there is confusion in roles in terms of senior Commissioners and management but that is something that the organisation committed to try to work out. On the whole the organisation views the experience of such changes as at 1996 as positive.

## Development strategy

Another major difference in the work of the Commission in recent years is that the Commissioners decided that it had to develop a follow up strategy to the Commission's investigatory work. The past has been traditionally fighting one-off cases, securing one-off victories in tribunals but those victories have not necessarily gone anywhere. The Commission has decided that for every case that it wins there should be follow-up with the individual respondent. That respondent should be revisited to ensure that the problem does not recur. And not only that, but the case should be looked at to see whether or not there are implications for that particular sector.

For instance, where a case is won against a caterer the CRE will be looking to see whether there are implications for the catering industry and indeed as part of the restructuring the CRE has a legal strategy unit whose job it is:

1. to set up an outcomes database so there is a centralised point for information on law enforcement outcomes;
2. to develop that database for disseminating information to its various networks and partnerships on law enforcement outcomes; and
3. to provide a centralised point to lead on following up successful outcomes

Indeed in following up successful outcomes the work is relatively new but the CRE is looking at situations where legal officers sit down with officers in its Communications Division, officers in its Research section and officers in its Campaigns to devise ways of getting messages across so that success is not just measured in terms of individual cases in court. The CRE is constantly looking to see how it can make the impact of decisions felt right across the board.

**Equality standards**

Together with that work should also be mentioned the Commission's work on equality standards, another main platform of the Commission's work. In essence, it is really a follow-up from the power to formulate codes of practice. The experience of the CRE has been that the codes of practice have only had a limited amount of success so the Commission has decided that it should work towards drawing up equality assurance standards which are actually trying to translate quality into action. The CRE is producing documentation based on defined standards which sets out realistic, measurable criteria which lead to results and which can be formulated and shared with employers and service providers so that they can take ownership and measure their own progress in terms of attaining racial equality. Indeed in the year 1994-1995 it has produced an equality standards assurance for employers and for local government and it has also produced a youth standards with further standards are expected.

**Communications strategy**

The Commission's communications strategy is a major plan in the work it does. The image and perceived role of the Commission has been very negative. It is perceived to be an organisation set up to protect the rights of minorities, it has been perceived as an inefficient, ineffective organisation, unable to tackle government properly, unable to make changes to the law and unable to fight effective cases in the courts.

One of the main duties of its Communications Division and its strategy development is to tackle those perceptions, not only in order to try and explain the difficulties that it has, but also proactively to promote good practice and to put the Commission in the best light.

One of the unfortunate side effects of successful cases is often negative publicity. The CRE has tried to combat this not only by putting its perspective on these successful cases but also by trying to engage with the media. Its Communications Division has regular meetings with the media and has briefings, particularly with the tabloid media, people from the likes of the Sun and the Daily Mail. The CRE felt that this won't have the desired effect until it tackled those organs of the media that did the commission and its cause most damage. Resources have been dedicated to developing a message, building campaigns with which everyone can identify and communicating that message.

## Campaigns

Successes in court are all very well but do they actually change behaviour? Unfortunately the CRE experience is that successful court cases do not, in themselves, change behaviour, or they change behaviour for short periods of time. An employer will change perhaps for a year or two but then complaints are seen again against the same employer.

Now the CRE is looking to use such campaigns to change public perceptions. it has a campaign 'Uniting Britain for a Just Society' which it is promoting with a number of major institutions and advertisers. it has another successful campaign, 'Let's Keep Racism Out of Football', and a third one 'All Different All Equal', as well as a news campaign across Europe. The Commission has seen its successes in terms of race equality as not only coming from the hard edge cases in courts and tribunals but also from winning the so-called hearts and minds.

In relation to publications the CRE is looking to move away from seeing all Commission activities ending up in a publication. One of the criticisms of enforcement agencies is that they spend a lot of time and money on academic endeavours producing interesting research and publications but such outcomes don't necessarily impact on individuals. The Commission is diverting resources from work that was seen as academic to more populist ways of getting messages and views across. Only time will tell whether that will bear fruit.

## Reviews of the Act

With reference to parliamentary work, the CRE has a duty to keep the Act under review and it has produced two reviews of the Race Relations Act which have been duly sent to the Home Secretary. The first review wasn't even acknowledged.[11] The second review was acknowledged but not a lot was given. In one sense all it managed to secure was an undertaking from the government to introduce a legally binding undertaking, that is a power which the Commission could use as an alternative to law enforcement action to get employers to agree to provide it with a course of conduct or behaviour which it could enforce in the courts. It is believed that that would be an advantage to the commission because at present the only way it can get binding agreements to take action is by issuing court proceedings or by issuing a Non-discrimination Notice after formal investigation.

If it had a power of issuing a binding undertaking the employer would have a choice. Rather than actually get into the business of issuing proceedings and creating a lot of acrimony, the CRE would offer an alternative: 'Look, we've got this facility and if you'll agree to do XYZ then we don't have to go down the road of litigation and lawyers and all the rest of it'. That idea has been sold to the government essentially on the grounds of costs, not surprisingly. It has been persuaded that that would be an advantageous power for the Commission to have because the perception is that the Commission will not have to flex its muscles so often if it has this new power. That is essentially all the government has given the CRE in real terms although in fairness, it have agreed to look at a number of other issues.

It has agreed to look at administrative ways of changing some of the difficulties the CRE has with the current arrangements. It is fair to say that the commission has quite a good working relationship with the civil servants in the Home Office who are charged with this area of work. Far from being negative about what the government has decided in relation to the review of the Act, the CRE has decided to make the most of what's been offered but to pursue its own strategy in terms of making other changes which need to happen.

## Confidential settlements

Two other developments have taken place recently in terms of law enforcement. The Commissioners felt that the Commission was entering into too many confidential settlements in cases. Again a strong view expressed by Commissioners is that one of the outcomes of successful cases, or even unsuccessful cases sometimes, is actually promoting what has happened, promoting any change that has been achieved. Consequently it is contrary to promoting change to accept confidential settlements. As a matter of policy, the Commission decided that it would not engage or enter into confidential settlements in cases supported by the Commission. The lawyers in particular will appreciate that there is a potential problem in applying that kind of policy. The policy is a general one but it is subject to the rider that if an applicant really insists on a confidential settlement, or indeed if officers of the CRE, think it is in the interest of the applicant to have a confidential settlement then it will enter into one but it will seek to send out a very strong and firm message that it is not in the business of sweeping breaches of the Act under the carpet. It wants to be able to promote outcomes in a positive way so it seeks to engage with respondents as to the best way of promoting an outcome where possible. Accordingly, it is not just a case of carpeting a respondent in terms of trying to project what has been achieved in the case.

## Funding casework

In relation to funding casework, the CRE had a problem a few years ago where it found its  legal commitment was over-committed because of the number of individual cases it were supporting. As a reaction to that problem it actually had to stop using lawyers and many solicitors in private practice from doing Commission cases because it found that the cost was prohibitive. What it is currently doing instead is using an in-house team of litigators in each region who prepare the case work but who instruct counsel directly. By doing that it is able to cut the cost of litigation, while retaining the quality and having greater  control over cases it is funding.

Often in discrimination cases it is found out just before the hearing that the case is not as strong as it was thought to be. In the past the experience has been that external lawyers have been very reluctant to advise the commission of that problem. Now this problem has largely been overcome by bring cases in-house. In terms of publicity, with in-house lawyers acting for the CRE in particular cases , then it has better control over publicity and it is able to promote publicity that enhances rather than puts a negative image on its work.

## Conclusions

### Promotions

Perhaps it would be helpful to end by giving a few examples of what the Commission has been able to achieve by way of the new approach. The 'Kick Racism out of Football', referred to above, is a campaign which seems to have gripped the footballing nation in a way in which was never expected. Indeed it is funded by outside funders and it has a gathered a momentum of its own. It is a campaign which is expected to last for quite some time. A spillover has come from it - there is talk of a campaign in cricket, in rugby, and other campaigns are seemingly springing from it.

In the 'Uniting Britain for a Just Society' it had some quite high profile advertisements designed by Saatchi & Saatchi which, according to research that it had done, had caused people to acknowledge the existence of the Commission, whereas before people don't seemed to have known much about the Commission. The commission is now finding from action research that some of the messages are beginning to sink through to the public.

### Cases and investigations

The CRE has had some successful cases. The case of Jenkins succeeded in highlighting the issue of racial harassment not only in the educational establishment but in the work-place in general. That gave birth to quite a successful publication on racial harassment that it was promoting. It had threatened formal investigation of the Police Federation which has led to the Police Federation now backing the cases of their members in racial discrimination. It has threatened formal investigation of a local authority which formally had a policy of rehousing victims of racial harassment as a last resort. Following a series of judicial reviews against the authority, it was contacted and only by threatening a formal investigation the CRE was able to get them to change their policy and to introduce a new policy.

The whole thrust of the Commission's law enforcement work is now to use legal action as a last resort both for reasons of expense and because the law is cumbersome. The Commission now has an expectation of using innovative, flexible, and new methods of securing racial equality.

## Observations

The relative success or failure of the changes which have taken place regarding the different emphases of the work of the CRE under its present chairman, Mr Herman Ouseley, must be judged against a backdrop of changing expectations of what the institution should aim to achieve.

The Race Relations Board set out, in its first annual report published in 1967, the role of legislation. The law was seen as promoting:

1) an unequivocal declaration of public policy;
2) the provision of support for those who do not wish to discriminate, but who feel compelled to do so by social pressure;
3) the provision of protection and redress to minority groups;
4) the provision for the peaceful and orderly adjustment of grievances and the release of tension; and
5) the reduction in prejudice by discouraging the behaviour in which prejudice finds expression.

While this is seen as a classic statement of institutional objectives and others have sought both to enlarge and refine this definition of the purposes of anti-discrimination provision, today the aims of the current CRE as quoted in the opening section are perhaps expressed in somewhat looser terms but are no less ambitious. In the 1975 White Paper, which heralded the current structure of the CRE, government acknowledged that racial equality in Britain could not be achieved by the actions of a commission alone but required a raft of supportive government initiatives to ensure that both attitudes and behaviour were changed.

Those supportive initiatives have included the urban aid programme, an ethnic minority grant, section 11 funding under the

171

Local Government (Social Services) Act 1966 for local authority staff and government voluntary monitoring of employees in the civil service. Nonetheless the commitment of central government has clearly waxed and waned over time and is today characterised as 'benign neglect' (McCrudden: 1995). Accordingly the necessary framework of policy support for the CRE and the law it administers is flawed.

There have been changes to the Race Relations Act 1976 since its inception: the Education Acts of 1980 and 1981 extended the duty of local education authorities not to discriminate in the exercise of all their functions and a similar provision was made in respect of planning authorities by way of the Housing & Planning Act 1986. The statutory authority of the CRE to provide Codes of Practice has been extended from employment to the housing sphere by reason of the Local Government and Housing Act 1986. These now apply to both the rented and non-rented sector. The new Higher Education Funding Councils (for England, for Wales and for Scotland) have duties to promote racial equality by reason of the Further and Higher Education Act of 1992. The Courts and Legal Services Act 1990 closed the loophole whereby the non-contractual relationship between barristers (and advocates) with solicitors had meant that discrimination between them was not covered by the 1976 Act.

In truth, however, while these amendments, together with the Race Relations (Remedies) Act 1994 which removed the limit on awards in racial discrimination cases which may be made by industrial tribunals, may be important in themselves cumulatively they do not represent a significant expansion of the powers of the CRE to meet the various criticisms identified in the two CRE reviews of the 1976 Act previously referred to.

In particular the CRE has argued that institutional discrimination requires a systemic approach: accordingly the requirement of major employers to monitor their work-force in the manner that such obligations are placed on employers in Northern Ireland in respect of religious discrimination, and for housing authorities to monitor housing allocations are overdue reforms. Such measures together with a more rigorous government approach to the use of contract compliance in order to promote equality of opportunity have proved to be requests which have fallen on deaf ears

Those who criticise the agency for being based on a liberal model of individualism and thus being largely unable to respond to legitimate aspirations of minority ethnic groups point to such failures by government to respond to requests for change to legitimise their argument. Other criticisms of the role of the enforcement agencies include the assertion that the law, in being 'colour blind', is essentially integrationist or assimilationist and ignores the reality of cultural diversity between different ethnic groups (T. Modood, 1991). Institutions such as the CRE are also prone to the charge that they are buffer agencies, there to protect the government from challenge by the black community to its monochrome authority (Katznelson, [1973] and Sivanandan [1976]).[12]

There is also a general criticism that the Race Relations legislation and the CRE as an enforcement agency represent the 'rights approach' to social change. Essentially this is characterised as a misplaced legalism in setting unrealistic goals within a framework which is ill-matched for their delivery.

Whatever the merits or demerits of this discourse, and it is clearly relevant to consider how it impinges on the performance of the agency, it remains evident that this government, in keeping with more general demands for accountability for the expenditure of public resources, sets expectations on the performance of its quangos that they will be both efficient and effective: from time to time the Home Affairs Committee and the Public Accounts Committee may provide their own view regarding such performance but ultimately, it is probably the general public, and perhaps more importantly, the minority ethnic groups most keenly affected, who will be the arbiters of how well the institution has performed within its acknowledged limitations.

[1] This legislation and the 1968 Act is fully described in context by Geoffrey Bindman and Anthony Lester, 1972, 'Race and Law', Pengiun Books: Harmonsworth. A useful review of the development of the law is found in Chis McCrudden, *Racial Discrimination* in Chis McCrudden and Gerald Chambers (1995), 'Individual Rights and the Law in Britain' Clarendon Press: Oxford.

[2] The Street Report, (1967),'Report on Anti-discrimination Legislation' was written by Goeffrey Howe, Geoffrey Bindman and Harry Street and published by the Home Office: London.

[3] Political and Economc Planning, (1967), 'Report on Racial Discrimination', PEP: London.

[4] See chapter by Michael O'Flaherty on ICERD and discussion by M. MacEwen in 'Tackling Racism in Europe' (chapter 2), Berg: Washington and Oxford.

[5] See Bindman and Lester (1971) above.

[6] The investigatory powers of the now CRE are examined by Chis McCrudden, *The Commission for Rqcial Equality: Formal Investigations in the Shadow of Judicial Review,* in Baldwin, R. and McCrudden, C. (1987), 'Regulation and Public Law' Weidenfeld and Nicolson: London.

[7] See Table 4.2 and commentary in chapter 4 in M. MacEwen, (1990), 'Housing, Race and Law', Routledge: London

[8] See discussion by McCrudden(1995), above.

[9] See Franks Committee Report 1957 (Committee on Administrative Tribunals and Inquiries), Cmnd 218, HMSO: London.

[10] MacEwen, M. (ed), (1994), 'Anti-discrimination Law on the Grounds of Race: a comparative survey of provisions in Australia, New Zealand, Canada and the USA', a report of a study for the Home Office, Commission for Racial Equality/Scottish Ethnic Minorities Research Unit: Edinburgh

[11] 'Review of the Race elations Act 1976: Proposals for Change', (1985), Commission for Racial Equality: London.

[12] Katznelson, I. "Black Men, White Cities" (1973), Oxford University Press: London and New York.
Sivanandan, A. ( 1976) "Race, Class and the State: The Black Experience in Britain" 17 Race and Class 347.

# 9 South Africa: legal institutions and fairness

*Sarah Christie*

## Introduction and problem-setting

The South African government is politically committed and legally obliged to promote equality as part of the social and economic transformation of the country. Its fundamental legal obligations are contained in its interim Bill of Rights, accession to the four major international conventions dealing with women and ratification of central ILO conventions but the absence of proper machinery makes one doubtful of their efficacy.[1] The Constitution obliges the state to establish a Human Rights Commission, a separate Commission on Gender Equality, a Public Protector (Ombudperson) and a Commission on the Restitution of Land Rights. This process has begun.[2] There are also increasing demands to compel the state to expropriate to provide arable land for redistribution.[3] Finally, major change to the core labour statute, the Labour Relations Act (LRA), will substantially change labour law and institutions.

In addition to these legal foundations, the government has proposed an extensive package of social reform in its White Paper on Reconstruction and Development (RDP).[4] Thus far the RDP has very little to show for itself, although there have been forums, strategic planning meetings and white papers. Some of the reasons for this are that the national and provincial governments are at times in conflict with each other, budgets are not always properly allocated, excessive bureaucracy has delayed project implementation, infrastructure is as yet poorly developed and the politics of consultation is enormously slow.[5]

This reconstruction process raises prodigious challenges for South Africa: first, the state is finding it difficult to balance social development claims of the unemployed poor against constitutionally protected property rights, yet if property is designated as a private zone of individual rights, general societal obligations may be held hostage to property owners.[6] Secondly, legislative reform of labour law and institutions has as its primary focus the unionised environment and although formal labour rights are extended to all employed people South Africa lacks institutions to deal with the predicament of the unemployed or underemployed; thirdly, state strategies for black empowerment are unlikely to reach much beyond the small black middle class to the majority who are very poor and who cling precariously to survival economic activity.[7]    South Africa faces prodigious problems in turning the country from a beleaguered, uncompetitive economy to one able to drive development in the sub-continent.

The final constitution is likely to suggest a social democratic rather than liberal model of development, in striking a balance between private interest and public need. Even so, this will not immunise the Constitutional Court from having to tackle really difficult issues in measuring legislative or executive action against economic development and the protection of individual rights.[8]

*Economic challenges and the labour market*

A compelling challenge to law and legal institutions as techniques for social and economic transformation is the persistent failure of the South African economy to generate employment. Only formal employment generates regular wages and ancillary benefits such as pension and medical aid schemes and in general, protective labour legislation covers only the formal employment sector. However, formal employment continues to decline. The total population increased from 24 million in 1980 to about 40 million in 1994 (growth rate: blacks 2.8%, Asians 1.7%, Coloured 1.7% and Whites 1.0%).[9] The economically-active population (EAP) increased from 8.4m in the same period to approximately 14.3m (an annual rate of 2.9%).  But formal job opportunities in the non-agricultural sectors barely moved, a mere 0.35% increase p.a.[10] Although total employment has recently begun to rise (1.3% in the last three quarters of 1994), this modest nominal growth is far below the

176

increase in the total labour force. Unemployment remains extremely high and nearly a third of the EAP was without formal employment in October 1994. Young people and rural women, among the worst off, remain impoverished through prolonged non-access to jobs or, at best, remain trapped in the informal 'illegal' economy and social security is wholly inadequate.[11] Paradoxically, average nominal labour costs increased by 11.9% in the first half of 1995 (10% in 1994).[12]

Although the South African economy is moving from its protectionist trading and import substitution policies, the process has been slow and is far from complete and labour market institutions have not managed mass retrenchment through the kind of retraining and development programmes which are commonplace in industrialised countries. Foreign investment has increased but we still have substantial domestic capital outflows. Savings are low and falling, aggravated by fiscal drag: the marginal tax rate has not risen for three years although the value of money has dropped by 26% in the same period and the ratio of net savings by the private sector to GDP fell from 9% in the second quarter of 1993 to 7.5% in the first two quarters of 1995. South Africa continues to compare poorly with South East Asia's developing economies which have high levels of foreign investment, high domestic savings and investment and a liberal trading environment. Its problems are compounded by very rapid rural to urban migration, high population growth and a poorly educated workforce.[13]

*Racial imbalances*

Overall economic imbalances are massive and very well known: white households earn more than six times black households; this disparity is exacerbated by sex. Thus earnings of male-headed white households are more than seven times those of female headed African households.

**Figure 9.1**
**Average monthly household income in rands**

| African | 1,005 |
|---|---|
| Coloured | 2,057 |
| Indian | 4,009 |
| White | 6,379 |
| Average | 2,089 |

Source: Table 13.1 *South Africa's Rich & Poor*: Baseline Household Statistics[14]

**Figure 9.2**
**Average monthly household income of female headed households in rands.[15]**

| | |
|---|---|
| African | 833 |
| Coloured | 1,576 |
| Indian | 2,199 |
| White | 3,269 |
| Average | 1,142 |

Black equity holdings are very low: black people have between 5% and 10% of total holdings. There would need to be growth of 6% pa or more, to double this in five years and reach the targets the state has set for itself.[16]   Although there has been some progress in achieving employment transformation across economic sectors, this has been mixed. Only 3% of managers are African and women form a little over 11% of managerial staff.  furthermore it has been pointed out that white domination of supervisory staff remains a barrier to internal development and promotion within undertakings.[17] Black advancement within organisations tends to be biased towards non-executive posititions within boards of directors and this usually through outside appointment, not promotion from within. Thus effective control of private sector business remains firmly white and male dominated.

At the same time there is even more dispiriting evidence of a widening disparity between rich and poor blacks. Large companies seem willing to pay black senior managers up to 50% more than whites for the same position.  Whereas a small, visible black elite, has been seen to benefit considerably from affirmation action programmes, sometimes implemented unilaterally by white management and occasionally negotiated with trade unions (particularly in large businesses) there is massive and persistent impoverishment. This is similar to certain societies in Latin and South America.[18]


**The challenge**

The challenge South Africa faces is stark: it must eliminate discrimination and promote equity in the workplace without jeopardising employment growth and it has to manage the tension between job creation and employment equity.  The state recognises that its policy and strategies must focus on equality of outcomes if anything useful will be achieved for the victims of past discrimination.[19] Labour and social security law will therefore need to focus on qualitative outcomes so that employers for instance will have positive obligations to remedy inequality, promote equality and prevent discrimination in the future.[20]

*Definitions*

The focus of this piece is not on conceptual problems of definition and it is taken as given that the substantive law should define discrimination in such a way that evasion is made difficult. The Labour Relations Act (LRA) of 1995[21] proscribes direct and indirect discrimination, as does the Bill of Rights.[22] Both instruments try to balance principles of inclusivity in specific declared grounds of impermissible discrimination as well as in a generic definition, but the LRA does not expressly include unfair treatment or sexual harassment as discrimination.[23] It is not yet clear how far civil rights legislation will reach, but unless it is wide it may well replicate the private/public or private/commercial divisions and complex and confusing jurisprudence of the USA.[24] A politically delicate matter, as yet unresolved, is the extent to which civil rights of general application may trump customary and religious law and practice.

> South Africans need to analyse the strong parallel between discrimination legalised within customary law, and for[sic] former system of legalised racial discrimination. Both involve dual systems of law. With racial discrimination, there was one set of laws for the whites, and another for the blacks. With gender discrimination there is a very similar dual legal system: statutory law where women are apparently equal, but customary law where they are not.[25]

*Enforcement* [26]

It is trite that unless enforcement mechanisms are accessible and comprehensive, the rights enshrined in substantive law and policy will be ineffective. Even more if the law against discrimination focuses on adjudication it is likely to benefit the few who have access to tribunal-justice. A number of different options have therefore been promoted in South Africa: labour and other specialist tribunals, ordinary courts, a Human Rights Commission and a separate Gender Equality Commission as well as a Constitutional Court.

## Civil rights legislation

South Africa does not yet have coherent civil rights legislation to complement its constitutionalised equality provisions. Various researchers and policy analysts are working in this area but no final proposals on substantive law have been proposed although the Ministry of Justice has published a green paper on Employment Equity in the middle of 1996.

### Existing enforcement mechanisms

The most useful legal mechanism we have had for dealing with discrimination is the unfair labour practice (ULP) incorporated in the Labour Relations Act.[27] This outlaws practices which *unfairly affect* workers and employers, create *labour unrest* or *adversely affect the relationship* between management and worker(s). The industrial court[28] has a broad equitable jurisdiction to determine unfair labour practices and to grant *any* relief it deems fit, including compensation and reinstatement. In the exercise of this open-textured jurisdiction the court has outlawed direct and occasionally indirect discrimination, but has been chary of reviewing negotiated agreements.[29] The loose language of the unfair labour practice is to be replaced by a statute which defines direct and indirect discrimination more sharply in a reformed employment statute.[30]

### Equal pay

Although discrimination in pay is outlawed there are no techniques or institutional arrangements for dealing with equal pay claims in any rational or systematic way, nor has South Africa ratified the ILO Convention No 100 on Equal Pay.[31] Work-place discrimination disputes are at present subsumed under the unfair labour practice jurisdiction but will in future be resolved by a restructured Labour Court; other unfair dismissal cases in which discrimination is not alleged will be conciliated and arbitrated by the Commissino for Conciliation Mediation and Arbitration.[32] The Commission is an autonomous state-funded institution, analogous to the UK's Advisory Conciliation and Arbitration Service but it is also to arbitrate much of the kinds of dismissal disputes which would in the UK be referred to industrial tribunals. It is also likely to have jurisdiction to review alleged breach of minimum employment standards.

Civil courts (inferior and superior) have no equity jurisdiction although they are constitutionally obliged to interpret common and statute law in the light of the Bill of Rights. Claims arising from non-employment-related discrimination claims will be adjudicated by the Supreme court, and the Labour Court will retain concurrent jurisdiction in employment-related claims. Individualised claims tend to be inadequate in dealing with indirect discrimination and it is a pity that the Labour Relations Act makes no provision for punitive or exemplary damages in relation to repeat offenders or in cases of egregious discrimination.

*Specialist tribunals*

There are demands for the establishment of a specialist equality tribunal free of narrow legal processes comprised of people with labour relations as well as human rights experience.[33] The long-term goal of fairness in employment must be weighed against harm caused by its attainment and in the context of employment this is an industrial standard of fairness and rationality. Discrimination claims are not purely legal claims and in our view procedures need to be qualitatively different from not merely simpler than civil court remedies.[34] UK process is probably unduly complex even for the more sophisticated user population and should almost certainly be avoided in South Africa[35] not least because discrimination victims seldom have easy access to legal services and this is exacerbated by formalistic procedures.

South Africa's Interim Constitution designates eleven official languages and provides that 'conditions shall be created for their development and for the promotion of their equal use and enjoyment' and 'the status of languages at the commencement of the constitution may not be diminished'.[36] The final Constitution retains the eleven languages but has a slightly different configuration ' Recognising the historically diminished use and status of the indegenous language sof ouyr people, the state must take practical and positive measures to elevate the status and advance the use of these languages.'[37] The Constitution recognises that for reasons of practicality and cost not all languages will be equally prominent in each of the nine provinces but all lanauges 'must enjoy parity of esteem and must be treated equally.'[38] and a Pan South African Language Board is to be established to promotion the use of all official languages, the Khoi, Nama and Sam languages, sign language.[39] Even more remarkable the constitution provides (s 6(5)) that the Pan South African Language Board must promote and ensure respect of languages, including German, Greek,

Gujarati, Kindi, Portuguese, Tamil, Telegu, Urdu, and others commmonly used by communities in South Africa, and Arabic, Hebrew, Sanskrit and others used for religious purposes.

Quite how these pious aspirations may be attained is anyone's guess; it does seem a little like legislative control of the moon and the stars. It is also obvious that whether one is in Nigeria, Kenya or Cape Town the way of the ghetto is through competence in the language of commerce and government.[40]

*Nature of enquiry*

Tribunals which deal with discrimination cases are probably able to issue clear determinations if the proceedings are based on full enquiry ie they are investigative rather than adversarial proceedings. This is particularly so where it appears that discrimination is systemic. The object of such enquiry would be to make factual findings, and help the parties find solutions to difficult problems and to give answers if the parties are not able to do so themselves.

*Representation at tribunal enquiry*

There is evidence to indicate a positive correlation between competent legal representation and success in a hearing and poorly or unrepresented complainants are likely to be at a disadvantage.[41] We have no reliable evidence to support this contention from South African experience, but a limited cursory survey of recent unfair labour practice applications suggests that access to legal representation does make a difference. During 1994 and the first two quarters of 1995, 141 determinations were published in the authoritative Industrial Law Journal. In 38 of these, worker claimants were represented by union officials (or para-legal advisers) and respondent employers by lawyers or industrial relations consultants. Applicants won 6 and lost 18 four of which were with costs; all these costs orders were expressly issued because of what the industrial court found to be incompetence or negligence in practice and procedure.[42]

*Funding for legal representation*

Legal costs are high and funding for litigation is increasingly difficult to come by. Whereas funding (almost exclusively from abroad) from for human rights litigation was relatively easy to come by in the 1980s, it has all but disappeared in South and Southern Africa. The only state funding for poor people is provided by the Legal Aid Board (LAB) and its support for labour matters is a derisory 0.6% of its total grant aid during 1993-4.[43]   If the Labour Court is to have jurisdiction in discrimination disputes legal assistance is vital, at least in test cases.

> Because employment discrimination is a sensitive area of the law, where victims are in need of a speedy and just remedy, the quickest and fairest means of resolving a dispute is essential.[44]

## Multi-forums and forum shopping

Special care needs to be taken to avoid inundating tribunals and people should be prevented from bringing or continuing claims in more than one forum. It is suggested that labour tribunals could enjoy concurrent jurisdiction with a specialist tribunal in employment claims especially as discrimination is seldom the sole issue in dispute.   One way of avoiding forum shopping would be if employer-employee claims could be resolved either by labour courts or a specialist tribunal.[45]   If the equality tribunal were able to grant similar remedies to those available in labour courts this would prevent equality tribunals from being manipulated into being litigation supermarkets. Recent proposals by the Ontario Law Reform Commission suggest that the registrar should manage the process very actively and direct a complaint so that it is handled fairly and expediently but once only and if a tribunal resorts to external law in making a determination, this should not be reviewable.[46]

## Case management

The more a tribunal is perceived to be claimant-friendly, the greater the tendency for it to be overwhelmed and popularity may become a cause of administrative overload. Poor case management has meant that labour courts established in Botswana and Lesotho as recently as a year ago are already undermined by inefficiencies in case handling.[47]

## Absence of class action

But no matter how simple, adjudicative processes are not appropriate to remedy systemic discrimination: repeat offenders are seldom liable to punitive measures such as exemplary or double damages and our civil procedure reflects its English background in restricting joinder. Thus, although discrimination arises because of 'group membership discrimination' and is experienced by individuals, class actions which are needed to enhance the impact of decisions are not available.

*Conciliating discrimination*

South Africa's experience of statutory mandatory conciliation has been poor. Although all labour disputes have to be remitted for conciliation it has failed lamentably and in 1994 only 11% disputes were resolved consensually through statutory conciliation.[48] To remedy this defect a conciliation institution, independent of, but funded by the state, will be established early in 1996 as a one-stop dispute settlement agency for individual and collective labour disputes.[49] The Commission will have jurisdiction to handle conciliate discrimination cases which if unresolved will be adjudicated in the Labour Court.

*Disadvantages of conciliating discrimination*

Desiderata of efficient case management urge conciliation to 'clear the decks' but the process may be bedevilled by a number of different, not always related problems, including the following:

* where mediator prestige is linked to settlement rates disputants are vulnerable to mediator manipulation;
* the settlement imperative is exacerbated in discrimination cases which have to do with power imbalances. Mediator pressure and early settlement is likely when disputants have unequal skills and very different needs;
* where the weaker party bears the burden of eventual litigation, conciliation may be unfair to individual complainants;
* if conciliation or mediation is promoted, let alone compelled, too early, conciliated settlements mask systemic discrimination;
* if the settlement process incorporates confidential mediation, defendants are unduly protected by confidentiality.
* mediation may be a waste of time if it is foisted on disputants who really do not want to settle.[50]

Conciliation may be more valuable after a complaint has been investigated, particularly in repeat claims, so that practices do not persist merely because an individual complaint has been settled.

## Pre-trial conferences

If conciliation fails to settle a matter and it is remitted to adjudication, pre-trial procedures need to assist parties to clarify disputed issues, guide evidence and discovery, burden of proof, duty to begin and other relevant matters both to expedite the hearing and explore settlement possibilities without jeopardising neutrality.

## Tribunal remedies

There is very little settled wisdom about what kinds of remedies are appropriate and for what kinds of problem or offence.

### Criminal sanctions

Although labour legislation criminalises 'differentiation on the basis of sex, race or colour'[51] the impact of criminal provisions in discouraging discriminatory behaviour is obscure: proceedings are rare and only the industrial court's unfair labour practice jurisdiction has had some, though limited impact.

### Reinstatement of unfairly dismissed workers

Unlike British industrial tribunals which seldom reinstate, it is now an accepted principle in South Africa that the primary remedy for unfair dismissal is reinstatement and this applies equally to discriminatory dismissals.[52]

### Damages and compensation

South African courts do not award damages for non-patrimonial loss in claims arising from breach of contract although the labour courts occasionally award compensation for non-patrimonial loss in unfair labour practice complaints.[53]  Compensation for patrimonial loss is generally expressed in the equivalent of monthly wages, which is almost certainly not suited to discrimination disputes.  Behaviour modification and structural change are needed, not compensation for individual complainants.[54] The 1995 LRA provides compensation for 'ordinary' unfair dismissal (capped at twelve months remuneration) and discrimination at twenty four months but as mentioned earlier, the Act no direct reference to exemplary or punitive damages. This is most unfortunate.

## Extension of international instruments on discrimination

At the ILO Conference in 1994 South Africa's Labour Minister Tito Mboweni declared strong support for universal acceptance of the core ILO conventions on forced and child labour, as well as equality of opportunity and income. Trade unions are watching the Ministry of Trade and Industry fairly closely in case of contradiction.[55] The ILO is perturbed by increasing disparity between the rich northern and poor southern hemispheres and urges the incorporation of a social charter in some form or another to deal with poverty within countries and unequal distribution of the world's resources between countries. It warns that 'inaction would be harmful for economic and social progress globally.'[56]

## Human Rights Commission and the Commission on Gender Equality

This chapter has in general terms set out procedural problems experienced by claimants in tribunals and some likely developments in these areas. It now turns to survey mechanisms which are being established in South Africa to redress discrimination, the most important of which are the Human Rights Commission and the Gender Equality Commission.

With the more blatant forms of discrimination now gone, the legislative endorsement of formal equality is proving an obstacle to tackling the more deeply ingrained and hidden forms of injustice. It is quite apparent that many employers, unionists and industrial council officials believe that, provided their agreements are gender-blind, they are relieved of the responsibility of having to do anything further to promote equality. Special treatment for women - necessary if real equality is the objective - is being resisted on the basis that such an approach would be in conflict with the law.'[57]

Institutionalised discrimination in South Africa against blacks and women has led to a hierarchical relationship between blacks and whites and between women and men and the state recognises that sex or gender discrimination should not be isolated from other forms of discrimination because strategies to improve the situation of women may ignore black women. Moreover race and gender discrimination is undoubtedly exacerbated by physical disability and sexual orientation.

Anti-discrimination law usually relies on a male comparator and as the ideal typical comparator is a middle-class white male with few domestic responsibilities, it has been argued that 'penalties for divergence from the norm fall disproportionately on women'.[58] The industrial court has furthermore, been loath to challenge indirectly discriminatory collective bargaining agreements.[59]

> [A]n investigation into the fairness or otherwise of the agreement concluded must necessarily be restricted, for even if the court did not approve of the agreement reached between the trade union and the respondent company, once such agreement had been reached, the court would be on dangerous ground if it sought to interfere with such agreement.[60]

There remains surprisingly little clear understanding of the nature of gender inequality in the labour market or of appropriate techniques for identifying direct and indirect discrimination. The proposed establishment of a Commission (GEC) to target gender discrimination is therefore overdue.[61]

Both Human Rights Commission (HRC) and GEC will monitor state policy and practices and evaluate legislation and compliance with international conventions. The HRC is empowered to administer human rights legislation and promote observance of human rights. Whereas the GEC will research equality and promote the elimination of gender bias, it will not itself prosecute complaints, although it may help to resolve conflict by mediation, conciliation or negotiation. If this fails, complaints will be directed to the HRC.[62] In summary, the objects of the commissions will be to monitor, liaise, research and educate or publicise. Neither of the commissions is to perform any adjudicative functions. The objectives of the HRC and GEQ are broad and their powers are extremely interventionist: if they determine to investigate an issue within the scope of the Commission, they may subpoena witnesses and compel them to answer questions (even if incriminating) and they enjoy police powers to enter premises, search and seize.[63] Although these powers may seem redolent of Joe McCarthy's House Committee on Un-american Activities these concerns may be ill-founded; it is also depressing that the most vociferous objections were made in relation to the GEQ, although the powers are the same in respect of both commissions.

Some protection is provided (although this may prove insufficient to escape constitutional challenge): evidence garnered in the course of commission investigations may not be used in any subsequent hearing, save on a charge of perjury.[64]  It is granted that these commissions should be high profile and have real powers; even so, individuals and the courts will not willingly submit to attacks on constitutional rights to privacy and the right to silence, unless accompanied by wisdom and fairness.

In the absence of substantive equal opportunity legalisation consideration of the possible success of these commissions is highly speculative. At the very least it is hoped that effective people are assigned to them, because if they are not competent and committed and their appointment is vulnerable to political barter, each will be resented or susceptible to trivialisation, or both.[65]  Therefore it would probably be undesirable for the Commissions to exercise its powers of investigation too early and if the ACAS experience is anything to go by, non-binding codes and publicity have been useful aids to shape best practice and promoting particular social goals.[66]

*The Constitutional Court*

The work of the GEQ, the HRC, the Public Protector and Land Rights Commission will be of less ultimate power than the Constitutional Court.[67]  The court has enormous power to rule on the legality of state executive and legislative action but it is a costly forum and in the absence of organisational support is unlikely to have much impact on executive action as it affects the poor at least outside criminal law.

**Beyond the agency pale: the poor and the law**

Enforcement tribunals to determine discrimination complaints and commissions to promote awareness are North American and European devices which may be irrelevant to the overwhelming majority of the really poor.

Policies and strategies need to have proper concern for the fact that hardship is greatest, and discrimination felt most acutely, by the rural poor rather than the urban employed. The really big divisions between the very rich and very poor are likely to get larger not smaller in the short to medium term.  One of the most difficult issues which the state has not managed to answer is how to disentangle massive numbers of poorly educated unemployed people and relatively high minimum wages in some industries (established through collective bargaining, not law).

Labour law reform is likely to continue to benefit urbanised workers in large corporations but have little impact on agricultural and domestic workers who are not organised and have little access to capital. If South Africans are really serious about changing the nature of society, we are going to need support for economic development linked to fair work and social security practices. The following are some suggestions:

*Access to credit not handouts*

Access to finance needs to be increased: for poor people the price of money is too high and access to economic activity too difficult. The ILO suggests that 'there is thus a strong case on efficiency and equity grounds for lending to the poor, not by providing subsidized credit but by increasingly the quantity of credit available at rates of interest determined by the market.'[68] South African agriculture was privileged over other sectors of the economy during the apartheid eras through easy money granted by the Land and Agricultural Bank. Financial support for the white farming community has gradually been withdrawn and the present government is likely to encourage black agricultural activity by allocation of land and other financial support. This is almost certainly to lead to new dependency on the state. The poorest of the poor do need access to start-up finance without conventional collateral but grants in aid to people who have little demonstrable agricultural competence is hardly desirable and models such as the Grameen Bank with its community backing for loans may be a more useful model than those which are likely to lead to welfare dependency and ghettoisation.

*Small business training*

Small businesses, street traders and home-based workers, formerly controlled through racially discriminatory licensing laws now find it difficult to cope with a wholly deregulated market place. Without skills to trade effectively they are vulnerable to competition from better organised white traders who are able to exploit deregulation. The Self Employed Women's Union (SEWU)[69] have begun to help women traders develop manufacturing and marketing skills. SEWU acknowledges that unsophisticated small traders need encouragement and skills but they do not need conventional protection which keeps them inefficient and cosy in their ghetto.

The scope of the employee concept for the purposes of statutory social security needs reform and to take cognisance of notionally atypical, but increasingly significant forms of economic activity. The ILO has been doing important work to create an appropriate convention on home-based work as a separate or companion piece to Convention 175 on Part Time Work. It must be noted that by the end of 1994 this had not been ratified by a single member state.[70]

Recent research into the conditions of South African home-based workers points to clear race and gender differences: 33% of the men but 64% of the women earned less than R200 per week; 59% of Africans, 53% of Indians and 39% of Coloureds earned less than R200 pw which is acknowledged as the absolute minimum subsistence survival level.[71]

It has been shown that anti-discrimination mechanisms which focus on formal sectors of employment are likely to reach urban employed people whereas what is needed is an integrated approach which does not focus unduly on the small black middle class since such an approach would do little more than fabricate visible elites. In the Southern African context structural inequalities must be addressed alongside equity programmes which are combined with broader social and economic policies at a national level.[72]

Policy needs to provide guarantees against race- and gender-based poverty but needs also to encourage people to take care of themselves as much as possible. The coverage of state and occupational programmes needs to link benefit (unemployment or disability) with a duty to seek training and work and the feasibility of trade-offs between welfare arrangements and private and public investment in infrastructure assessed. Development economist Guy Mhone argues for policies which promote 'redistribution alongside growth with equity within the context of an all-embracing development strategy aimed at economic transformation and within which affirmative action and equal opportunity polices are a component.'[73] At the same time we need to avoid continuing debilitating dependency on some benefactor, the state, the employer, the clan or the party for benefits and instead to encourage labour participation and social citizenship. This is a long trail.

¹ A proviso to the equality clause enables special measures to be adopted to achieve the adequate protection and advancement of persons or groups or categories of persons disadvantaged by unfair discrimination, in order to enable their full and equal enjoyment of all rights and freedoms.' Article 8 (3) Section s33(1) (a) & (b) also allows limitations which are reasonable and justifiable in an open and democratic society based on freedom and equality and do not negate the essential content of the right, similar to article 8(2) of the European Convention on Human Rights. Fundamental rights apply only as between state and individuals, not horizontally between groups in the private sector, *De Klerk & Ano v Du Plessis & Others* 1995 (2) SALR 40 (T) but may be extended by s33(4). On the dangers of inadequate machinery see the *Report of the Commonwealth Advisory Mission on National Machinery for Advancing Gender Equality*, Commonwealth Secretariat, 1995.

² The Human Rights Commission has been appointed, as has the Public Protector who may investigate complaints of maladministration, abuse of power and corruption in public life. It could be useful in exposing endemic corruption amongst poorly paid, ill-trained and often badly managed civil servants ie those most vulnerable to corruption. A Gender Equality Commission is en route to establishment.

³ Section 121(2)(b) directs parliament to enact legislation to enable individuals or communities to claim restitution of rights in land from the state if dispossessed under apartheid. A Land Claims Commissioner and Land Claims Court has been established to entertain claims emanating as far back as 1913 when the Land Act reserved 87% of the land for whites. Between May and August 1995 4,740 claims had been lodged; none has yet been processed. *Sunday Times* 27 August 1995.

⁴ WPJ/1994 in GN 1954 of 1994.

⁵ A draft report prepared by the Senate and the parliamentary select committee on Labour point to lack of co-operation between RDP structures, unresolved conflict between civic structures and other infrastructural problems, which could lead to the collapse of RDP projects. *Cape Times* 31 August 1995.

[6] The Interim Constitution protects property rights which may only be expropriated 'for public purposes' and subject to fair compensation with reference to 'the use the history of its acquisition, market value and the value of investment in it by those affected.' s (3). It is not yet clear to what extent property rights will be enshrined in the final constitution which is to be promulgated at the end of the life of the interim Constitution in April 1999.

[7] Debbie Budlender & Jan Theron 'Working from home: the plight of home-based workers' (1995) 19 *South African Labour Bulletin* 14.

[8] Unless attacks on private property rights are 'disproportional' either by reference to means or ends. See Laurence Tribe *American Constitutional Law* 2nd The Foundation Press, New York, 1988, 589, Edward McWhinney *Supreme Courts and Judicial Law-Making: Constitutional Tribunals and Constitutional Review* Martinus Nijhoff Dordrecht, 1986, 20.

[9] Source: Central Statistical Service in National Manpower Commission Report 1979-1995, p7; other researchers note slightly slower increase in population since 1991: Blacks 2.4%, Asians 1.3%, Coloureds 1.4% and Whites 0.7% p.a. Source: SA Bureau of Market Research, August 1995.

[10] During the period 1980 to 1993.

[11] Labour Statistics 1995, South African Central Statistical Services.

[12] Taking into account inflation, this indicates a rise of about 3%. Chris Stals Governor of South African Reserve Bank, Address 22 August 1995, Cape Times 23 August, 1995.

[13] Only about 17% of all Black, Coloured and Indian workers have at least 10 years of schooling whereas more than 60% of whites have 12 years. F Barker, *The South African Labour Market: Critical Issues for Transition* van Schaik, Pretoria, 1992, p107.

[14] SA Labour & Development Research Unit School of Economic UCT, August 1994.

[15] ibid., table 13.2.

[16] Ian Emsley *The Malaysian Experience of Affirmative Action: Lessons for South Africa*, cited in Business Times 16 April 1995. See also *Breakwater Monitor*. This is a human resource development database project jointly managed by the University of Cape Town Graduate School of Business and 130 leading South African organisations collectively employing more than 1 million people. Data is captured and analysed by reference to region and sector and focuses on understanding and anticipating the links between business efficacy and human resource practices. See P Wright, G McMahan & A Williams 'Human Resources and sustained Competitive Advantage: a Resource-based Perspective' (1994) 5 *International Journal of Human Resource Management*.

[17] Paterson C Band - 77% white, Breakwater Monitor, op cit.

[18] FSA-Contact Survey 1994.

[19] Sara Hlupekile Longwe shows that development projects which are consistent with existing social systems tend to make no effort to remedy structural inequality between men and women. 'The Lack of National Machinery for Women's Advancement in Zambia and Implications for South Africa' in *Report of the Commonwealth Advisory Mission on National Machinery for Advancing Gender Equality*, Commonwealth Secretariat, 1995.

[20] As in the Swedish *Act Concerning Equality Between Men and Women* 1991:433.

[21] This will probably be promulgated on 1 May 1995.

[22] Interestingly the Bill of Rights enshrined in the final constitution outlaws discrimination on the ground of sexual orientation.

[23] See Sydney J Key 'Sex-Based Pension Plans in Perspective: *City of Los Angeles, Department of Water & Power v Manhart*' (1979) 2 *Harvard Women's LJ* 1.

[24] For instance to include employers (against employees and applicants), employment agencies, partnerships, trade unions, employers' associations, pension funds, medical aid schemes, friendly societies, occupational controlling bodies educational institutions (against students and applicants), the state, statutory authorities, local authorities or other persons exercising power to permit, licence or register; see the UK Sex Discrimination Act, 1975. David Pannick, op cit., 71-74. *Dockers Labour Club and Institute Ltd v Race Relations Boards* [1976] AC 285 (HL) and *Charter v Race Relations Board* [1973] AC 868 (HL). Section s25 Race Relations Act, similar to the Sex Discrimination Act, was at first interpreted narrowly. S25 now prohibits race discrimination by '*any* association of more than twenty five members' where admission is regulated by a constitution.

[25] Longwe, op cit. 49. There is increasing tension between the notion that indigenous 'culture' is synonymous with rural value and that traditional, non-elected chiefs should be bolstered by the state and that modernist-urban values are antithetical to African purity.

[26] This piece draws heavily on Christie et al 'Submissions on the Promotion of Equal Opportunities Draft Bill' *Current Labour Law* 1993 Juta, 123.

[27] Act 28 of 1956.

[28] The jurisdiction of the Industrial Court extends to workers in the public and agricultural sectors through The Public Service LRA (1993), the Education LRA (1993) and the Agricultural Labour Act (1993).

[29] *SACWU v Sentrachem* (1988) 9 *ILJ* 410 (IC), race discrimination; *Mineworkers Union v East Rand Gold* (1990) 11 1070 (IC) all white union seeking recognition, employer entitled to refuse; *Randall v Progress Knitting Textiles Ltd* (1992) 13 ILJ 200 (IC), dismissal for pregnancy not justified unless operational requirement; *Transport & General Workers' Union v v SA Stevedores* (1993) 14 ILJ 1068 (IC) 1072, age discrimination; *Rademan v Ministers of Education and Finance & Ano* unrep Industrial Court NH 27/2/00001 23 June 1995, discriminatory benefits married women. *Collins v Volkskas Bank (Westonaria Branch)* (1994) 15 *ILJ* 1398 (IC), dismissal for pregnancy. Curiously, in *Collins* the court treated dismissal for pregnancy as indirect rather than direct discrimination, in contrast to the European Court of Justice in *Dekker* and the European Pregnant workers Directive 92/85/EEC.
See Janet Kentridge 'Banking on Maternity Leave - the Case of Collins v Volkskas Bank' (1994) 15 *ILJ* 1195; Sarah Christie, 'Majoritarianism, Collective Bargaining and Discrimination' (1994) 15 *ILJ* 708. See also Gillian Lester, 'The Feminization of Collective Bargaining' (1991) 36 *McGill Law Journal* 1181. Christie et al op cit., 143/4.

[30] It will almost certainly be consistent with the constitutional definition of discrimination and the 1995 Labour Relations Act which outlaws dismissal on any of the following grounds: 'race, gender, sex, ethnic or social origin, colour, sexual orientation, disability, religion, conscience, belief, political opinion, culture, language marital status, family responsibility or any other arbitrary ground'; pregnancy is a separate ground. A green paper on minimum Employment Standards was published for comment early in 1996 and is likely to be tabled in Parliament late in 1996.

[31] Although these could be advanced under the residual unfair labour practice jurisdiction in terms of which the Labour Court may make any 'determination as it may deem reasonable'; Section 4 Schedule 3 Draft Labour Relations Bill February 1995.

[32] To be established in terms of the Labour Relations Act 1995 which is likely to be promulgated late in 1996..

[33] Alice M Leonard *Judging Inequality: The Effectiveness of the Industrial Tribunal System in Sex Discrimination and Equal Pay Cases* (1987: Cobden Trust, London) at 137. The other problem was lack of legal representation. See the Equal Opportunities Commission report *Legislating for Change* (1986) paras 2.14 and 2.21. David Pannick, op cit., 312; see also Michael Makes op cit.

[34] ILO: General Survey by the Committee of Experts on the Application of Conventions and Recommendations *Equal Remuneration* (1986) at 28-45. 'An expert in the field of industrial relations, in contrast to a federal judge, would be able to more accurately decide when an employer's action constituted a business necessity simply based on his or her familiarity with the field.' Mankes 'Combatting Employment Discrimination' (1994) 41 *Comp Labor L J* 67, 83, fn107. One could draw on legislation of Canada, France, Ireland, The United Kingdom and The Netherlands so that evaluation could consider general and particular differences in relevant undertakings, see, for example, Netherlands *Equal Wages for Women and Men Act.* (1975). On the danger of equity tribunals being dedicated to the needs of metropolitan users thereby prejudicing the legitimate interests of the rural poor, the Ontario Labour Relations Board offers fast-track determinations in Toronto and slower circuit courts, linked to conciliation procedures for the country. Chris Albertyn 'Expediting Labour Court Hearings', unpublished paper delivered to the 8th Annual Labour Law Conference Durban South Africa, 1995.

[35] Schedule 2 of the Industrial Tribunals Rules of Procedure Regulations 1985 *British Coal Corporation v Smith* [1993] IRLR 30 demonstrates the inadequacy of some aspect of the UK system.
See also PR Orazem, JP Mattila & SK Meikum 'Comparable Worth and Factor Point Pay Analysis in State Government (1992) 31 *Industrial Relations* 195 and detailed bibliography cited there.

[36] Section 3; this must be read with constitutional principle 12. These 'Constitutional Principles' were negotiated between the political parties as part of the multi-party negotiations in 1993 and as they are obliged to be incorporated into the final constitution they bind the Constitutional Assembly which is charged with the duty of drafting the final constitution.

[37] Section 6(2) Constituion 1996. The Constitution must be verified by the constitutional court to determine whether it complies with certain specific 'constitutional principles' which were negotiated at the end of 1993 and incorporated into the interim constituion and which bound the Constitutional Assembly in drafting the final constitution. This process is not yet complete.

[38] Section 6(4).

[39] Which version is not stated.

[40] The lingua franca is quite simply English and anyone who commands ten of the official languages and all fourteen others mentioned in the Constitution, but not English, would have difficulty communicating generally with the populace.

[41] Alice Leonard of the UK EOC, see chapter 2, indicates that complainants represented by lawyers had a 46% success rate, but where not represented had only 23% success rate; furthermore in cases she monitored between 1980 and 1982, complainants were represented by lawyers in half of the cases but respondents in 90%; Leonard, op cit p89. In the context of South African reform, see Peter Buirski 'The Draft Labour Relations Bill 1995 - Case for Legal Representation at its Proposed Fora for Dispute Resolution' (1995) 16 *ILJ* 529, esp 534.

[42] *Industrial Law Journal* volume 15 parts 1 - 6 and 1995 parts 1 & 2. Costs orders are not do not, in the ordinary way orderd in the Industrial Court. Costs do not therefore generally follow the event, as is commonplace in civil cases. Its jurisdiction to order costs is expressly limited to frivolous or vexatious litigation s (9) LRA.

[43] Established in 1969 in terms of Legal Aid Act No 22 1969 it has a statutory mission to make legal services available to poor people. Although the accounting periods for the Industrial Court are for the calendar year and the Legal Aid Board runs from April 1993 to March 1994 this is probably not significant.

The means test is abysmally low: a single person with a maximum calculated monthly income of R500 and R150 per dependent is deemed to be indigent. The Legal Aid Board acknowledges that its current means test is too low and probably conflicts with individual's constitutional right to legal representation, but it lacks funding to service the need. *Annual Report* Legal Aid Board 93/94 p7-8. It is instructive that on 31 March 1994 all LAB members were men and, with a single exception, white.

[44] Mankes, op cit.

[45] As in the UK where industrial tribunals have jurisdiction over matters other than discrimination claims; ss 62 and 63 of Sex Discrimination Act 1975. Jurisdictional 'competition' as in the USA and Canada should be avoided. See *Gilmer v Interstate/Johnson* Lane Corporation US 111 S Ct 1647 (1991); comment in L Stallworth & C Hernandez 'Labor Arbitration and Alternative Methods of resolving employment discrimination disputes' (1992) 2 AFL-CIO, *Workplace Topics*, 33. R G Silberman, SE Murphy & SP Adams 'Alternative Dispute Resolution of Employment Discrimination Claims' (1994) 54 *Louisiana Law Review* 1533. RH Abramsky 'Grievance Arbitration, External Law & the Problem of Multiple Forums' in Kaplan, Sack & Gunderson (eds) 1944-5 *Labour Arbitration Yearbook*, Lancaster House, Toronto, 41 canvasses some of the problems which flow from the extensive juridification of labour rights where a single dispute could generate litigation for alleged breach of contract, arbitration proceedings arising from collective bargaining, a human rights complaint and in more limited circumstances a claim to the Workers' Compensation Board.

[46] *Report on Avoiding Delay and Multiple Proceedings in the Adjudication of Workplace Disputes* Toronto, 1995. The report examines the inordinate time spent in resolving disputes under the *Labour Relations Act*, the *Industrial Standards Act*, the *Occupational Health and Safety Act*, the *Human Rights Code*, and the *Pay Equity Act*,.

[47] The Industrial Court in South Africa has a backlog of more than 6000 cases and in the busiest court in Gauteng, the delay in ULP determinations is a year or more. 'Although the court is committed to the introduction of all feasible mechanisms for alleviating the backlog of cases on the roll, in the final instance, the only solution lies in the provision by the State of the services or more and able and experienced judicial officers on a permanent and ad hoc basis and the provision of the necessary infrasructure.' Adolph Landman President Industrial Court 'The Industrial Court: A Time to Look Back' (1995) 4 *Industrial Democracy Review*, 16, 19. In Namibia more labour disputes are generated by domestic workers than any other sector. Ministry of Labour Annual Report 1994.

[48] This applies both to interim and final relief. Applicant may only secure interim relief if *application* for conciliation has been made (s (3) and final relief if conciliation has failed: s (9)(a) read with (d) of the Labour Relations Act 28 of 1956.

[49] Commission for Conciliation Mediation & Arbitration (CCMA). Disputants may negotiate private dispute resolution processes and so by-pass the CCMA, eg private final and binding arbitration subject to the proviso that such agreement would be vulnerable to review if the agreement to arbitrate were itself discriminatory.

[50] Conciliated settlement is either driven by case management problems or a desire for more comfortable dispute resolution; mediation works best when the parties have equal power and this is preternaturally not so in discrimination cases. Whereas its value is not denied it should be encouraged rather than mandated; participation could be rewarded eg by accelerated court processing and registrars and other case management officials could play a useful role.

Generally on mandatory mediation, see RH Mnookin & L Kornhauser 'Bargaining in the Shadow of the Law: The Case of Divorce' (1970) 88 *Yale LJ* 950; on the need for adjudication not settlement, Owen Fiss 'Against Settlement' (1984) 93 *Yale LJ* 1073; Carrie Menkel-Meadow 'For and Against Settlement: Uses and Abuses of the Mandatory Settlement Conference' (1985) 33 *UCLA LR* 488; in the context of women and wife abuse, see Lisa G Lerman 'Mediation of Wife Abuse Cases: The Adverse Impact of Informal Dispute Resolution on Women' 7 (1984) *Harvard Women's LJ* 57; Tina Grillo 'The Mediation Alternative: Process Dangers for Women' (1991) 100 *Yale LJ* 1545; and Margaret Thornton 'Equivocation or Conciliation: Resolution of Discrimination Complaints in Australia' (1989) 52 *Modern Law Review* 733.

[51] The Wage Act No 5 of 1965 s19 (6) and s (2) LRA No 28 of 1956; both statutes were amended in 1981 to deracialise them. 1995 LRA decriminalises labour law.

[52] *Sentraalwes (Ko-op) Bpk v FAWU* (1990) 11 *ILJ* 977 (LAC) at 994E; *Collins v Volkskas Bank* op cit.

[53] *Harmony Furnishers v Prinsloo* (1993) 14 ILJ (LAC).

[54] UK: Commission for Racial Equality; in the USA: EEOC; Michael Mankes 'Combatting Employment Discrimination in the United States and Great Britain: A Novel Remedial Approach' (1994) 16 *Comparative Labor Law Journal* 67, 81.

[55] Auret van Heerden 'ILO Conference: Setting new standards' (1995) 19 *South Africa Labour Bulletin*, 73, 74.

[56] World Employment 1995: an ILO Report, Geneva 1995, 74.

[57] C O'Regan and C Thompson *Equality for Women in Employment: An interdepartmental Project working Paper: Collective Bargaining and the Promotion of Equality: the Case of South Africa* ILO 1993.

See Blumrosen et al, 'An Affirmative Action Statute for Employment and Contracting: Some Proposals' (1994) 15 *ILJ* 217.

[58] Sandra Fredman 'European Community Discrimination Law: A Critique' (1992) 21 *ILJ* 119 at 121. *Rummler* Case 235/84 [1986] ECR 2101; *Ntsangani v Golden Lay Farms (Pty) Ltd* (1992) 13 ILJ 1199 (IC); Fredman *op cit* at 123.

[59] O'Regan & Thompson op cit.

[60] *Ntsangani* at 1206C; comment by SH Christie, 'Majoritarianism, collective bargaining and discrimination' (1994) 15 ILJ 708. For instance the court failed to consider *Rimmer Kuhn*.

[61] It is to comprise people committed to promoting gender equity, have knowledge (or experience) of matters connected with the objectives of the commission and should reflect the regional diversity of the country, s (1), Draft Commission on Gender Equality Act [C2-95].

[62] Sections 4 and 7(d)(aa).

[63] Section 5; protection against the consequences of self-incrimination is founded on the fact that information derived directly or indirectly from questioning (though not apparently from search) is inadmissible in 'criminal proceedings or before any body or institution established by or under any law' (s (a). Presumably the word 'or' is disjunctive so that the information would be inadmissible in any statutory proceedings and probably any non-statutory fora which has legal consequences. It is suggested that even if the general scope of enquiry is permissible, this does not mean automatic validation of all requests and subpoenas. The demands of privacy and enquiry will require balance and delicacy.

[64] Section 6(a) draft GEQ; see Report of the *ad hoc* select committee on the Establishment of Commission on Gender Equality C2-95 and s (a) HRC Act 54/1994.

[65] Elizabeth Meehan *Women's Rights at Work: Campaigns and Policy in Britain and the United States* Macmillan, Basingstoke, 1985 Chs 4 and 5.

[66] Section 6 Employment Protection Act 1975. See Lord Wedderburn *The Worker and the Law* (1986: Penguin, Harmondsworth) 3rd ed 247 and 308. It is therefore surprising that the UK's EOC has not issued codes. See Meehan at 114.

[67] The first judgement of the Court ruled the death penalty unconstitutional under the right to life provision in the bill of rights; it has recently ruled on the legality of the Publications Act in the context of the free speech provisions in the constitution and class with the right to dignity. Most of its decisions address criminal procedure.

[68] ILO World Employment 1995 p . See also R Meier & M Pilgrim 'Policy-induced constraints on small enterprise development in Asian developing countries' in (1994) *Small Enterprise Development*, 32-38.

[69] Modelled on the Indian Self employed Women's Association whose general secretary Ela Bhatt has long recognised the crucial link between economic activity, access to finance and organisation.

[70] ILO *Lists of Ratifications by Convention and by country*, ILO Geneva 1995.

[71] Debbie Budlender & Jan Theron op cit.

[72] Evance Kalula, & David Woolfrey, *The new labour market: Reconstruction, development and equality*, Labour Law Unit University of Cape Town 1995.

[73] Guy Mhone 'Factor utilisation structures and affirmative action', in Kalula and Woolfrey, ibid 95.

# 10 The Fair Employment Commission in Northern Ireland

*Bob Cooper*

The first Fair Employment legislation in Northern Ireland was introduced in 1976 following the suspension of the Stormont Parliament and the introduction of direct rule. One of the major complaints of the Civil Rights movement, which grew up in the 1960s, was that of discrimination in employment against Catholics. The legislation was designed to solve that problem. Unfortunately, those who promulgated the Civil Rights demands, as well as those who responded in legislative form, had a very simplistic view about the nature of the inequality experienced by Roman Catholics in Northern Ireland. They saw that Catholics were badly represented in the public sector and in particular in the middle and senior parts of the public sector, badly represented in the professions and in the more prestigious service sector. They were badly represented in white collar and also in skilled manual employment. They were over-represented in insecure employment, in unskilled employment and among the unemployed.

The perception was that all of these disadvantages arose because of direct discrimination. The legislation was, therefore, designed to prevent employers from directly discriminating. Although the legislation was introduced at around the same time as the sex discrimination legislation and the amendment to race discrimination legislation in Britain, it did not follow those acts in outlawing indirect discrimination.

The Fair Employment Agency established under the 1976 Act was given wider powers of investigation than in the case of the Equal Opportunities Commission or the Commission for Racial Equality but there was considerable confusion about how far the Agency could go to enforce any form of affirmative action for which there was no express provision.

One of the investigations carried out by the Agency was into the Northern Ireland Civil Service where, by looking through files of all Civil Servants, the Agency was able to develop a compositional analysis which showed the level of under-representation of Roman Catholics in middle and senior grades.

One of the recommendations which the Agency made and which was accepted was that, in future, there should be detailed monitoring of the religious composition of the whole of the Civil Service. Until this was installed, the concept of monitoring on a religious basis was widely regarded as an anathema to both public and private sector employers. As a result of the regime of monitoring in the Civil Service, the attitude among civil servants changed dramatically. Senior civil servants were unable to see why if they had to monitor the religious composition of their own labour force, other employers should not do the same.

Slightly later, great pressure started to be exerted on the government from the Irish government under the terms of the Anglo-Irish Agreement and particularly the Irish American lobby to strengthen the fair employment legislation.

The Northern Ireland Standing Advisory Commission on Human Rights, a body set up under the 1973 Constitution Act to advise the Secretary of State on human rights, under the Chairmanship of James O'Hara, who had had a life-time commitment to the cause of Fair Employment, and including in its membership Dr Christopher McCrudden, one of the major legal experts in the field, as well as Professor Tom Hadden, an outstanding scholar in the field of human rights, recommended substantial strengthening of the fair employment legislation.

Government accepted many but not all of the recommendations and in 1989 a new Fair Employment Act was established which came into force on 1 January 1990.

The legislation created the Fair Employment Commission and gave it statutory duties of:

a. promoting equality of opportunity on grounds of religion in Northern Ireland
b. promoting affirmative action
c. working for the elimination of religious discrimination.

The Commission deals solely with discrimination on the grounds of religion or politics and inequality in terms of religion. It has a staff of approximately 80 employees and a budget of £2.5m to £3m.

The legislation provided that all employers with more than 10 employees should monitor the religious composition of their labour force by 9 standard occupational categories and report this information on a yearly basis to the Commission.

In addition, the Commission was given wider investigative powers and all employers were required every 3 years to carry out a fair employment review to establish whether the company was providing fair participation in employment.

The concept of fair participation is one of the most novel in the legislation. It is not, however, defined in the legislation as such but in the Code of Practice drawn up to advise employers on how to implement the legislation.

It stated:

> What is required is that you afford opportunities to both communities and, where a community is under-represented, you take affirmative action steps to remedy that under-representation. Accordingly you must ask yourself whether, in the light of all factors known to you, and including advice from the Commission, the composition of the workforce and your recent recruits as revealed by monitoring is broadly in line with what might reasonably be expected. If it is out of line then you must ask yourself why this is so and what affirmative action is needed in order to bring about fair participation by both Protestants and Roman Catholics.

The concept of fair participation has been most valuable and while it may cause difficulties to operate, it is the main tool which has forced employers to ask themselves the right questions.

In its Corporate Strategy for the three year period 1993 - 1996, the Fair Employment Commission set out its policy aims in the following terms:

> The Commission will work for a situation of fair participation in Northern Ireland, where there is proportionate representation of both communities in all types of employment and in the extent of employment, while working for the removal of segregation in the labour force by eliminating religious and political discrimination, promoting affirmative action and promoting equality of opportunity.

The extent to which progress towards achieving those aims has been made will form a central part of the current Employment Equality Review being carried out for Government by the Standing Advisory Commission on Human Rights (SACHR). What is clear, however, both from the FEC's experience and from independent research is that the issue of fair employment and equality of opportunity is on the agenda of many more employers than would have been the case even 10 years ago. More employers are seeking advice on equality training, on developing greater professionalism in recruitment and selection and in creating harmonious working environments in which all employees regardless of community background, can feel comfortable.

There is also no question that decisions from the Fair Employment Tribunal have established clear guidance for employers on the importance of the Fair Employment Code of Practice and have focused awareness on important areas of unlawful discrimination such as sectarian harassment. An increasing number of cases are now being settled before reaching the Tribunal and in addition to an element of financial redress for the complainant, the Commission presses for settlement terms that practically address the issues that gave rise to the complaint. When the Commission receives a complaint of discrimination it carries out a preliminary investigation and then decides whether or not the complaint should be supported to the Fair Employment Tribunal, which is an independent Tribunal similar to the Industrial Tribunals.

The Fair Employment Tribunal is a specialist body with a structure similar to the Industrial Tribunal with a legal Chair and a representative of each side of industry. The representatives are chosen from panels of people believed to have expertise in anti-discrimination methods. The advantage of this system over the Industrial Tribunal system is that panel members and indeed legal chairs are able to build up specialist expertise in fair employment which would not be available to members of Industrial Tribunals, the majority of whose work is taken up with industrial rather than discrimination matters.

If the Commission decides to support the case, further investigatory work is done and at any stage, depending on the information which becomes available, the Commission may decide to withdraw its support. At the Tribunal full legal representation is provided for a Complainant who is supported by the FEC. The following are some of the figures:

|                     | 94/95 | 93/94 | 92/93 |
|---------------------|-------|-------|-------|
| General Enquiries   | 2,027 | 1,227 | 711   |
| Complaints Lodged   | 315   | 301   | 259   |

Of the proceedings lodged with the Fair Employment Tribunal (assisted by the FEC), the make up is as follows:

| Recruitment/selection/promotion | 57% |
|---------------------------------|-----|
| Dismissal/Redundancy            | 17% |
| Sectarian Harassment            | 15% |
| Victimisation                   | 3%  |
| Other Detriment                 | 8%  |

Proceedings disposed of:

|                          | 94/95 | 93/94 |
|--------------------------|-------|-------|
| Settlements              | 57    | 35    |
| Withdrawals              | 79    | 78    |
| No Further Assistance    | 37    | 17    |
| FET decisions - upheld   | 8     | 10    |
| FET decisions - dismissed| 6     | 8     |

The total compensation recovered in the 57 settled applications during 1994/95 was £579,640. A total of £87,294.70 compensation was recovered by the Complainant in the eight complaints upheld by the Fair Employment Tribunal.

While the progress towards creating an equality culture is welcome there is no room for complacency. The Commission has consistently taken the view that action to remove discriminatory employment practices would not be sufficient in itself to ensure fair participation. The Commission has a statutory duty to promote affirmative action and considerable efforts have been made to place affirmative action at the centre of employment practices in Northern Ireland and to promote the use of goals and timetables.

There is evidence to suggest that there has been considerable success in encouraging employers to develop formal equal opportunities policies but fewer employers have addressed the need to review practices which have the potential for indirect discrimination or to adopt open and visible forms of outreach affirmative action. It is encouraging, however, that an increasing number of larger employers ie. those in the 250 plus employee sector are actively encouraging applications from the under-represented community.

It is clear from the Commission's experience that the scope for affirmative action permitted under current legislation should be a key area for consideration during the Employment Equality Review. The Commission would identify religion specific training, presently not permitted - unlike the position regarding race and gender legislation - and recruitment from those not currently in employment as additional measures which should be a protected forms of affirmative action.

In terms of the extent to which there has been measurable progress towards fair participation, analysis of the 1991 census and FEC monitoring data since 1990 shows significant positive change. It is estimated that the Roman Catholic share of the economically active population is 40%. Since 1990, the Roman Catholic percentage of the workforce has risen by 2.4 percentage points to 37.3 %. In the past Roman Catholics were disadvantaged not only in terms of their place in the overall labour force but also by their substantial under-representation in the more prestigious occupations. The largest increase in the Roman Catholic proportion has been in the managerial and professional occupations. Roman Catholic managers and administrators have increased from 30.5% to 34.4% (3.9 percentage points) and among professionals from 33.4% to 38.8% (5.4 percentage points), encouraging evidence that the 'glass ceiling' is being cracked.

All of these figures and the progress they represent however should be seen in the context of an annual increase in the Roman Catholic share of the economically active population, a factor often missed by those who argue that the pendulum of inequality has swung the other way. In fact these figures indicate that there is still some way to go to bring the equality pendulum to equilibrium.

The progress that has been made, often in the most unpromising economic and political circumstances over the past five years, is important. But the most striking difference between Protestant and Roman Catholic workers remains their differential unemployment rates. Over 50% of the male unemployed are Roman Catholic and almost 65% of the long term unemployed are Roman Catholic. Over the past 20 years, the reduction in the male unemployment differential has been small, from 2.5:1 to 2.2:1. The `concrete floor' that keeps so many in the unemployment basement is much harder to breach.

A marked weakness of equality legislation the world over is that the benefits of increased opportunity are felt by the most advantaged section of minority communities while the most disadvantaged are left largely untouched. This would seem to be the experience of American civil rights legislation which predates fair employment legislation by more than a decade. It is for this reason that the FEC has always argued for a two pronged attack on employment inequality: well enforced fair employment action allied to well-funded government measures directed at areas of high unemployment and social disadvantage. Such an approach should not only assist in reducing the disparities between the two communities, but also redress the problems of disadvantage and deprivation to be found in both communities in Northern Ireland.

In this context the effectiveness of the government policies of Targeting Social Need and Policy Appraisal and Fair Treatment will also need to be keep under close review.

Only by combining government policy to assist the disadvantaged, together with effective fair employment legislation can the unemployment discrepancies be removed.

# 11 The UN Committee on the Elimination of Racial Discrimination as an implementation agency

*Michael  O 'Flaherty*

The United Nations' Committee on the Elimination of Racial Discrimination (CERD) is the supervisory body under the International Convention on the Elimination of All Forms of Racial Discrimination, mandated to supervise implementation of that instrument by the States parties.[1] The Committee is comprised of eighteen independent experts, elected by the States parties for terms of office of four years.[2]   At present the qualifications of members include law, diplomacy, anthropology, social sciences and philosophy.  CERD meets for two three-week sessions each year, in Geneva.

As an implementation agency, within the understanding of the term for the present volume, CERD can best be described as being of the 'second line', in that the primary obligation to implement the Convention falls to the States parties.[3] CERD undertakes its implementation task by means of its various procedures to encourage States parties to improve the extent to which they abide by the Convention.

A thorough effort to determine the effectiveness of CERD in promoting implementation of the Convention would require an examination of the extent to which the Convention is respected in the practice of each of the States parties and the measure in which such practice is related to the work of the Committee. The present survey is considerably more modest and focuses attention only on Committee procedures. In so doing, however, it examines a *sine qua non* for effective implementation - the inherent efficiency of the international supervision machinery.

## The International Convention on the Elimination of All Forms of Racial Discrimination

The International Convention on the Elimination of Racial Discrimination is the principal United Nations instrument imposing internationally binding obligations concerning racial and related forms of discrimination.[4] It was adopted by the General Assembly in 1965 and entered into force on 4 January 1969. As of 1 October 1995 there were 145 State parties. Seven of the articles of the Convention address substantive matters. Article 1 contains the definition of 'racial discrimination' for purposes of the instrument:

> the term....shall mean any distinction, exclusion, restriction or preference based on race, colour, descent or national or ethnic origin which has the purpose or effect of nullifying or impairing the recognition, enjoyment or exercise, on an equal footing, of human rights and fundamental freedoms in the political, economic, social, cultural or any other field of public life

Article 2 imposes a heavy implementation burden on States parties to take effective measures to review governmental, national and local policies and to amend, rescind or nullify any laws and regulations which have the effect of creating or perpetuating racial discrimination. The obligation is to root out racial discrimination in society by all the lawful means at the State's disposal. Thus, in subsection two of the article, there is an obligation to take 'affirmative action' in situations which 'so warrant'. The latter important provision has considerable potential but its significance has been  somewhat neglected by commentators, States parties and the Committee itself.[5] Implementation of article two has been held to require  the ongoing collation by States of comprehensive data on the racial and ethnic composition of the population and on their needs.[6]

Article 3, which seems to be primarily about *apartheid* was effectively resuscitated in 1995 in order to draw attention to the obligation on States to combat any tendencies in society towards the creation of involuntary ghettoes.[7]

Article 4 contains a strict and unconditional obligation on States to outlaw racist utterances and racist groupings or organisations. In its absolute nature the article gives cause for considerable debate regarding the mutual balancing of rights such as those of freedom of expression and of the enjoyment of freedom from racial abuse.[8]

Article 5 contains a non-exhaustive list of rights which States must ensure are enjoyed in a non-discriminatory manner. It seems to be the view of the Committee[9] that the obligation extends beyond the enumerated list of issues to all those other issues which might be considered as human rights in a given society. Where rights are considered to be fundamental, the obligation to eradicate racially discriminatory enjoyment extends to citizens and non-citizens alike.

Article 6 imposes an obligation on States to provide adequate remedies against acts of racial discrimination.

Article 7 contains the obligation to combat racial discrimination and prejudice by way of education, information and promotion of a 'culture of human rights'. The provision has an exceptionally wide scope but its potential remains to be fully explored.[10]

## International supervision of the Convention

In supervising implementation of the Convention, CERD devotes the greatest part of its time to examination of reports submitted periodically by States parties detailing their compliance with the Convention.[11] CERD also, within certain limits, examines and issues opinions on complaints taken against States parties by individuals and groups.[12] A third implementation action of CERD is to be found in its rapidly evolving procedure to address situations of impending or actual crises occurring in States parties and which have a racial or ethnic dimension.[13]

## The reporting process

The reporting process is intended to promote compliance with the Convention by means of the periodic preparation by the state of an analysis of its record under the Convention, the examination of that analysis by the Committee in dialogue with representatives of the State, and the subsequent implementation by the State of whatever advice it might be offered by the Committee.[14]

Under article 9 of the Convention, States are obliged to submit reports to CERD one year after yhe Convention comes into effect for the State and thereafter every two years, on the legislative, judicial, administrative or other measures which they have adopted and which give effect to the provisions of the Convention.[15] Consonant with the State's implementation obligation as stated in the Convention, the Committee has indicated that the reporting requirement is a substantial one requiring that the report provide exhaustive information on a very wide range of Government activities and that it comprehensively indicate the actual situation within the State even with regard to issues and circumstances which may appear to be beyond the appropriate or normal purview of Governmental interference.[16] In July of 1993 the Committee stated that reports, to be comprehensible, must also contain detailed information concerning the racial and ethnic configuration of society.[17]

Reports are considered by the Committee in public session and in dialogue with representatives of the State.[18] At the end of the scrutiny, which usually extends over two consecutive three-hour meetings, the Committee adopts its 'Concluding Observations'. The Concluding Observations comprise a critique of the State report and of the response of the State representative to the scrutiny of the Committee, noting positive factors, drawing attention to matters of concern and making suggestions and recommendations. Concluding Observations are issued as public documents at the end of each session of the Committee and included in the annual report to the General Assembly of the United Nations.

The significance of the reporting procedure may be scrutinised by means of the identification of the key protagonists and an examination of the effectiveness of the manner in which they carry out their roles.[19]

The first actor in the reporting process is the State. Its primary responsibility is to produce a clear and comprehensive report.

Ideally it should do so following a process of national consultation which draws on as wide a range of sources of information as possible and which provokes a climate of reflection on issues pertaining to the convention. The state is also called on to look on the reporting process as constructive and advisory rather than adversarial or litigious. The reporting procedure affords a unique opportunity for expert international scrutiny of its record. If participated in enthusiastically and received with a willingness to learn, the process provides many insights which may elude the domestic observer.

The second actor is the Committee, which is called on to carry out its tasks in a reasoned, non-confrontational, systematic, efficient and speedy manner. Essential to its task is its willingness to make use of reliable independently sourced information which can complement the government reports. One source of such information is the range of United Nations and related inter-governmental organisations, such as ILO and UNESCO. Another is the record of the deliberations of other human rights treaty bodies[20] together with the corpus of relevant reports which may have been issued by UN investigative procedures, such as Special Rapporteurs and Working Groups of the Commission on Human Rights.

Most important of all as sources of independent information are the range of non-governmental organisations (NGOs) and they can be seen to constitute the third category of actor in the reporting process.[21] Information provided by, particularly, national or local NGOs, can serve to balance Government input, often pointing to inaccuracies or *lacunae* in the report, and providing the Committee with specific local information. Non Governmental Organisations do not have rights of audience before the Committee and their submissions remain informal and addressed to individual committee members only.[22]

It is crucial that the proceedings attract adequate publicity and this is the task of the fourth actor, the media. The activities of the Committee do not attract attention unaided. It is important, above all that local media be alerted to the consideration of State reports and that news be speedily transmitted back to the general public in the country concerned. Absence of such publicity seriously diminishes the potential long-term domestic impact of Committee proceedings, as well as the possibility of informing the local political agenda.

213

The gravest problem facing the reporting process is the extent of overdue reports. As of August 1995, 88 States were overdue in submitting two or more and of these 12 had not yet submitted initial reports.[23] A wilful disregard for the process may motivate a certain number of States in failing to report. A more important factor is a lack of the necessary technical skills in many Governments to gather appropriate information and draft reports in accordance with the Committee's guidelines. A third element is the periodicity requirement itself, which at two years, is onerous.[24] By comparison, it may be noted that the periodicity for reporting to the Human Rights Committee is five years. Finally, many States express concern that the combined extent of reporting obligations under the various human rights instruments can impose heavy burdens on hard-pressed public servants.[25]

The Committee has responded to the situation by permitting overdue States to consolidate all their reports in one document covering the entire overdue period rather than insisting on submission of a series of reports each referring to a two year period in the past.[26] They have also attempted to ameliorate the two year periodicity rule by occasionally stipulating, on the occasion of the examination of a report, that the next report be of an up-dating rather than a comprehensive nature.[27] For chronically overdue states CERD has instituted a procedure to review the situation in States which have in the past at least submitted an initial report. Between 15 August 1994 and 18 August 1995 the Committee received 59 periodic reports consolidated into 19 documents.[28]

With regard to the quality of submitted reports, some are excellent and most at the very least serve as an adequate starting point for the deliberations of the Committee. However, very few states involve non-Governmental groups in the drafting process or otherwise draw public attention to the procedure. One recent development has been the practice whereby in States which have autonomous Anti-Discrimination agencies it is common for these to be invited to comment on the drafts before publication.[29]

In recent years there has been a notable improvement in the quality of participation of representatives of the State in the Committee's examination of reports.[30] Most States now send high level delegations from their capitals, often representing a range of relevant Government ministries.[31] Delegations also occasionally include representatives of racial or ethnic groups. The delegations tend to enter into substantive dialogue with the Committee, frequently proffering additional information and generally attempting to respond to concerns expressed by members.

*The Committee*

Note has already been taken of various initiatives of the Committee to encourage States to submit overdue reports. One of the most innovative is that whereby the situation will be reviewed in the most recalcitrant of States, based formally on the last report submitted. By August 1995 the procedure had been employed for 49 States and had resulted in 13 of them re-establishing dialogue with the Committee.[32] Other attempts by the Committee to assist States in submitting reports have caused some confusion through inconsistent application. Thus, members of the Committee have, on occasion, presented the practice of requesting alternate updating and comprehensive reports as a standard one[33], and on other occasions as a matter to be decided on a case by case basis.[34]

Once reports are submitted, CERD takes them up within a relatively short period of time, and it was decided at the second session of 1995 that all outstanding reports would be considered during 1996.[35] With the present workload of the Committee this is just possible. However, recent years have seen a significant expansion in the range of activities undertaken by the Committeeand, it may not be able for much longer to dispose so effectively of its backlog. The point has indeed already been reached where the Committee must choose between speedily taking up submitted reports or affording adequate time for their consideration. Ironically, also, were more than a trickle of recalcitrant States to decide at any one time to submit overdue reports, CERD's programme of work would become unmanageable.

An issue related to the issues of scheduling is the extent to which notice is given to States and to the non-governmental community. At present it is possible to provide such notice at least three months in advance of the consideration of a report. However only the State party is so advised in an automatic manner and a system has yet to be put in place whereby the Committee would systematically bring the information to the attention of the media, the general public and relevant NGOs.

At the present time, the Committee carries out its examination of

215

reports in a thorough manner. The public meetings during which it meets with the State representatives extend, on average, for some six hours. The subsequent ad-hoc and formal meetings to draft the Concluding Observations can extend to ten hours. CERD, unlike the Human Rights Committee, does not stream-line its work practices by holding pre-sessional working group meetings to formulate questions to be put to State representatives. Instead, each report receives the focused attention of one Committee member, the country rapporteur, who undertakes to thoroughly examine all relevant materials and to lead the questioning of the members.[36] The rapporteur, as the Committee member assumed to have the most comprehensive grasp of the information and the issues, is also responsible for preparation of the first draft of the Concluding Observations.

A wide range of background materials are consulted by the rapporteur and the other members. These include reports of previous considerations by CERD of the State concerned, all such recent considerations by other human rights treaty bodies and as many relevant references as can be detected by the secretariat in the documentation of mechanisms of the Commission on Human Rights and of projects under the auspices of the High Commissioner for Human Rights. Other agencies making information available include the ILO and UNHCR. During 1995 the Committee commenced the practice of meeting with certain of the sources of information. Thus, for example, in the context of consideration of the situation in three countries of the former Yugoslavia, it met with the then Special Rapporteur of the Commission on Human Rights for former Yugoslavia, Mr. Mazowiecki. The subsequent exchange of views was lively and helped the participants to more clearly identify the ethnic dimension to the range of actual and potential conflicts in the region.[37]

The quantity of information originating with non governmental organisations has also grown considerably in recent years.[38] Many members have also proved willing to meet informally with representatives of NGOs both before and during consideration of reports. CERD has shown a particular respect for one NGO, the Anti Racism Information Service.[39]

The growing volume of country-specific material before members is such that it is becoming increasingly difficult to absorb all the information. The problem is common to all the human rights treaty bodies, which, cumulatively, considered some 1,000,000 pages of documentation in 1995. One response to the problem has been the appointment of country rapporteurs. Another, not yet in place for CERD, might be the preparation by its secretariat of background briefing papers and analyses of the material. However, for this to be done for all countries considered in each session would be beyond the resources of the secretariat at its present size.[40]

In order to verify and effectively assimilate facts concerning the actual situation in States under examination, the conducting of missions to the territories might prove most useful. Already CERD has indicated its willingness to nominate members to undertake such trips and, as of late 1995 the mission of one member to Guatemala was being planned. It is difficult to envisage the extent to which missions might become part of the regular work practices of the Committee as they may only occur on invitation of the State concerned and are usually dependent on funding from the regular UN budget. Difficulty might also be found in finding members willing to travel in that they all have responsibilities outside the Committee.

Essential to the usefulness of the reporting procedure is the quality of the Concluding Observations. These have developed quite dramatically since their inception in 1991[41] and now tend to contain a high level of detailed analysis.[42] They are also, on occasion, forthright in condemning violations of the Convention and quite specific in the recommendations made to the states parties. There remains however a certain inconsistency of quality and length.[43]

The formulation of Concluding Observations will be carried out in public meetings commencing with the first session of 1996. This decision, which is unique in the practice of human rights treaty bodies, will render it possible to closely study the drafting and adoption methodology, including the relative weight given to various sources of information available to the Committee. Clarification should also be forthcoming as to the *de facto* understanding which members have of the function of Concluding Observations, i.e., identifying the relative weight accorded to the detailing of problems and achievements, and the criteria actually applied in choosing whether to adopt forceful and direct recommendations as opposed to exhortatory uncontroversial suggestions.

As has been noted above, a willingness by the Committee members to receive NGO materials has led to an increasing participation by such groups in the reporting procedure. The establishment of the Anti Racism Information Service (ARIS) has also proved useful. This NGO which exists only to service CERD, strives to promote knowledge of the process in the countries concerned, is willing to serve as a 'postbox' for submissions to the Committee, and provides some summaries (but not analysis) of such material for the members. The activities of ARIS in no way preclude other NGOs from directly contacting members.

Another useful activity of NGOs is the occasional provision by well-informed organisations of advice and assistance to assist other groups in getting information to the Committee and also in attempting to coordinate submissions and representation in Geneva. This has occurred, for instance, in the United Kingdom, where an NGO, 'Liberty' has provided training for groups in England and Wales which might wish to make submissions for the then forthcoming consideration of that country's report, and which has facilitated discussion of NGO strategies for that occasion.

There remains considerable room for improvement in the level of participation of NGOs in the reporting procedure. Firstly, there have been many occasions when no national NGOs whatsoever have made submissions regarding a particular country.[44] Second, there is scope for significant improvement in the quality of submissions. Too often they are excessively long, in a language not understood by many Committee members, or not sufficiently related to specific provisions of the Convention. Third, very few national NGOs travel to Geneva for the meetings of the Committee and what submissions they do make are thus rendered considerably less effective. Absence from the meetings also deprives NGOs of the opportunity to speedily relay the results of the proceedings to the national media and other interested parties.[45]

Some of the responsibility for a less than optimal participation by NGOs certainly lies with the Committee and its secretariat which has yet to develop satisfactory public information services.[46] However, the States parties themselves could also do much more to promote the necessary knowledge of the procedures[47] and facilitate NGOs in being represented at the proceedings. The large international NGOs also have an as yet incompletely exploited role in promoting awareness and skills in local and national organisations.[48]

*The media*

The UN secretariat systematically reports the day to day proceedings of the Committee through the issuing of regular and detailed press releases which are distributed to the press corp at the UN in Geneva. Each session also concludes with a press conference. Despite such efforts, proceedings before the Committee are very inadequately reflected in the international and relevant national media. The causes for the neglect are legion, ranging from ignorance of the existence of the proceedings to a lack of understanding of their significance and a failure to detect their 'newsworthy' aspects. The neglect may also reflect general cynicism regarding the ability of an international committee without enforcement powers to change anything within a State.

The attraction of media interest will require strenuous efforts from the other actors in the process, States, Committee (and its secretariat) and the NGO community. All of these have appropriate roles in improving flows of public information, changing public perception, alerting key journalists to relevant proceedings and relaying information effectively and speedily while it is still newsworthy.

### The early warning and urgent procedure

Commencing in 1993, the Committee has developed a procedure whereby it examines the situation in States parties in circumstances where it considers that there is particular cause for concern on the basis of actual or potential circumstances.[49] The procedure has two defining elements : (a) it is not dependent on the State having submitted a report for consideration, and (b) there are as yet no relevant rules of procedure and matters are dealt with on an *ad-hoc* case by case basis.

By the end of 1995, the procedure has been invoked concerning eleven States parties.[50] In each case members named the States in public session of the Committee and then or later in the session the situation was considered. Consideration has taken place in both public and private sessions and, on occasions, the Committee has invited participation in the discussion of State representatives and experts such as Rapporteurs of the Commission on Human Rights. On occasion the consideration by the Committee has included examination of the question of whether a particular situation actually raises issues under the Convention or not, and requests for further information have been made to States with a view to clarifying the matter.[51]

Among the outcomes of the consideration by the Committee have been formal Decisions expressing the views of the Committee and usually requesting the immediate submission by the State of a report[52], the bringing of particular situations to the attention of the High Commissioner for Human Rights and, or, the Secretary-General[53], and to the General Assembly and the Security Council[54], and the undertaking, with the consent of the Governments concerned, of missions to the territory concerned.[55]

Once a State is placed under the procedure it remains indefinitely on the agenda of the Committee and may receive attention at forthcoming sessions. Accordingly there has been a series of Committee initiatives concerning a number of the named States.

The procedure has proved potentially useful as a device whereby increased international attention can be paid to situations which give cause for particular concern. In particular, the referral of matters to the High Commissioner and the Secretary-General is a way of formally seising their programmes of work in order that they might explore the issues in the course of their good-offices missions and their other forms of 'quiet diplomacy'. It is however too early to assess the extent to which the High Commissioner and the Secretary-General do take up matters as referred.[56] It is also worth recalling that the sort of crisis matters which CERD might refer to them are already engaging their attention and it is not clear what if any extra atypical practical significance can be attributed to references made by a human rights treaty body. In these regards it might be appropriate for the Committee, as a guide for future action, to precisely identify the unique role which it might play in informing the work practices of the High Commissioner and the Secretary-General.[57]

The requests which the Committee usually inserts into its Decisions for commencement of a dialogue with the State concerned are proving effective. Thus in 1995, two States submitted requested reports[58], three sent representatives to meet with the Committee[59] and two promised that reports would be submitted in time for the first session of 1996.[60] This willingness to dialogue with the Committee is especially significant in circumstances where a State may be reluctant to otherwise facilitate international consideration of a situation and it can ensure that international legal implications not be overlooked. It also suggests possibilities for the emergence of CERD as a body with a mediating and even reconciling role in a range of conflict situations.[61]

In its development of the early warning and urgent procedure, the Committee must address the lack of clarity as to its legislative basis for action under the Convention[62] (presumably article 9 which permits the Committee to request reports whenever it so wishes[63]). This matter arises most acutely in circumstances where the Committee addresses issues which do not appear to fall clearly under the Convention and when decisions adopted do not call for submission of a report or of 'additional information.'[64] Another concern derives from the somewhat erratic application of the procedure in the absence of relevant standing rules. The lack of rules has, for instance, led to confusion in certain cases as to whether a matter was being dealt with in the context of regular reporting or the urgent procedure.[65] The absence of clarity as to the operation of the procedure also impedes efforts to publicise it and limits the roles which might usefully be played by third party States, NGOs and the media.

### The system of individual petition

The procedure permits individuals and groups to complain directly or through representatives to the Committee about a State party in circumstances where they are the alleged victims of violations of the Convention and the State party has made the necessary declaration under article 14.[66] The function of the Committee is to gather all necessary information, primarily by means of written exchanges with the parties (the State and the complainant), to consider the admissibility and merits of complaints and to issue its 'opinion' accordingly.

It should be noted that the Committee is not a court, does not issue 'judgements' and has no means to enforce any views which it might adopt. Furthermore all exchanges with the Committee currently take only written form. There is no provision for the awarding of any financial assistance to needy applicants to assist them in taking a case to the Committee.

All steps of the procedure under article 14 are confidential until the point where the Committee adopts its Opinion or otherwise concludes a case. As a matter of practice Opinions are reported in the Committee's annual report together with a summary of the information made available to the Committee. Decisions on non - admissibility are also reported.

Before a case can be considered on its merits it is necessary for it to have been found admissible. The conditions for admissibility are as follows :

i. A case may only be taken against a State and never an individual. The State must be a party to the Convention and have accepted the individual communication jurisdiction of article 14. Furthermore, the alleged violation of the Convention must have occurred since the date when article 14 came into force for that State.

ii. Anonymous communications will not be accepted. However the wish of the complainant to have his name withheld will be respected.[67]

iii. Communications may be submitted by or on behalf of alleged victims and persons acting as representatives must display their authority to act given them by the alleged victim.[68]

iv. Communications will be considered inadmissible if they are deemed to be an abuse of the rights of petition or incompatible with the provisions of the Convention. These provisions are sufficiently unclear to allow for an overlapping of concern with other admissibility requirements. It is clear that they may cover a wide range of fact situations and would certainly preclude communications designed to subvert the work of the Committee, containing allegations of a frivolous nature or abusive of the Committee or the Convention. Cases will also be deemed inadmissible if the complainant fails to provide a minimum amount of information indicating a possible violation of the Convention.

v. Before a case can be taken to the Committee all domestic remedies should have been exhausted. However, this rule does not apply where the application of domestic remedies is unreasonably prolonged or is unlikely to bring effective relief to the victim.[69] Article 14 makes provision for the establishment of national bodies to consider petitions concerning allegations of racial discrimination and for the subsequent submission of such patitions to the Committee in given circumstances. This provision, which has not been implemented by States parties, is probably not an obligatory one and the absence of such bodies may not be seen as an impediment to the exercise of the right of petition to the Committee. Certainly the Committee in its jurisprudence and its Rules of Procedure[70] has not understood the provision in an obstructive manner.

vi. The Rules of Procedure indicate that communications must be submitted within six months after available domestic remedies have been exhausted, 'except in the case of duly verified exceptional circumstances'.[71] It would appear from an examination of article 14 that this time restriction is not stipulated therein. The rule instead has its origins[72] in the Committee's desire to adequately acknowledge the provisions of article 14 concerning the role in the complaints procedure of national bodies while at the same time not allowing them to obstruct the right of petition. Perhaps a reformulation of the Rules of Procedure could continue to achieve this purpose while at the same time removing the six month time limit for those petitions emanating from the jurisdiction of States parties which have not established such bodies.

The rules of procedure allow for the appointment by the Committee of working groups or special rapporteurs to gather and assess all information relevant to a determination of the admissability of a case[73] but the actual decisions in these regards must be taken by the Committee itself. The Committee may also choose to consider both the admissability and merits issues together.[74]

Decisions on admissibility are communicated immediately to the State party and the complainant. If the matter has been found admissible and the merits have not been considered, the State party is forwarded any new material which may have been provided by the complainant and is requested to offer its views.

In its consideration of the merits the committee may defer decision pending receipt of further information. In all cases where further information is requested the State party and the complainant are kept fully informed.

The rules of procedure of the Committee allow for the conducting of confidential oral hearings by the Committee in cases where they are of the view these that would be of assistance to them in gathering necessary information concerning the merits of a case.[75] There is no such provision with regard to cases which are only at the admissibility stage. No hearings have as yet occurred.

When the Committee is of the view that it has gathered sufficient information it proceeds to a consideration of the merits and the adoption of its Opinion.

The practice of the committee is to adopt Opinions by consensus. Members are free however to append individual views to those of the committee. Though the Committee has no power to make awards, pecuniary or otherwise, it is free to make recommendations to the state party regarding such matters. The Opinion of the Committee is communicated to the State party and the complainant. Further to the rules of procedure the State party is invited to inform the Committee in due course of the action it takes in conformity with the Committee's Opinion.

The Committee has not as yet developed a procedure for the follow-up of cases subsequent to the adoption of its views.

By the end of 1995, the Committee had adopted Opinions concerning only four communications, three of which it stated to indicate no violation of the Convention. One other communication has been declared inadmissible. Two cases currently await decisions on admissibility. All complaints taken to the Committee have originated with individuals rather than groups.

The article 14 procedure is clearly under-utilised and it has not yet been allowed to operate as an effective tool for implementation of the Convention. First among the reasons for this neglect is the relatively small number of States which have made the necessary declaration under article 14 when compared to analogous procedures under other instruments. Thus, at 1 October 1995, 22 States had made the declaration, while 85 States had accepted the relevant jurisdiction of the Human Rights Committee[76], and 36 that of the Committee Against Torture. States may be reluctant to accept the jurisdiction of CERD because of concern about the right accorded to groups and the extent to which this might be exploited by a range of minority interests. Also, some States have expressed the view that access for alleged victims to multiple international procedures is superfluous and so they opt only for the Human

Rights Committee's procedure.[77]

Concerning those States which have accepted the article 14 jurisdiction it is more difficult to comprehend the lack of recourse. Perhaps the greatest problem is a lack of information whereby those who might most benefit know of neither the mechanism nor the procedure. Another impeding factor may be the practice of 'forum shopping' whereby potential complainants, where their Governments have also accepted the jurisdiction of the Human Rights Committee, opt for that procedure because of the greater range of issues which can then be argued. In this regard it may be noted that all States which have made the article 14 declaration have also accepted the procedure before the Human Rights Committee. Complainants may also be attracted to the Human Rights Committee by its substantial body of jurisprudence and the related possibilities to assess chances of success.[78]

There is immediate need for a comprehensive study which would both identify precisely the causes of the neglect of the article 14 procedure and indicate realisable strategies for its widespread utilisation.


## Conclusion

In its consideration of each of the three principal implementation procedures of the Committee, this paper has identified useful practices as well as structural and functional weaknesses. With regard to the reporting procedure, a significant process of ongoing improvement can be detected in the actions of States parties, the Committee and NGOs. However the number of recalcitrant States remains high and there is a serious problem concerning flows of information and strategies for its assimilation. The second of the examined procedures, the early warning and urgent response mechanism, is an important innovation in the work of treaty bodies and holds much promise in drawing attention to and promoting rectification of egregious problems of racial discrimination. As a tool for the implementation of the Covenant the procedure is, however, more interesting in its potential than in successes achieved. Finally, the article 14 procedure must be acknowledged to be a forlorn and utterly neglected device, currently playing almost no role whatsoever in promotion of the Convention -protected rights of its target-beneficiaries, both groups and individuals.

It may be concluded, within the narrow terms that this chapter sets for itself, both that the Committee plays a significant role in promoting implementation of the rights enshrined in the Convention and that the possibilities are far from realised. From the range of impediments obstructing the Committee's progress perhaps one can be acknowledged as paramount : the extent of lack of knowledge and understanding of its purpose and working practices by all the concerned parties, States, non governmental organisations and actual or potential victims of racial discrimination. The redressal of this 'deficit of comprehension' must then become an urgent priority for all concerned with the struggle against racial discrimination in general and promotion of the Convention in particular.

[1] For an overview of the role and activities of the Committee see K. Partsch, 'The Racial Discrimination Committee', in P. Alston ed., *The United Nations and Human Rights*, Oxford, 1992; N. Lerner, *The U.N. Convention on the Elimination of all Forms of Racial Discrimination*, Alphen aan den Rijn, 1980, at part iv; N. Lerner, 'Curbing Racial Discrimination-Fifteen Years' CERD, 13 *Israel Yearbook on Human Rights* 1983; T. Buergenthal, 'Implementing the UN Racial Convention', *Texas Journal of International Law*, 121:141, (1977), 187-221; M. Banton, 'Effective Implementation of the U.N. Racial Convention', in *New Community* vol 20/3 (1994) 475-487.

[2] As of 6 November 1995 the members and their nationalities were, Mr. Aboul-Nasr (Egypt), Mr. Ahmadu (Nigeria), Mr. Banton (United Kingdom), Mr. van Boven* (Netherlands), Mr. Chigovera (Zimbabwe), Mr. Diaconu* (Romania), Mr. Ferrero Costa* (Peru), Mr. Garvalov* (Bulgaria), Mr. de Gouttes (France), Mr. Lechuga Hevia (Cuba), Mr. Rechetov* (Russian Federation), Mrs. Sadiq Ali* (India), Mr. Agha Shahi (Pakistan), Mr. Sherifis (Cyprus), Mr. Song* (China), Mr. Valencia Rodriguez* (Ecuador), Mr. Wolfrum (Germany), Mr. Yutzis* (Argentina). The membership of those indicated with an asterisk were due to expire in January 1996, though these members were eligible to be nominated as candidates for re-election at the meeting of States parties scheduled to take place in 1996.

[3] Article 2, International Convention on the Elimination of All Forms of Racial Discrimination (hereinafter ICERD).

[4] For a recent review of the substantive provisions, see M. O'Flaherty, 'The International Convention on the Elimination of All Forms of Racial Discrimination, the Substantive Provisions' in, S. Pritchard and O. Havnen (eds.) *United Nations Human Rights Procedures and Indigenous Australians*, 1996 (forthcoming). Reference may also be had to, E. Schwelb, 'The International Convention on the Elimination of All Forms of Racial Discrimination', 15 *I.C.L.Q.* (1966), T. Meron, 'The meaning and Reach of the International Convention on the Elimination of All Forms of Racial Discrimination', 79 *American Yearbook of International Law*, 283, K. Partsch, 'Elimination of Racial Discrimination in the Enjoyment of Civil and Political Rights', 14 *Texas International Law Journal* (1979), N. Lerner, op cit.

[5] See M.O'Flaherty, Secretary of the Committee on the Elimination of Racial Discrimination. op cit.

[6] General Guidelines for the Preparation of State Reports, UN Doc. CERD/ C/70/rev. 3, at para 8.

[7] General Recommendation XIX (47), adopted on 17 August 1995. Reproduced in UN Doc A/50/18, Report of the Committee on the Elimination of Racial Discrimination

[8] See M. O'Flaherty, op cit.

[9] id.

[10] id.

[11] Article 9 ICERD. The relevant rules of procedure of the Committee are Rules 63 to 69 (UN Doc CERD/C/35/Rev.3)

[12] Article 14 ICERD. The relevant rules of procedure are Rules 80-97.

[13] For the legislative basis see discussion infra.

[14] See P.Alston, 'The Purposes of Reporting', in *Manual on Human Rights Reporting*, United Nations, New York, 1991; M.O'Flaherty, *Human Rights and the UN: Practice before the Treaty Bodies*, London, 1996, at chapter 1.

[15] See, L.Valencia Rodriguez, 'The International Convention on the Elimination of All Forms of Racial Discrimination', in *Manual on Human Rights Reporting*, op cit at part II, ch. 3.

[16] General Guidelines for the preparation of State Reports, op cit. See K.Partsch, *The Racial Discrimination Committee*, op cit., at pages 350-351. The Committee also provides guidance to States in implementing their reporting obligations in the series of General Recommendations which it has issued which serve to explicate the content of the various substantive and other articles of the Convention. For a recent examination of the General recommendations concerning substantive articles, see M. O'Flaherty, The International Convention on the Elimination of All Forms of Racial Discrimination - the Substantive Provisions, op cit.

[17] *General Guidelines*, op cit at at para. 8

[18] Rules of Procedure of the Committee on the Elimination of Racial Discrimination, Rules 63-68, UN Doc CERD/C/65/rev.3

[19] See the use of an analagous model by the present writer to examine the reporting procedure under the International Covenant on Civil and Political Rights, see, M. O'Flaherty, 'The Reporting Obligation under Article 40 of the International Covenant on Civil and Political Rights: lessons to be learned from consideration by the Human Rights Committee of Ireland's First Report', *Human Rights Quarterly*, 16 (1994), 515-538. See also the interim report, commissioned by the United Nations : P. Alston, 'Interim Report on the Operation of the Human Rights Instruments', in UN Doc A/CONF.157/PC/62/Add.11/rev.1, (1993) (hereafter, Alston, The Interim Report). For an interesting insight into early perception of the role and effectiveness of the reporting procedure see T. Buerganthal, *Implementing the UN Racial Convention*, op cit.

[20] The Human Rights Committee, the Committee on Economic, Social and Cultural Rights, the Committee on the Rights of the Child, the Committee Against Torture, the Committee on the Elimination of Discrimination Against Women.

[21] See M. O'Flaherty, 'Human Rights and the U.N.: Practice before the Treaty Bodies', op cit., at chapter 4.

[22] However the Committee, in Decision 1 (XI) of 1991 stated that, 'members of the Committee must have access, as independent experts, to all (other) available sources of information, governmental and non-governmental'. See UN Doc A/46/18 at Annex VII.

[23] Information abstracted from UN Doc A/50/18, chapter 7.

[24] The Committee, in 1984, indicated its opposition to any relaxing of the two-year periodicity requirement. UN Doc A/39/18, paras 127-128. But see note 26.

[25] See, inter-alia, the references and citations found in the Report of the Sixth Meeting of Chairpersons of Human Rights Treaty Bodies, HRI/MC/1995/2 at para 37; and, Alston, *The Interim Report*, op cit, at paras 123-138.

[26] See, e.g., 1995 Report of the Committee on the Elimination of Racial Discrimination, UN Doc A/50/18 at para 693.

[27] At its 38th session in 1988, the Committee decided to accept the proposal of the States parties that States parties submit a comprehensive report every four years and a brief updating report in the two-year interim (see L. Valencia Rodriguez, op cit. at page 141). However, this practice has not been followed in all cases. See infra.

[28] Information abstracted from UN Doc A/50/18 at chapter 7.

[29] This is, for instance, the practice in the United Kingdom and Australia

[30] The practice whereby representatives of the State participate in the proceedings of the Committee was only established after much deliberation and hestitation. For an account see K. Partsch, 'The Racial Discrimination Committee', op cit., at page 354.

[31] Of the States whose reports were considered under the regular periodic report system in 1995 (i.e. excluding States under the urgent procedure or the 'seriously overdue States procedure') only one out of 17 failed to send a delegation from its capital.

[32] Informal note of the CERD secretariat distributed at the 47th session of the Committee, August 1995

[33] See note 26 above

[34] See, for instance the Committee's suggestion to El Salvador, on the ocassion of consideration of a comprehensive report from that State, that its next report be a comprehensive one. UN Doc A/50/18 at para 498.

[35] UN Doc CERD/C/SR 1125

[36] The practice, initiated in 1988, is decribed in L. Valencia Rodriguez, op cit. The annual reports of the Committee list country rapporteurs for State reports considered during the reporting period.

[37] See UN Doc CERD/C/SR 1071

[38] In Decision 1 (XL) adopted at its 40th session in 1991, the committee stated that, 'members of the Committee must have access, as independent experts, to all....available sources of information, governmental and non-governmental'. Reported in UN Doc A/46/18 at chapter 7. The important role of NGOs in the work of treaty bodies has been forcefully restated by the sixth meeting of chairpersons (September 1995), UN Doc A/50/505 at para 23.

[39] See, for instance, comments recorded in UN Docs CERD/C/SR 1070 and 1126.

[40] One professional officer assisted by a secretary and one to two vulontary intern students. For a vigorous critique of secretariat support to human rights treaty bodies, published in 1993, see Alston, *The Interim Study*, op cit, at paras 197-206

[41] In that year Concluding Observations were expressed in a high degree of generality, none exceeded thirty lines of text in the English language version of the documents and a number comprised from four to five lines.

[42] In 1995 Concluding Observations in the English language version of the text tended to be of some 150 to 200 lines in length.

[43] Compare, for example, the various concluding Observations adopted in 1995, particularly those concerning States which are well known to have grave problems of ethnic or racial tension or discrimination. For all the Concluding Observations adopted in that year see UN Doc A/50/18 at chapter 3.

[44] In 1995 this was, for instance, the case with regard to the examination of 6 States.

[45] For an examination of options and possibilities for NGOs before human rights treaty bodies see, M. O'Flaherty, *International Covenant on Civil and Political Rights, Guide for making an Independent Submission*, Irish Commission for Justice and Peace, Dublin, 1992.

[46] See UN Doc A/50/505 at para 23. The Secretariat is currently in the process of systematising its procedures for the flow of information to and from the NGO community.

[47] Suggestions to this effect form a constant theme in Concluding Observations of CERD and the other human rights treaty bodies.

[48] See R. Brett, 'The Role and Limits of Human Rights NGOs at the United Nations', *Political Studies* (1995), XLIII, pp101-103

[49] Reported in UN Doc A/48/18 at paras 15-19 and annex 3.

[50] Papua New Guinea, Rwanda, Burundi, Israel, Mexico, the Former Yugoslav Republic of Macedonia, the Russian Federation, Algeria, Bosnia and Herzegovina, Croatia and the Federal Republic of Yugoslavia (Serbia and Montenegro)

[51] The case of Algeria, UN Doc A/50/18 at para 29.

[52] Such Decisions have been adopted in almost all cases so far considered.

[53] In 1995 this action was taken with regard to situations in the Russian Federation, Rwanda, Bosnia and Herzegovina, Papua New Guinea.

[54] Burundi and Bosnia and Herzegovina (1995)

[55] Missions have taken place to Croatia and the Federal Republic of Yugoslavia (Serbia and Montenegro)

[56] At a meeting with the chairpersons of the human rights treaty bodies on 19 June 1995 the Secretary-General stated that he welcomed the initiative to have appropriate matters brought to his attention by treaty bodies. There is slight reference to this meeing in UN Doc A/50/505 at para 13. The High Commissioner for Human Rights has also repeatedly welcomes the practice, see, for instance, UN Doc CERD/C/SR 1061.

[57] The paper on the procedure, adopted by the Committee in 1993, does not address this question in any depth. UN Doc A/48/18 at annex 3.

[58] Mexico and the Russian Federation

[59] Bosnia and Herzegovina (twice, once in the context of consideration of a periodic report), Algeria and Mexico (in the context also of consideration of a periodic report). Croatia sent representatives to meet with the Committee in the context of consideration of a periodic report.

[60] The Former Yugoslav Republic of Macedonia and Algeria

[61] There is one mediatory role envisaged for CERD in the Convention, contained in Articles 11-13 concerning settlement of disputes between States parties. These procedures have never been employed.

[62] It may, however, be noted that the development of the procedure has been welcomed by the United Nations General Assembly in, *inter-alia* , Resolution 49/145 of 23 December 1994

[63] In 1992 the Committee indicated this as the legislative basis for its requests to Burundi, Rwanda and Papua New Guinea to submit additional information. See UN Doc A/47/18 para 40.

[64] See, for instance, Decision 2(47) on Bosnia and Herzegovina, reported in UN Doc A/50/18 at chapter 2.

[65] Such was the situation regarding Mexico in 1995.

[66] For a recent examination of the procedure see M. O'Flaherty, 'The Individual Complaints Procedures under the Convention Against Torture and the International Convention on the Elimination of All Forms of Racial Discrimination' in S. Pritchard and O. Havnen (eds) *United Nations Human Rights Procedures and Indigenous Australians* op cit.

[67] Article 14(6)a, of the Convention

[68] See N. Lerner, *Curbing Racial Discrimination - Fifteen Years of CERD*, 13 Israel Yearbook of Human Rights, 1983, pp180ff.

[69] See A. Byrnes,'The Committee Against Torture', in P. Alston, ed, The United Nations and Human Rights, Oxford, 1992

[70] UN Doc CERD/C/35/Rev.3 as amended

[71] Rule 91(f)

[72] E. Schwelb, The International Convention on the Elimination of All Forms of Racial Discrimination, *I.C.L.Q.* 1966, at page 1043.

[73] Rule 87 (as amended)

[74] Rule 94 as amended.

[75] Rule 94(b)

[76] The Human Rights Committee is the treaty body responsible for international supervision of implementation by the States parties of the International Covenant on Civil and Political Rights. It excercises an individual petition procedure pursuant to the terms if the (first) Optional Protocol to the Covenant. See M.O'Flaherty and L. Heffernan, *International Covenant on Civil and Political Rights : International Human Rights law in Ireland*, Dublin, 1995 at chapter 4 and the references cited therein.

[77] See for instance the views expressed by a representative of the Government of the United Kingdom before the Human Rights Committee, UN Doc CCPR/C/SR 1432.

[78] See M.O'Flaherty and L. Heffernan, *International Covenant on Civil and Political Rights : International Human Rights law in Ireland*, op cit. at chapter 4 and the references cited therein.

# 12  Concluding remarks

*Martin  MacEwen*

## Introduction

The previous chapters have described the experience of an array of
agencies operating under differing conditions including the social
and economic context, the functions and powers allocated by the
legislation and the expectations both explicit and implicit which the
governments in office place on their performance. In the opening
chapter it was acknowledged that these constraints tempered the
confidence with which comparisons could be made and conclusions
drawn. Nonetheless, it was hoped that the making of such
comparisons was not merely an idle narrative on inevitable
difference but would prove stimulating and provocative in
demonstrating that each of the particular models examined  was
neither ineluctably driven by circumstances nor of necessity a
reflection of the distilled essence of comparative wisdom.

## Critical evaluation

In deciding what lessons are to be learnt form these comparisons,
the experience, interests and, perhaps, the predispositions of the
reader will have influenced the interpretation. Consequently this
chapter will also be selective and partial but it will attempt to re-
evaluate the basic questions posed.

*Value added*

First, do such agencies justify their existence? Theoretically this study cannot begin to look at this question because it has not examined the experience of countries which have similar anti-discrimination laws but no dedicated agency or agencies to enforce them. In reality, however, there are no comparables in this respect. In itself, this suggests either that those passing progressive legislation have failed to analyse alternatives or that they have been convinced of the benefits of an 'agency' model. While it is always possible to argue that a lack of complaints reflects a lack of discrimination, there is sufficient evidence outside this study to indicate that the absence of comparable agencies in countries such as Greece, Denmark and Germany inhibits effective enforcement of anti-discrimination provisions.[1]

*Single or multi focus agency*

Second, should agencies be single focus, such as the CRE or multifocus such as the Canadian Human Rights Agency? The argument appears fairly polarised in that each type justifies it own benefits and the objectivity of interests is questionable. It does seem possible, however, to marry the benefits of both arguments in a single agency with specialist sections thus enabling the development of coherent policy on a general human rights platform, informed by the specialist interests harnessed by individual sections. However Doyle argues in chapter 4 that it is of particular importance that a disability enforcement agency has a strong presence on its governing body of disabled people: too frequently organisations have been for disabled people and not of them. That argument would attract considerable support from minorities and women in respect of their interests. Boothman [chapter 8] points to the importance of the chairperson in stamping a particular personality on the commission and in effecting a change in priority and culture for his or her period of office.

If there were to be a single commission, therefore, it would be necessary for the chair to have a clear vision encompassing all interests and to ensure that the development of one sector, say disability, was not advanced at the expense of another such as racial equality. It may also be important to spell out the differing roles of commissioners and staff with greater clarity than has been the case in the past so that the responsibilities of the former are confined to major policy issues and do not interfere with operational matters.[2] With that important proviso, it is certainly arguable that the commonality of interest across sectors is sufficient for single campaigns in have multiple benefits.

## The human rights approach

Third, the one stop agency has advantages for the complainant not only in respect of ease of referral but also in relation to support for multiple discrimination. Moreover, economies of scale for the agency together with a single base for developing coherent strategies of enforcement from shared experience across the sectors would also feed in to promotional work heightening a more general awareness of civic, economic and social rights.

The CRE (1991: 62) in its second review of the Race Relations Act 1976 listed 10 advantages of a Human Rights Agency including the rationalisation of commissioners, senior staff, research, publications and library resources, the greater public support likely to ensue and the specific advantage to law enforcement in the better range of material from which to select and test legal issues. The Standing Advisory Committee on Human Rights in Northern Ireland (SACHR) also see advantages in the Human Rights approach, viewing it as a natural development of the existing provisions.[3] While Doyle questions the practical advantage of this approach Hucker, in chapter 6, hints at the narrow vision of its critics and emphasises the mutuality of interest that it promotes.

## Stratification of state provision

Four, are there advantages in having a federal structure and having different agencies operating at federal and state level? The experience of the Canadian and Australian Human Rights Commissions, as described by Hucker [chapter 6] and Wilkie [chapter 5], provide models which have their own strengths but these are not of uncontested merit. In each the constitutional framework provides for sister agencies to operate in the 'states': such federal structures seem to add to the complexity of arrangements without evident benefit. Where choice is available in the agency from which to seek a remedy of assistance, the advantage is not transparent. Such a conclusion is not to criticise the method of

236

approach adopted in federal states but it does raise issues about the advantages of geographically devolved structures in the UK. The existence of the Fair Employment Commission in Northern Ireland (Cooper, chapter 10) illustrates the potential for different approaches and the strength gained from local knowledge and commitment.

If Scotland achieves an assembly with its own legislative powers it would be possible to extend its jurisdiction to human rights. In the absence of a UK Bill of Rights, there is no constitutional inhibition on such a development nor on placing similar responsibilities on a Welsh assembly or on regional assemblies in England. Although the argument for local accountability [and even national accountability] is a strong one, there is also a case for controlling the delivery of fundamental obligations, often related to international conventions, through a central state agency. The existing structures of the EOC and the CRE enable a local voice to influence policy development through national and regional offices and it may be preferable to build on these structures than to invite a multiplicity of law and practice by legislative devolution.

*Subject focus*

Five, is the agency more effective in enforcing anti-discrimination law in one area of concern such as employment or is a holistic coverage preferable? The division of responsibilities exemplified in Australia and Canada, while subject based, owe more to historical and constitutional issues of state autonomy and federal jurisdiction than to a view that subject specialism is desirable in itself nor in the commentaries by Hucker and Wilkie is there a suggestion that the particular split described has advantages for the complainant.

In the UK the N.I. Fair Employment Commission does exemplify a conscious decision to provide a remedy in the single area of employment in respect of religious discrimination. Cooper in chapter 10 clearly demonstrates that the Commission has had a significant impact on accountability and employment practices in Northern Ireland, opening up job opportunities for the Catholic population which would not otherwise have happened. But much of this success may have depended as much on the strength of the legal obligations as the commitment of the Commission itself. In the absence of a parallel organisation in another country with a religious focus but not restricted to the area of employment one is wary of drawing lessons from this experience. The Northern Ireland Housing Executive has statutory obligations to allocate housing without discrimination but has been somewhat less successful in gaining the confidence of the Catholic minority. While this may reflect the fact that it inherited a legacy of discriminatory practice in the exercise of its own functions and an impossible task of dealing with de facto spatial segregation in housing increased by sectarian intimidation of minorities in mixed areas, there are distinct problems associated with areas of discrimination that the single agency appears no better able to solve than the those with general powers. Where the adjudicating body is established on a subject base, such as the industrial tribunals which deal with all employment cases in the UK, the division of responsibility to enforcement agencies to mirror these structures has a more evident rationale. Conversely there is a lobby, illustrated in the 1991 CRE discussion  document on the Race Relation Act 1976 [4] to create a special discrimination court to handle all cases, perhaps building on the experience of the specialist employment tribunals in Northern Ireland. Moreover, the arguments for both a human rights approach and a one-stop shop for the complainant support a multi-disciplinary agency.

### Key functions of an agency

What are the key functions of an enforcement agency? One suspects that this question is one of the 57 varieties of spouse beating alternatives, and may lead to much hot and fetid air.

Critical to this debate is the question of whether the agency should deal with the adjudication of complaints, a feature of the system in the Netherlands and Australia. The experience of the Dutch in respect of the Equal Treatment Commission, as Goncalves and Goldschmidt describe in chapter 7, is embryonic and the decisions of the commission appear to be advisory, at least until endorsed by the courts. Consequently it may be premature to pronounce judgement. In Australia, the Human Rights Commission and many agencies at state level, are empowered to pass judgements enforceable by the courts but they must strive to distance themselves from representing the complainant. In Canada the rulings of the Human Rights Commission exclude formal adjudication but include the interpretation of the the law which it enforces: this has binding

238

effect until overruled by a court judgement. The evident advantage of this process and of formal adjudication is that the experience and expert knowledge of the commission informs the interpretations made in the first instance and, as a consequence, these interpretations are likely to be more sympathetic to the complainant than those made by a court of law.

Courts and tribunals may frequently lack the personnel, experience and possibly even the expertise in an area of relatively unpracticed law. The most obvious disadvantage of the agency having power to adjudicate is that it may not represent complainants or, alternatively, that there must be an evident distinction between the role of agency officials who inform the investigatory process and that of the commissioners who decide cases. When the Race Relations Board had power to investigate and conciliate complaints under the 1968 Act, its conciliation committees and its Board were charged with coming to decisions ('opinions') and in doing so they had to keep at arms length from complainants and the process of investigation undertaken by employees.

Even so, the public were not convinced regarding the objectivity of the system[5] and such criticisms are similarly made against other jurisdictions. The Commission for Racial Equality in its second review of the 1976 Act expressed concern about its power to issue non-discrimination notices when a severance of the functions of investigation and adjudication are possible.[6] There appears to be, on the one hand, a desire to facilitate investigation, conciliation and 'reconciliation' by the enforcement agency and, on the other hand, a recognition that such processes when accompanied by unchallengeable decisions may constitute an abuse of power. Thus while there is no objection to the agency entering into legally binding undertakings on a voluntary basis there is concern that it is prosecutor and judge its own cause.

With that proviso, there seems little doubt about the need for an agency to have the formal capacity to assist complainants in the investigation of complaints.

Another key concern in respect of the powers of an agency is the extent to which enforcement should be matched with promotion. The developing strategies of most of the agencies discussed in this book illustrate that this linkage is seen as instrumental. Promotion without effective sanctions for breaches of the legislation may render equal opportunities a paper tiger but the reverse, law enforcement without a strategic policy to apply individual case law to promote cultural change appears to be not only a waste of a valuable tool but also to run counter to the presumption that prevention is better than cure. The various campaigns adopted by the CRE, for example the promotion of equal opportunities in local authority and housing association tenure, were built on both individual cases and on investigations. These informed the agency regarding the nature and extent of discriminatory practice and also provided reference points, relevancy and weight to the arguments for positive action.

Similarly the requirement of the public sectors in Canada and Australia to submit returns monitoring employment practices gives a poignant weapon and focused target to the agency in its promotional activities. The provisions in the Netherlands, while strongly opposed by both employers and unions, as Rodrigues illustrates in chapter 3, require monitoring of the work force and a direct linkage to an action plan.

The power of the Fair Employment Commission in Northern Ireland mirrors that in the Netherlands in requiring employers to make annual returns and adopt programmes of goals and timetables to counter underrepresentation on religious grounds. It is the most proactive measure to be found in UK anti-discrimination law going well beyond the traditional model of powers. The measures found in the other Acts, principally the Sex Discrimination Act 1975, the Race Relations Act 1976 and the Disability Discrimination Act 1995 largely estew the imposition of obligations which demonstrate compliance with the law: for the most part the obligations arise only when a breach is suspected by reason of an individual complaint or a formal investigation.

It is, on the face of it, ironic that the Disability Discrimination Act which imposes the most demanding requirements in financial terms- the requirements to meet reasonable access needs for example- has the weakest support role for the agency. Indeed it is a misnomer to consider the Disability Council an enforcement agency as it has no power to support or aid complainants or to investigate complaints of its own initiative. But clearly the government was not prepared to replicate the practical powers placed in the sister commissions. Doyle (chapter 4) points to the ambivalence of government towards the concept of disability rights legislation itself, its conversion being a matter of political pragmatism rather than a re-evaluation of the underlying principles. Consequently powers of the Council are advisory only: on matters relevant to the elimination of discrimination, on measures likely to reduce discrimination and on matters relating to the operation of the Act. Even these advisory powers are limited. Government intents to set up a National Advisory Council on the Employment of Disabled People under the Disabled Persons (Employment) Acts 1944-1958 which will assume responsibility for advice in this area.

## Institutional or systemic discrimination

While some impact on practice may be achieved by the Disability Council and the advisory function relating to codes of practice may prove of value in this respect, the failure to give explicit enforcement powers to the Council endorses a major criticism of the legislation. In common with its sister legislation in the UK, the Disability Discrimination Act 1995 is based on individual complaints and, particularly in the absence of class action, it fails to recognise the fact that discrimination is systemic.

Some author's (eg McCrudden, 1995) have argued that the legislation in the UK does provide a limited recognition of the systemic nature of discrimination, the power to investigate broad areas of concern such as mortgage lending and the power to issue codes of practice being cases in point. But there is little doubt that the rights of minority groups to pursue specialist interests whether of a cultural, social linguistic or religious nature are not the focus of concern of the legislation any more than the provision of group remedies for historical, social or economic disadvantage when this is not evidently linked to present and particular acts of discrimination.

To an extent, the powers of some enforcement agencies from outside the UK do demonstrate a more obvious acknowledgement of systemic discrimination and its linkage with minority group interests. Thus the Canadian, Australian and Dutch provisions relating to record keeping and monitoring of the work force of certain employers and the separate legal rights given to the Inuit and the Aboriginal peoples in Canada and Australia respectively go beyond the isolated and somewhat idiosyncratic recognition of difference found in the UK and reflected in provisions, for example, which allow Sikhs not to wear motor cycle crash helmets.

The argument that major 'concessions' to systemic discrimination promotes reverse discrimination is a recurrent theme in the equality debate (see Edwards, 1987). Some of the problems associated with this discourse are semantic. The expressions 'systemic', 'institutional' or 'structural' discrimination are seldom defined by the user and consequently they may have different but unexplained connotations. However, most would subscribe to a definition which refers to conduct 'unconciously embedded in the social fabric giving rise to indirect acts of discrimination'. In other words individuals are socialised into making unconcious judgements about members of minority ethnic groups which are prejudicial and disadvantagious to their interests. In reality the 'white' norms imposed as acceptable behaviour result in both direct and indirect discrimination. This results in two different patterns of behaviour. In the first, the majority expect minorities to behave differently on the assumption that their aspirations differ. Thus the assumptions of the need for community support, to be near a mosque or temple or to require access to specialist shops may each result in the allocation by officials of public housing to meet assumed rather than expressed preferences (see Henderson and Karn, 1987). It is also common for assumptions to be made about the commonality of ethnic minority interests when there is substantial evidence to demonstrate that there are significant difference between distinct minority ethnic groups: by way of illustration the 1996 survey of the UK Office for National Statistics showed the following:

1.  One in eight black households in England and Wales was burgled in 1993- twice the proportion in the Pakistani, the Bangladeshi and the white groups.
2.  Black, Pakistani and Bangladeshi groups had unemployment rates of 24%: this compared with 12% for Indians and 8% for whites.
3.  Bangladeshi women are on average 21 years on marriage, compared with 27 for white and 33 for black Caribbean women. ( source: *Independent*,   8 August 1996, p5).

In the second, rules and practices are established which make similarly untested assumptions but in this case which totally ignore the aspirations of the minority communities. Thus housing development programmes which provide only for small starter homes to reflect dominant demand including single parent families, treat other needs, including that for larger houses to meet extended family requirements, as peripheral: this is not unique to

242

ethnic minorities but cumulatively these processes reinforce disadvantage. Cooper ( chapter 10) demonstrates that the economic disadvantage of the catholic population in Northern Ireland is so entrenched that the fair employment opportunities promoted by the legislation have not impacted on the experience of cyclical disadvantage where one generation inherits the relative poverty of the previous one.

Leonard in chapter 2 emphasises that low pay is central to the issue of achieving equal opportunity for women in the UK whose experience of offering disproportionately less well paid part-time employment to women is a feature of structural sex discrimination in many western economies. But the 'tremendous progress on gender equality in past twenty years', referred to by Leonard, suggests that, however embedded, institutional or structural discrimination is, it is still amenable to change and the enforcement agency may play a vital role both in identifying important issues and in developing strategies to focus attention on them.

## International obligations

On 4th and 5th March 1996 the UN Committee on the Elimination of Racial Discrimination (CERD) considered the thirteenth periodic report of the United Kingdom. CERD were critical of the failure to entrench the race relations legislation rendering it subordinate to a wide range of other legislation and vulnerable to being superseded by new provision.[7] In its view the legal framework is further weakened by the non-incorporation of the Convention into domestic law, the absence of a Bill of Rights espousing the principle of equality before the law and non-discrimination, the lack of rights for individual petition to CERD and the lack of uniformity of protection against discrimination throughout the UK. Commentators have asserted that such advancements in civil liberties that have been achieved in recent years have come about more as a result of Britain's obligations under the European Convention on Human Rights and the Treaty of Rome than by its own Government or its elected members of parliament.[8] The discussion by O'Flaherty in chapter 11 together with the recent response from CERD demonstrates that other international conventions and their machinery have a capacity to influence the performance of state parties. In Australia the Human Rights and

243

Equal Opportunity Commission Act 1986 and related human rights legislation expressly attempts to implement international obligations relating to discrimination on the grounds of sex, race, religion, political opinion, disability, age and marital status.[9] The fact that the relevant convention is scheduled to certain domestic legislation reinforces this reference point and promotes awareness regarding the nature and extent of the obligations which are being addressed.[10] But the number of recalcitrant states remains high in respect of the submission of periodic reports to CERD and the utility of Article 14 which permits individual petition is seen by O'Flaherty to be a 'forlorn and utterly neglected device' not least because there are relatively few state parties who permit such reference.

Unlike the European Convention on Human Rights whose enforcement provisions are well developed although the convention itself is woefully weak on certain aspects of discrimination, the UN instruments on human rights do not provide strong machinery for monitoring or enforcement, owning neither standing tribunals nor courts. While the incorporation of international conventions into domestic or municipal law is no guarantee of their more effective application[11] it represents a symbol and a reference point at minimum and a genuine commitment by government and practical remedy for discrimination when it is accompanied by appropriate machinery for enforcement.

The UK government has been opposed both to the creation of a Bill of Rights as a constitutional framework to anchor a raft of rights floating in a sea of international conventions and also the incorporation of such conventions. In respect of the latter the oppositional argument is frequently based on the assertion that the language of such conventions is too imprecise to be enforceable in UK where courts which estew principle and logic in favour of precision and precedent. It is better, therefore, to provide London designed law of a cut and style fashioned to the prejudices of our insular courts.

The ability of our courts to deal with the law of the European Union, including the requirements of Article 119 of the Treaty of Rome not to discriminate on the grounds of sex, and to incorporate rulings of the European Court into domestic law, however, suggests that such problems are not insurmountable.

There is some truth, nonetheless, in the view that the designer law for the local market - the Race Relations Act 1976 and the Sex discrimination Act 1975 being examples - may provide broader

244

protection and better articulate the processes of enforcement to the benefit of a complainant than an international convention is able to do. To that extent, the role of the enforcement agency is more effectively served by local provision than by the incorporation of conventions simpliciter.


## A Bill of Rights

The argument for a Bill of Rights has much in common with that for the creation of a Human Rights Commission. Do we favour a structured approach or does piecemeal accrual better meet evolving needs. The new constitutional provisions in South Africa are wrought from a history of entrenched and systematic discrimination and the consequent economic disadvantage of the black communities has become a barrier to an effective constitutional approach based in the individuation of rights in contrast to the promotion of group remedies. While it may be argued that human rights are absolute and indivisible, that truth, one suspects, is dependent on how vaguely the right is stated. Even the most evident of these, the right to life, is not unqualified. Is there a right, for example, to terminate the life of someone in a permanent vegetative state? But the UK is unique in not having a written constitution and in professing to provide protection to its citizens and denizens by way of internal and mostly unwritten conventions, the common law and ordinary statutory provision all of which may be annulled by one Act passed by a simple parliamentary majority.

Consequently although a Bill of Rights need not prove indelible, it should be designed to express a core set of rights and to provide a framework for their promotion and protection which would not be subject to the vagaries of parliamentary concern. Government sees this development as a threat to parliamentary sovereignty-ministers should be accountable to parliament for abuse of power in any of the labyrinthian recesses of the civil service. But many central services have now been privitised or quangofied: ministers are not accountable for the former and are not responsible for operational matters of the latter. Moreover, the fiction that ministers always assume responsibility and resign when they or others have transgressed has been defenestrated: in the UK the refusal of Mr. Waldergrave to resign in 1995 after the Scott Inquiry into the sale of arms to Iraq provides an example. The inquiry found that the covert and deliberate alteration by the minister of the interpretation of guidelines approved by parliament was acceptable on the grounds that there was 'no dublicitous intent'. Thus although he clearly misled parliament he was not obliged to resign because he did not understand what he was doing. One is only surprised that a recent resignation, that of Mr. Rod Richards on 2nd June 1996 from a ministerial appointment in the Welsh Office on the grounds of an extramarital affair, was not resisted on the same basis.

In short, the arguments against a Bill of Rights forming a framework for anti-discrimination law are not entirely convincing but the bare bones of protection would require to be adumbrated by more specific provision which would spell out the powers and responsibilities of an enforcement agency.

## Conciliation

The issues of whether the agency should have power to conciliate is explored by Wilkie (chapter 5, p.l). The Australian model was built on the experience of UK and New Zealand and assumes that the conduct of the discriminator 'invariably arises out of unconscious racism or sexism, rather than from a conscious animus' (Thornton,1990:37-38). It is felt that the processes of conciliation and persuasion are more effective in changing  unlawful behaviour than any more punitive means of enforcement. While there is clear evidence that the criminalisation of discrimination has proved of little value to the complainant- under the 1966 South Australian Act only ten prosecutions were brought in ten years- the explanation given to ICERD that conciliation confronts the complainant with the immorality of discrimination and is more accessible than other forms of redress is not beyond challenge. In particular the extent to which 'rights' are compromised by the process, the individuation of complaints (the model tends to characterise the complaint as being a single aberration rather than an institutionalised practice), and the fact that the process is not open to public scrutiny constitute serious shortcomings in the conciliation model.

Nonetheless the evidence available suggests that conciliation does offer an acceptable alternative for many victims as well as respondents. In that the South Australian Equal Opportunity Commission has attempted to attach equal opportunity programmes to conciliation settlements, there is clearly scope for developing this model. It must also be recognised that informal conciliation is practised in jurisdictions were the agency has no formal powers. The Equal Opportunities Commission and the Commission for Racial Equality in the UK are examples.

## Comparative experiential prognostications

If any other author has employed this terminology, the reader must forgive us both, not merely for obfuscation but, in all probability, for self-delusion. In large measure the preceding chapters have described the powers, practices and experiences of agencies designed to combat discrimination- thus the importance of the particular 'experiential' narrative. The 'comparative' element comprises three particles, that expressed by each contributor, that contributed by the editor and that edited, consciously or unconsciously, by the reader. In truth it is likely that the last will be of greatest benefit: we all make sense of others of that which makes sense to ourselves and it is often the particular insights of the observer, adding his or her intelligence to the written text, that highlights nuances otherwise overlooked.

Deciding 'prognostications' is more difficult. When does prediction advance beyond the intelligent guess? Hopefully when it is informed by the experience of the past described.

The experience of the agencies in all the countries examined is dynamic: whatever the legislative powers of the agency, practical experience informs goal setting and the revision of processes and approaches. There is a growing acknowledgement of the need to establish priorities and to develop, monitor and revise programmes to promote efficiency and effectiveness in their achievement. The contribution of the various authors provides merely a snapshot of activities in a fairly narrow selection of countries and agencies. Without comparable statistical data it is not fair to pass unqualified judgement as to the merits of one form of agency over another.

Despite greater attention now being paid to record keeping, to performance indicators, such as success rates in supported cases and satisfaction rates in the conciliation process, and of the increasing recognition of the need to articulate the work of enforcement with that of education and promotional activities, it seems improbable that the comparative evaluation of the kind examined in this book will progress from art form to science.

It is to be hoped, however, that comparisons in the field of discrimination law and practice will continue and that they will make some small but increasingly significant contribution to the improvement of human relations.

1   See MacEwen, M. 1995, 'Tackling Racism in Europe', Berg: Oxford and Washington

2   Vera Sacks [1986, 'The Equal Opportunities Commission -Ten Years On', Modern Law Review, September, 560-592] points to the fact that weak management in this commission in its early years led to the commissioners being involved in operational matters at the expense of policy development. Similarly the Home Affairs select Committee [Commission for Racial Equality, H.C. 46 (1986)] advised the commissioners to step back and allow management to manage without undue interference: the commissioners role should be a parallel to that of non-executive directors on the board of a company.

3   Also referred in CRE, 1991 at page 62. The SACHR saw this agency subsuming the responsibilities of the Fair Employment Agency and the Equal Opportunity Agency when protection against racial discrimination was extended to Northern Ireland

4   CRE, 1991,'Second Review of the Race Relations Act 1976' recommendation 10 at paragraph 37 suggests that a discrimination division be established within the tribunal system to hear not only sex and race cases in employment but also any other category of discrimination complaint, thus doing away with the non-employment jurisdiction of the County Courts in England and Wales and the Sheriff Courts in Scotland.

5   See the Home Office (1975) observations in 'Racial Discrimination', Cmnd. 6234, HMSO; London. This referred to the lack of confidence amongst ethnic minorities in the effectiveness of the law and the lack of credibility they had in the work of both the Race Relations Board and the Community Relations Commission (par. 33, page 8). There was also reference to the advantages of giving the agency discretion regarding the support of complaints and the preference for an independent agency to conciliate complaints but there was no explicit discussion of conflict of interest in this white paper which intimated the Government's decision to replace the 1968 Act.

6   see CRE (1991) recommendation 14, para. 72 at page 37.

7   The UK's report constitutes CERD/C/263/ADD.7 [parts 1 and 2]

8   Robertson, Geoffrey, 'Freedom the Individual and the Law', 7th Edition at page 497, Penguin Books: London

[9] See HREOC,1994,'HREOC: Summary of Responsibilities and Functions': Sydney.

[10] See Wilkie, above. But note that 'scheduling' is short of incorporating the convention into domestic law.

[11] See MacEwen, M, 1995, 'Tackling Racism in Europe' at chapter 4, Berg: Washington and Oxford. Here the discussion of the experience of Denmark, Greece and Ireland illustrates this point. Greece has incorporated ICERD but its domestic remedies for racism and discrimination are probably worse than Denmark which passed its own legislation but did examine its obligations under ICERD. Ireland was not a signatory and had no domestic provision.

# Bibliography

Abram, M.B. (1986), 'Affirmative Action: Fair Shakers and Social Engineers' 99 *Harvard Law Review*, 1312-1326

Abrams, P. (1992), *Historical Sociology*, Shepton Mallet, Open Books; London

Alston, Philip (ed), (1995), *The United Nations and Human Rights: a Critical Appraisal*, Clarendon Paperbacks: Oxford

Bailey, P. (1990), *Human Rights: Australia in an International Context*, Butterworths: Sydney.

Baldwin, J.R. & McCrudden, C. (1987), *Regulation and Public Law*, Weidenfeld & Nicolson: London

Banton, M. (1994), *Discrimination*, Open University Press: Buckingham and Philadelphia

Banton, M. (1994), 'Effective Implementation of UN Racial Convention' in *New Community*, Vol. 20 No. 3 pp 475-487

Bell, D (1992), 'An Allegorical Critique of the United States Civil Rights Model' in Hepple, B. and Szyszczak, E., (eds), (1992) *Discrimination: the Limits of the Law*, Mansell Publications: London

Bindman, G. (1994), 'How can EC Law confront Racism?' in *New Law Journal*, 11 March 1994, pp 352-353

Blom, J.A.H. (1994), *De effectiviteit vander wet gelijke behandeling dem/v Eerste deel onderzoek*: Den Haag

Bocker, A. (1991), 'A Pyramid of Complaints: the Handling of Complaints about Racial Discrimination in the Netherlands' in *New Community*, 1991, Vol. 17, pp 603-616

Bovenkerk, F., Gras, M.J.I. and Ramsoedh, D. (1994),*Discrimination against migrant workers and ethnic minorities in access to the labour market*, International Labour Office: Geneva

Brett, R. (1995), 'The Role and Limits of Human Rights NGOs at the United Nations', in Political Studies

Brownlie, Ian, (ed), (1992), *Basic Documents on Human Rights,* 3rd Edition, Clarendon Press: Oxford

Burgenthal, T. (1977), 'Implementing the UN Racial Convention' in *Texas Journal of International Law,* 121-141 at pp 187-221

Byrne, A. and Lovenduski, J. (1978), 'The Equal Opportunities Commission', 1*Women's Studies International Quarterly*, 131

CCH Australia (1995), *Australian and New Zealand Equal Opportunity Law and Practice,* CCH Australia: Sydney.

CERD (1979), *Summary Record of the 444th Meeting, 6 August 1979,* UN Doc:.CERD/C/SR.444.

Commission for Racial Equality (1984a), *Report of Formal Investigation into Liverpool City Council Housing Department,* CRE: London

Commission for Racial Equality (1984b), *Report of Formal Investigation into Hackney Borough Council,* CRE: London

Commission for Racial Equality (1985), *Report of Formal Investigation into the Immigration and Nationality Department of the Home Office,* CRE: London

Commission for Racial Equality (1988), *Homelessness and Discrimination: Report of a Formal Investigation into the London Borough of Tower Hamlets',* CRE: London

Commission for Racial Equality (1989), *Racial Discrimination in Liverpool City Council: Report of a Formal Investigation into the Housing Department,* CRE; London

Commission for Racial Equality (1992), *'Second Review of the Race Relations Act 1976'*, CRE: London

Commission for Racial Equality (1994), *'Annual Report for 1993',* CRE: London

Crenshaw, K (1988), 'Race, Reform and Retrenchment: Transformation and Legitimation in Anti-discrimination Law', 101 *Harvard Law Review* 1331

Cranston, Ross (1995), *The Legal Foundations of the Welfare State*, Weidenfeld and Nicolson: London

Cross, M (1993), Racism, Racial Inequality: the British case in a European context', unpublished paper presented to the conference on *Discrimination, Racism and Citizenship: inclusion and exclusion in Britain and Germany*: Berlin 25-27 November 1993

Delgado, R. (1987), 'The Ethereal Scholar: Does Critical Legal

Studies have what minorities want', 22 *Harvard Civil Rights - Civil Liberties Law Review* 312-322

Department of Economic Development (1986), *Equality of Opportunity in Employment in Northern Ireland: Future Strategic Options: A Consultation Paper*, HMSO: Belfast

Department of Social Security, (1990) *A Consultation on Government Measures to tackle Discrimination against Disabled People*, HMSO: London

Donovan, Lord (1969), *Royal Commission on Industrial Relations* (The Donovan Report), HMSO: London

Doyle, B. (1995), *Disability, Discrimination and Equal Opportunities: A Comparative Study of the Employment Rights of Disabled Persons*, Mansell Publishing Ltd: London

Doyle, B. (1996), *Disability Discrimination: The New Law*, Jordan Publishing Ltd: Bristol

Doyle, B. (1996), 'Disabled Workers Rights, the Disability Discrimination Act and the UN Standard Rules' in 25 *Industrial Law Journal*, pp 1-14

Federal Race Discrimination Commission of Australia (1993), *State of the Nation: Report on people of non-English speaking backgrounds*, (Irene Moss: Federal Race Discrimination Commissioner), HREOC: Canberra

Fiss, O (1971), 'A Theory of Fair Employment Laws', 38 *University of Chicago Law Review* 235; Chicago

Flick, G. A. (1984), *Natural Justice*, 2nd ed, Butterworths: Sydney.

Forbes, I. and Mead, G. (1992), *Measure for Measure*, Department of Employment: London

Franks (1957), *The Report of the Committee on Administrative Tribunals and Inquiries*, Cmnd 218, HMSO; London

Freeman, A. (1982), 'Legitimating Racial Discrimination through Anti-discrimination Law', 62 *Minnesota Law Review* 96

Freeman, A. (1986), 'Racism, Rights and the Quests for Equality of Opportunity: A Critical Legal Essay', 23 *Harvard Civil Rights - Civil Liberties Law Review* 295

Frenk, N. and Hondius, E.H. (1991), 'Collective Action in Consumer Affairs' in *European Consumer Law Journal*, No. 1, pp 17-34

Gardner, J. (1989), 'Liberals and Unlawful Discrimination', 9 *Oxford Journal of Legal Studies* 1

Heilbroner (1971), 'The Routes of Social Neglect in the United States' in Rostow, E. (ed) (1971) *'Is Law Dead?'*, Simon and Chuster; New York

Hepple, B. (1990), 'Discrimination and Equality of Opportunity: Northern Ireland Lessons', 10 *Oxford Journal of Legal Studies* 408

Hochschild, J (1984), *The New American Dilemma,,* Yale University Press: Newhaven

Home Office (1975), *Racial Discrimination,* Cmnd 6234, HMSO: London

Home Affairs Committee (1981), *Commission for Racial Equality: Home Affairs Committee Session 1981-82, vol. 1, Report with Minutes of Proceedings ,* HC 46-I, HMSO: London

Home Office (1985), *Ending Discrimination against Disabled People,* Cm 2729, HMSO: London

House of Commons Employment Committee (1990), *The Work of the Equal Opportunities Commission: Minutes of Evidence, Session 1989-1990,* HC Paper 364-I, HMSO: London

House of Commons Employment Committee (1995), *The Operation of the Disabled Persons Employment Act 1944,* HC Paper 383, HMSO: London

Hucker, J. (1995), 'Towards Equal Opportunity in Canada: New Approaches, Mixed Results', 26 *St Mary's Law Journal* 841

Hucker, J. (1994), 'Moving Towards the Elusive Goal of Equality: Reflections on Canada's System of Human Rights Enforcement', 25 *Cambrian Law Review* 33

Human Rights and Equal Opportunity Commission (1993), *Human Rights and Equal Opportunity Commission Annual Report 1992-93,* Australian Government Publishing Service: Canberra

Human Rights and Equal Opportunity Commission, (1994), *State of the Nation: A report on people of non-English speaking backgrounds,* HREOC: Sydney

Human Rights Commission (1983), *Proposal for Amendments to the Racial Discrimination Act to Cover Incitement to Racial Hatred and Racial Defamation,* Report No. 7, HRC: Canberra.

Hunter, R. and Leonard, A. (1995), *The Outcomes of Conciliation in Sex Discrimination Cases,* Centre for Employment and Labour Relations Law, Melbourne University: Melbourne.

Husband, C. (1982), *Race in Britain*: London

ICERD (1990), *Ninth Periodic Report to the Committee for the Elimination of all forms of Racial Discrimination: New Zealand,* United Nations: Geneva

Jayasuriya, L. (1989), *Legislating Against Racial Incitement:*

*Strategies and Rationales,* University of Western Australia: Perth

Katznelson, I (1973), *Black Men, White Cities: Race, Politics and Migration in the United States 1900-1930 and Britain 1948-1968,* Oxford University Press: London.

Kirby, M.D. (1993), 'Discrimination - The Australian Response' *Commonwealth Law Bulletin,* Vol. 19, No. 4 Labour Party (1991), 'Charter of Rights', *New Law Journal* , 13 September 1991 p. 1214

Law, Sylvia A. (1989), 'Girls can't be Plumbers: Affirmative Action for Women in Construction - Beyond Goals and Quotas', *Harvard Civil Rights - Civil Liberties Law Review,* Vol. 24 pp 45-77

Lerner, N. (1980), *The UN Convention on the Elimination of All Forms of Racial Discrimination,* Sijthof and Noordhoff: Alphen aan den Rijn and Rockville

Lerner, N. (1983), 'Curbing Racial Discrimination - 15 years of CERD' in 13 *Israel Yearbook on Human Rights:* Tel Aviv

Lustgarten, L. (1986), 'Racial Inequality and the Limits of the Law', 49 *Modern Law Review* ,68

MacEwen et al (1994), *Anti-discrimination Law on the grounds of race: a comparative literature survey of the provisions in Australia, New Zealand, Canada and the USA,* Commission for Racial Equality/Scottish Ethnic Minority Research Unit: London and Edinburgh.

MacEwen, M. (1986), *Community Relations Councils: Scotch Mist, Domestic Colonialism or What?,* Scottish Ethnic Minorities Research Unit: Edinburgh

MacEwen, M. (1991), *Housing, Race and Law,* Routledge: London

MacEwen, M. (1994), Anti-discrimination law in Great Britain', in *New Community,* Vol. 20, No. 3, pp 353-370.

MacEwen, M. (1995), *Tackling Racism in Europe: An Examination of Anti-Discrimination Law in Practice,* Berg: Oxford and Washington.

Mai Chen (1994), 'Eliminating Race Discrimination in New Zealand: Generating the political will and improving laws', in *New Community* , Vol. 20 no 3, pp 455-474.

Matheson, A. (1995), 'Gathering Dust', *Sydney Morning Herald,* October 3, p.13.

Mayhew, L.H., (1968) *Law and Equal Opportunity: a Study of the Massachusetts Commission Against Discrimination,* Harvard University Press: Cambridge, Mass.

McCrudden, C. and Chambers, Gerald (1995), *Individual Rights and the Law in Britain,* Clarendon Press: Oxford

McCrudden, C. et al (1991), *Racial Discrimination at Work* , Report of Inquiry by Policy Studies Institute (McCrudden, C., Smith, D., and Brown, C.), PSI: London

McCrudden, C. (1988) 'Codes in a Cold Climate: Administrative Rule Making by the Commission for Racial Equality', 51 *Modern Law Review* 409

McKenna, Iain B. (1994), 'Legal Protection against Racial Discrimination in Canada', in *New Community,* Vol. 20 (3); 415-436: London

McNamara L. (1995), *Responding to Hate in a Multicultural Society: Forms of Legal Intervention,* Unpublished Paper, Australian Law Teachers' Association Conference: Melbourne

Minister for Aboriginal and Torres Strait Islander Affairs (1993), *Social Justice for Indigenous Australians 1993-94,* Australian Government Publishing Service; Canberra

Modood, T. (1991), 'The Indian Economic Success: A Challenge to Some Race Relations Assumptions', 19 *Policy and Politics* 177-189

Myrdal, G (1944), *An American Dilemma,* Harper & Brothers Publishers: New York and London

O'Flaherty, M. (1996), 'The International Convention on the Elimination of All Forms of Racial Discrimination: The Substantive Provisions' in Pritchard, S. and Havnen, O. (eds.) *United Nations Human Rights Procedures and Indigenous Australians*: Sydney

O'Flaherty, M. and Heffernan, L. (1995), *The International Convenant on Civil and Political Rights: International Human Rights Law in Ireland*: Dublin

OEEO (1993), *The Office of Equal Employment Opportunity Annual Report 1992-93,* , OEEO: Perth, Western Australia

Office of Multicultural Affairs (1993), *Community Relations Strategy: and Evaluation,,* OMA, Federal Department of the Prime Minister and Cabinet: Canberra, Australia

Partsch, K. (1992) 'The Racial Discrimination Committee' in Alston, P. (ed) *The United Nations on Human Rights,* Clarendon Press: Oxford

Pentony, P. (1986), 'Conciliation Under the Racial Discrimination Act 1975: A Study in Theory and Practice', *Human Rights Commission Occasional Paper No. 15,* Australian Government

Publishing Service: Canberra

Race Relations Board (1969), *Race Relations Board Report for the year 1968*, Race Relations Board: London

Human Rights and Equal Opportunity Commission (1991) *Racist Violence*, HREOC: Sydney

Robertson, Geoffrey, *Freedom the Individual and the Law*, 7th Edition, Penguin Books: London

Rodrigues, P.R. (1991), 'Consumer Boycotts, New Activism in the European Consumer Movement', in Bourgoignie, T. (ed) *Group Actions and Consumer Protection*: Brussels

Rodrigues, P.R. (1994), *Kleurrijke kansen, Medezeggen-shaapsorganen en de WBEAA, Kort and Bondig*: Amsterdam

Rodrigues, P.R. (1994), 'Racial Discrimination and the Law in the Netherlands', in *New Community*, Vol. 20, No. 3 April 1994 pages 381-391

Rubenstein, C. (1995), 'Legislating an end to racism', *Sydney Morning Herald*, May 23, p.13

Sacks, Vera (1986), 'The Equal Opportunities Commission -Ten Years On', *Modern Law Review*, September, 560-592]

Scales, A.C. (1989), 'The Emergence of Feminist Jurisprudence: An Essay' in *Yale Law Journal* 95, pages 1373-1403

Scarff, A. M. (1995), *The Costs of Equality: N.S.W. Anti-Discrimination Law in Practice*, Unpublished Paper, Australian Law Teachers' Association Conference: Melbourne

Scarman, Lord (1981), *The Brixton Disorders, 10-12 April 1981: Report of an Inquiry by the Rt Hon the Lord Scarman OBE*, Cmnd 8427, HMSO: London

Schwelb, E. (1966) 'The International Convention on the Elimination of All Forms of Racial Discrimination', 15, *ICLQ*, (1966)

Sivanandan, A. (1976), 'Race, Class and the State: The Black Experience in Britain', 17, *Race and Class*, 347

Solomos, J. (1989), 'Equal Opportunities Policies and Racial Inequality: The Role of Public Policy', 67, *Public Administration*, 79

Standing Advisory Commission on Human Rights in Northern Ireland, (1990) *Religious and Political Discrimination and Equality of Opportunity in Northern Ireland: Second Report*, Cm1107, HMSO: London

Tarnopolsky and Pentney (1994), *Discrimination and the Law*, revised edition, Carswell Publishing: Toronto

Thornton, M. (1990), *The Liberal Promise: Anti-Discrimination Legislation in Australia,* Oxford University Press: Melbourne.

ten Berge Koolen, J. (1987),*The (Ab)use of Summary Proceedings,* Eighth World Conference on Procedural Law: Utrecht.

van Beek, K.W.H. (1993), *To be hired or not to be hired : the employer decides*: Amsterdam.

Wilkie, M. (1990), 'Victims of Neutrality, Race Discrimination in Denmark', *Nordic Journal of International Law,* Vol. 59, No. 1

Wilkie, M. (1994), 'Anti-discrimination Law in Australia' in *New Community,* Vol. 20 No 3 April pp 437-453; London

POLICE
STAFF
COLLEGE
LIBRARY
BRAMSHILL